# WordStar
# on the
# Amstrad PC1512

John M. Hughes

Sigma Press ● Wilmslow

First published in 1987 by

**Sigma Press**
98a Water Lane, Wilmslow, SK9 5BB, England.

**British Library Cataloguing in Publication Data**

Hughes, John M.
    WordStar on the Amstrad PC 1512
    1. WordStar (Computer program)   2. Amstrad
    PC 1512 (Computer)
    I. Title
    652'.5'02855369 Z52.5.W67

    ISBN 1-85058-079-0

**Distributed by**
John Wiley & Sons Ltd., Baffins Lane, Chichester, West Sussex, England.

Printed and bound in Great Britain
at The Camelot Press plc, Southampton

# CONTENTS

# INTRODUCTION

## Getting serious about word processing

This book is for everyone who needs to put words tidily onto paper, and especially for those who find many things more enjoyable than messing with correcting fluid and typewriter erasers.

With this book in your hand and any IBM-compatible computer on your desk, and your own natural curiosity and determination, you already have all you need to set yourself on the road to professional and effective word processing and document preparation.

What you certainly *don't* need is previous experience of word processing or computing, or any notion of how a computer or word processor works. You don't even need the natural caution with which most people approach computers for the first time, for a modern personal computer is far more difficult to damage (unless you drop it or attack it with a hatchet!) than almost anything else.

One of the problems which always plagues books about computing is that a computer program is dynamic, whereas a book is not. The display on the computer screen may change completely at the touch of a key, and it would obviously be impractical to fill a complete book with representations of how the screen will appear after every key-press you make. Because of this, the best way to use the book is to keep it open in front of you while you have the computer turned on, and to try out the different things which are suggested to see how they work.

The sure key to success is to take things a step at a time. If you expect to be producing complex documents within a week of starting, then you will certainly be disappointed; better to familiarise yourself with the machine and the various facilities which it offers, remembering that a modest investment of time at the start will pay handsome dividends later.

As you work through the book, sooner or later you will come to a topic that doesn't interest you, or that you feel is beyond what you can cope with. When that happens, skip that section. One day, when your needs change or your confidence increases, you may come back to it; but if not, no matter.

# Which word processing program?

This book deals with two different approaches to word processing. In the first section, we introduce the powerful and easy-to-use WordStar 1512, an up-to-date version of the standard WordStar program which is specifically designed to make the most of the advanced features of the Amstrad PC1512 and other modern IBM-compatible computers. If you are new to word processing, or if word processing is only a small part of your computing work, then its tremendous ease of use and its rapid spelling-checker combine to make this is an ideal program to use; and the built-in mail-merge database program makes it very easy to maintain up-to-date mailing lists, send out form-letters, address envelopes and the like.

The second part of the book is about 'standard' WordStar, specifically versions 3.2 and later, and its powerful relative NewWord. These programs are not as easy to use as WordStar 1512, and lack that program's built-in database facility; in many ways, however, they are even more powerful, and if word processing forms an important part of your work, then it may well be to these programs that you will turn. And going beyond the facilities of WordStar, NewWord 3, the most recent development of NewWord, has indexing and tables-of-contents facilities which make it ideal for the professional writer.

However, the main differences between WordStar 1512 on the one hand and 'standard' WordStar and NewWord on the other lie not so much in *what* they do as in *how* they do it. WordStar 1512 is a 'menu-driven program', with the various choices which you can make at any time clearly displayed on the screen; the other programs are predominantly 'command-driven', using special key-sequences to achieve their results.

Despite the differences between them, many of the commands which we shall meet are common to all the programs, and documents prepared using one program can be edited with any one of the others. This makes it easy to move from one program to another as your needs change; it also makes it possible to exchange work between your own computer system and someone else's.

## The equipment

The bare minimum of equipment which you need in order to benefit from this book is any IBM or IBM-compatible Personal Computer running under PC-DOS or MS-DOS. However, a second floppy disc drive is so useful that it is really almost a necessity for serious work; a hard disc, often called a 'Winchester', will make life even easier.

There is really no such thing as the 'best' sort of printer to use, and the whole question of printer choice is in any case dealt with at length in Chapter One. Briefly, if you are interested in printing graphic work as well as ordinary text documents, you will probably need a dot-matrix printer; if your aim is to generate high-quality text output indistinguishable from that produced by a good typewriter, you will want a daisy-wheel printer; and if expense is no object and you want to produce work of the highest calibre, freely mixing graphic and text output, then a laser printer will be most suitable.

## A note on presentation

In this book, **bold type** is used whenever an important new term is introduced for the first time; an explanation follows. Output from the computer is almost always represented by 'screen dumps', which are direct representations on paper of exactly what appears on the computer screen.

From time to time, you will be told to press particular keys on your computer keyboard; key-names are shown in square brackets, thus: [a]. Sometimes, keys are given names, although the key-tops may have symbols on them; the tabulator key is called [Tab], for example, although the keytop often has an arrow-symbol on it, and the Carriage Return key is called [Return], although on some computers it is known as 'Enter', and on others is marked with a bent arrow symbol.

It is often necessary to hold down one key while a second is being pressed; this is shown by printing both key-names separated by a slash, '/'. For example, to get a capital 'A', you would hold down the [Shift] key and tap the [a] key; this is represented as [Shift]/[a].

## Where to go from here

If you are already familiar with computers, then skip Chapter One and move straight on to beginning word processing with WordStar 1512 in Chapter Two; otherwise, we suggest that you sit down with Chapter One open in front of you and with the computer on your desk. As the various steps are outlined in the text, try them out. Word processing is a 'hands-on' affair, and this is a far more effective way of learning than reading through the book first and trying to remember everything it said.

To help you find your way round the book, each chapter starts with a short Preview of the material to be covered in that chapter, and ends with a brief Postscript. When you reach the Postscript to each chapter, take time to check it over and make sure that you really are comfortable with the various items that you need to know; there is no advantage in racing on to the next section if you are not tolerably sure of what you have already read.

If you do get really stuck, perhaps you can find a friend or associate who will be able to help. But if you take things gently, you will assuredly not get stuck very often.

# CHAPTER ONE

# Getting Started

## Preview

This chapter is intended for raw beginners to word processing, as well as for those who have a little practical experience of using a word processor but who don't really understand how it all works.

In the next few pages we shall look at the various items of equipment of which a typical word processing system is made up; these include both 'hardware' items, such as computer and printer, and programs, such as WordStar and WordStar 1512. We introduce the different types of printer which are commonly used for word processing, and describe the advantages and disadvantages of each, as well as different types of floppy disc.

Many newcomers to word processing and computing find that terms like 'floppy disc' send them into a flat spin. What is a floppy disc anyway? Where does it come from? How many different kinds are there and what is the difference between them? Is a floppy disc the same as 'software'– it is 'soft' after all.

Most of these questions, and many others like them, will be answered in this first chapter; as you read, you should find that other things also begin to fall into place, and by the end of the chapter you should understand most of what you will need to know about the equipment you will be using, and what you should look for when buying discs, printers and other items.

## Some useful concepts

When you create a document with a typewriter, every key which you press places a character on paper; editing your work and correcting mistakes is slow and unpleasant, calling for correcting fluid and erasers, and an absolutely perfect document is difficult to achieve.

1

With a word processor, text is created not on paper, but rather on a special screen, or **monitor**, on which corrections and alterations can be made with a minimum of effort. You can do some work on a document and then put it aside for a while and come back to it later, and when you have finished editing it you can print it out using any margin settings and on any size of paper which you like. Such a document can be of almost any length, ranging from a simple memo to a full-length book, although in reality most very long documents are actually created as a succession of short ones which are then joined together.

This basic concept has been the subject of a vast amount of sophistication in recent years, and three main developments are mentioned here.

The first of these is the use of **mail merge** programs. At its simplest mail merging is a technique which makes it possible to take the text of a letter and reproduce it several times, personalising each letter with such individual details as the name and address of the recipient; there are, however, several variations on this basic idea, and we shall be looking at these in detail later.

The second important change has been the development of **spelling checker** programs. At their simplest, these enable the spelling of a document to be checked against one or more special dictionaries, held on disc, so that any typing errors or mistakes in spelling can be corrected before the document is finally printed; many spelling checkers are also able to find anagrams, identify homonyms and do similar dictionary work.

Finally, interest has also grown in the production of work which never appears in traditional printed form: many documents now are sent by **electronic mail** over the public telephone system, and it is becoming relatively common for books and articles to be typeset directly from word processed text held on floppy discs. This is precisely the way in which this book was created, and the day may soon come when publishers will expect to receive all material in this way, and when conventional typed work will be as unusual, and as unwelcome to a publisher, as a handwritten manuscript would be today.

In this chapter, we shall be looking first at the equipment required for word processing and then at the different types of word processing program which are available.

# Looking at the machinery

Every personal computer or word processor is made up of a number of separate component parts. At the heart of any system is the **processor**, the 'silicon chip' which actually does the real work involved in word processing and computing. Associated with this is the computer's internal memory, which is, to all intents and purposes, blank when the machine is first switched on.

The first job of the user at switch-on, therefore, is to put enough information into the computer to enable it to begin doing its job. This typically entails inserting a floppy disc in the disc drive immediately after the computer has been turned on;

once this has been done, the computer will be ready to work. Remember that the information which you have loaded in will stay there only until you replace it with something else or the computer is switched off; next time you use it, you will have to repeat the procedure.

**Programs and Data** Two kinds of information can be fed into the processor. The first kind is a set of instructions for the processor to obey, which is called a **program** (note the un-British spelling, by the way); the second is **data**, such as the text of a document which you are preparing.

An expression which is often used in computing circles as a sort of shorthand for 'programs' is **software**. A computing or word processing system can thus be said to consist of both **hardware** – the actual physical equipment – and software.

## A little about the operating system

The disc which is used when the computer is started up at the beginning of a session contains a special program called the **operating system**. You need to understand almost nothing about this, except to know that it is the operating system which tells the computer such things as where to look for a particular file on disc, or what information is to be sent to the screen and what is to be sent to the printer. Just as a junior officer in the army takes the commands of the commanding officer and passes them on to individual units as appropriate, so the operating system takes your orders to the computer and sends them to the screen, the keyboard, the disc drive or wherever else is appropriate.

**MS-DOS and PC-DOS** The operating system which is used on, and supplied with, IBM Personal Computers is called PC-DOS – DOS is an abbreviation for *D*isc *O*perating *S*ystem; on IBM-compatible computers from other manufacturers, the same operating system is called MS-DOS. In general, any program which works 'under' MS-DOS, as the saying has it, will also work under PC-DOS, and *vice-versa*; however, not all computers sold as 'IBM-compatibles' are actually 100% compatible with the IBM PC.

## Using the computer

Once a word processing program has been loaded into the computer, you are ready to type in at the keyboard whatever text you wish. The processor will know what to do with it because it will simply be following its program of instructions.

In the majority of cases, this will involve displaying on the screen the text you have entered; at the same time it will be stored in the memory – known in computer circles as **RAM**, standing for **Random Access Memory**. Alternatively you might give instructions for text to be deleted, or moved from one part of the document on which you are working to another – or even moved from one document to a different one.

When you are ready, the typed-in data can be passed from the processor to the printer, giving what is often called 'hard copy' or 'printout'.

In computer terms, the keyboard is an **input device**, by which information is fed into the processor, and the monitor screen and the printer are both **output devices** on which the results of the processor's operation can be displayed.

# Files and how to keep them

We have already seen that when the computer is turned off, everything stored in it – program and data alike – will be lost. All computers therefore need some form of permanent 'external storage' on which information can be kept until the next time the computer is used.

This external storage most commonly takes the form of floppy discs which fit into the computer's disc drives. Anything of which you want to keep a permanent record can be recorded (**saved** is the usual computer jargon) onto a disc, and the disc is then removed and kept separately from the computer until the information is needed. Whenever such information is saved on a disc, the computer will ask you to give it an identifying name. A named set of data kept on a disc is called a **file**.

This is a term which causes problems to a lot of people. Essentially a computer file is not very different from any collection of documents kept in a conventional card folder; just as a folder is given a name which identifies its contents and which makes it possible to store and retrieve it among the other files in an office filing system, so a document which you have word processed and stored on a floppy disc is given a name so that it can be found again when you need it.

## How many disc drives?

Until quite recently, most personal computers were fitted with only a single disc drive. Most programs can be used fairly satisfactorily on a single-drive machine, but there are many reasons why two are more satisfactory.

The most important of these is that using a single disc drive will entail you in a good deal of 'disc swapping'– taking one disc out of the drive and replacing it with another in order to carry out a particular operation, then replacing the first disc when that operation is completed. It is also far easier to make **backups** if you have two disc drives – a backup is a second disc on which is kept which a copy of all your files, so that if you lose the original disc, or it is damaged in some way, you will not have to start working again from scratch.

Some programs either cannot be used at all or are very unsatisfactory on a single drive machine.

**Hard discs** An expensive, but ultimately very satisfactory, way of storing files is to have a **hard disc** in addition to one or more floppy disc drives. Unlike floppy discs, which are put into the disc drives or removed from them as the need arises, a hard disc remains permanently sealed inside its case, usually physically inside the computer itself. Because it is a sealed unit, it is able to store much more information than a floppy disc – typically as much as 30 or more 'floppies'– and although it is located physically inside the computer cabinet, it retains this information even after the machine has been turned off, and thus is really 'external storage'.

Information stored on a hard disc can be loaded into the computer's internal memory very much faster than information stored on floppy discs. A few programs cannot be run at all without a hard disc.

Hard discs are sometimes referred to as 'Winchesters'; this is not a trade name, as you might suppose, but a joking reference to the famous Winchester 30-30 rifle, as the first hard discs for personal computers had 30 **megabytes** of storage on 30 tracks – a megabyte is a measure of storage equivalent to one million characters.

Whether you have only floppy discs or a hard disc as well, you do not need to concern yourself about how or where information is stored. In this regard, recording material onto a disc is quite different from recording onto a video or audio cassette tape, where you may have to advance the tape to the right place before recording to avoid erasing some other material.

All these details are automatically taken care of by the computer, and a simple instruction to save information onto the disc is all that is required – you must give the file a name by which it will be known, and the computer will then know exactly where on the disc it is best to store it, as well as how to find it again when the time comes. When you need to gain access to that information in the future, you can simply 'read' it back into the memory off the same disc.

# About floppy discs

Floppy discs can be obtained in several different sizes and types, and usually only one type can be used in any given computer – generally 5¼", though 3½" discs are also becoming popular. Both designs are illustrated in Fig. 1.

Despite superficial differences between different types of disc, they all work on the same principles and are constructed of similar materials. Essentially they consist of a thin disc, usually made of Mylar, with magnetic oxide material similar to that used on audio and video tape bonded to both sides.

The Mylar disc is permanently enclosed either in a square flexible jacket in the case of 5¼" discs, or, for 3½" discs, in a rigid plastic case; the latter are thus not really 'floppy' at all. The jackets which protect 5¼" discs, have open 'windows' in them, one on each side, through which the magnetic material of the disc can be seen, and through which the disc drives' **read/write heads** pass when the disc is in use. To avoid accidental damage to discs of this sort, it is important to always replace them after use in the paper envelope in which they were supplied.

On 3½" discs the surfaces of the disc are concealed behind a sliding metal shutter when the disc is not actually in a disc drive. Consequently, there is less chance of these discs being damaged.

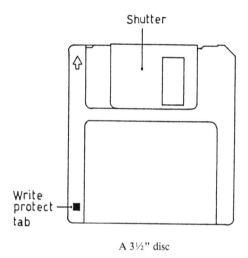

Shutter

Write
protect
tab

A 3½" disc

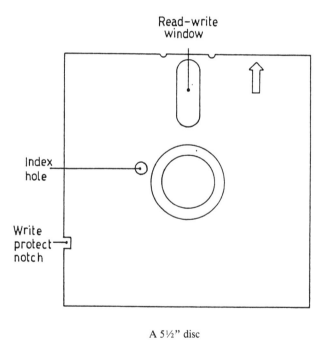

Read–write
window

Index
hole

Write
protect
notch

A 5½" disc

**Fig. 1.1** Floppy discs

In use, 5¼″ discs are placed in the disc drive as shown in Fig. 1.2, with the 'window' innermost and the manufacturer's label uppermost; the same rules apply to 3½″ discs.

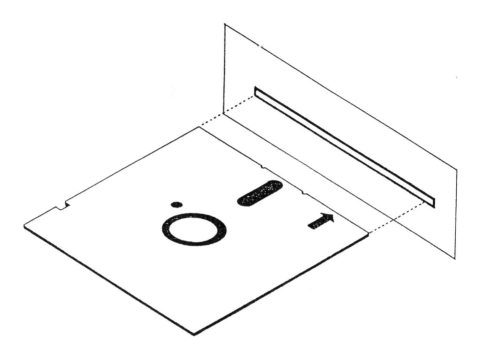

**Fig. 1.2** Placing a disc in the disc drive

## Tracks, sectors, sides and densities

Each side of a floppy disc is laid out in a series of concentric **tracks**, usually 40, numbered from the outside towards the centre, so that Tracks 0–39 are on one side and Tracks 40–79 are on the other. Additionally, the surface of the disc is divided into a series of (usually) 9 'pie slices' called **sectors**, as shown in Fig. 1.3. Sectors and tracks exist so that the computer can find the data stored on the disc; they are not apparent to the eye.

IBM-compatible personal computers generally use soft-sectored, double-sided, double-density 5¼″ discs, 48 tpi (tracks per inch), and if you buy such discs made by a reputable manufacturer you should have very few problems with them.

People are sometimes tempted to buy cheap unlabelled discs. This is a false economy, for at the worst cheap discs may not only corrupt your data and programs, but can actually damage your disc drives. Nor is it worth buying the cheaper discs which are intended for single-side disc drives. Typically, single-sided discs are double-sided discs one side of which has failed the manufacturer's quality control tests; they are therefore not to be relied on to keep your data securely.

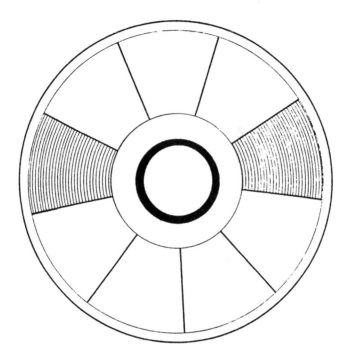

**Fig. 1.3** How a disc is laid out

**Density** refers to how 'thickly' the data on your discs can be packed together. Again, it is not worthwhile buying other than the recommended type of discs.

**Bytes and kilobytes** Just as written documents are often measured in terms of how many words they contain, the capacity of floppy discs – and, indeed, of computing equipment generally – is generally reckoned in **bytes** and **kilobytes**.

A byte is the amount of space necessary to store one character – a single digit, a space or a letter of the alphabet, for instance. One kilobyte, usually abbreviated to 1K, is equal to 1024 bytes, and not 1000 as you might imagine. A **megabyte** is equal to one million bytes.

Most word processing programs will make it clear to you how much space you have left on a floppy disc which you are using to store documents, but you can always carry out a check on this with the MS-DOS S H O W command.

## Formatting discs

A newly-bought blank floppy disc is not unlike a new car-park: before you can park cars on it in an orderly and sensible way, there must be white lines to mark the individual parking places. Similarly, a floppy disc needs to have the equivalent of electronic lines placed on it, so that your data can be stored and recovered properly. Indeed, *an unformatted disc is completely useless.*

You should use the MS-DOS FORMAT program, or equivalent, to format your new discs. Full details of how to do this should be in your computer's manual; the usual procedure is to put a working copy of the MS-DOS disc supplied with your computer into Drive A, the disc you want to format into Drive B, and then to type

FORMAT B:

then press the [Return] key and follow the directions displayed on screen. However, there are many variations of this command, and you should check your manual, especially if you only have a single disc drive or if you need to format the disc in some special way – as a single-sided disc, or with a non-standard number of sectors, for example.

It is a good idea to make a habit of formatting new discs in bulk, rather than in ones and twos as you need them. There is no advantage in keeping discs unformatted, and sooner or later an occasion will arise when you suddenly discover an urgent need for a formatted disc and don't have one to hand. Alternatively, discs can be bought ready-formatted if you prefer.

There is nothing to prevent you from reformatting an old disc, but if you do so, all the information stored on it will be irretrievably lost; indeed, this is one of the standard ways of destroying information you no longer need.

# Looking after discs

Because floppy discs of all sorts are vulnerable to physical and magnetic damage, it is important that everyone who uses them should know how to handle them, as well as how to minimise any accidental losses that may occur. The main rules for disc use are as follows:

1. Before turning a computer on or off, double-check that both disc drives are empty. *Powering up with a disc in the drive is the most common cause of disc damage.* In the event of a power failure, remove discs from the drives immediately.

2. Keep discs away from all potential sources of magnetism. Telephones, transformers and loudspeakers can all cause damage.

3. Because dust and moisture can ruin a disc, it is vital that any disc which is not actually in a disc drive should be replaced in its envelope. Don't smoke when handling discs.

4. Never take a disc out of a disc drive while the drive is working, as this can damage both the disc and the drive; an 'activity light' will come on when a drive is in use.

9

5. Never touch or blow on the magnetic surface of a disc; even a drop of moisture from your breath can cause data to be lost.

6. Discs must be kept in moderate temperatures; do not leave them in direct sunlight or near radiators, or in unheated areas.

7. Although discs are 'floppy', every care should be taken to avoid twisting or bending them.

8. When labelling 5¼″ discs, write out the label first and then stick it on the disc jacket – the pressure of a ball-point pen can easily ruin a disc. If you *have* to write on a label which is already stuck in place on a disc, use a soft felt-tip pen and be careful not to press down.

9. Keep a back-up copy of *everything*, and make sure that every disc is accurately labelled.

**Keeping copies** There is an established procedure for protecting data stored on discs from accidental loss: *When you prepare an updated version of a file, always keep a copy of the most recent update-but-one.* This ensures that at the worst you will lose only one session's work, as the previous version of the file will still be available.

Many programs do this automatically, keeping the old copy of the file, with the letters BAK, for *BAcKup*, added to its name, as well as the new version. Useful though this is, it is not an absolute guarantee of security, as the disc itself might be lost or damaged. It is wise, therefore, to keep a backup file on a separate disc, and to store that disc in a different place. Remember, the workings of fate are such that you will always lose the one thing of which you don't have a back-up copy.

**Write protecting discs** Unintentional erasure of disc-files can be prevented with the write-protect slot on your discs. On 5¼″ discs, this takes the form of a notch at the edge of the disc, and when an opaque adhesive tab is fastened over this, the disc is said to be 'write-protected' and the files on it are safe from erasure or alteration. It is also impossible for any other files to be saved on such a disc unless the tab is removed.

On 3½″ discs, there is a plastic slider which can be positioned to block or to reveal a hole in the case. The disc is write-protected when this is open.

# RAM discs

It is common for a portion of the RAM – the computer's internal memory – to be treated as a sort of imaginary disc drive, enabling material to be stored there, loaded from there into the 'normal' memory, and so on. Such a device is called a **RAM disc** or a **virtual disc**.

The advantages of this approach are that data and programs can be loaded from the RAM disc very much quicker than they could be loaded from a real disc. The disadvantages are that whatever is stored in the RAM disc must be saved on a real disc before the computer is turned off, or it will be lost like everything else in the memory.

The RAM disc is generally blank when the computer is turned on, and any files which you want to place on it must be copied there from a real disc. On some machines, such as the Amstrad PC1512, an area of RAM is supplied with electricity from batteries, and thus is constantly on, regardless of whether the computer is plugged in at the mains or not. This is known as 'battery-backed RAM'. Usually the amount of memory which is permanently on is too small to use for the storage of programs and data; its most frequent use is to enable the computer to keep track of the time and date even when it has been switched off.

# Files and file-names

We have seen that before a file can be saved on a disc or loaded back into the computer, it must be given a name by which it can be identified. The rules for creating these names are quite strict, and may vary somewhat between different types of computer, but as this is one of the areas where a certain measure of standardisation exists between different types of computer you will probably not have many problems.

MS-DOS file-names consist of two parts. The first part, consisting of not more than eight characters, is usually called the **file-name**, and the second, which is optional, but which if present must be separated from the first part by a full-stop, is called either the **file-type** or the **extension**. This terminology can be a little confusing at times, as the expression *file-name* is also used to mean the complete name including the extension.

File-names may contain any letter or number together with any of the following symbols:

> ! @ # $ % & ( ) – __ { } '

**File extensions** MS-DOS treats certain extensions in special ways –.COM and .EXE both identify programs, for example – but generally speaking you can use pretty-much any extension that makes sense to you, such as .DOC for a DOCument, perhaps, or .TXT for TeXT. Or, if you prefer, you can simply leave the extension blank, and use only the file-name part.

A few programs automatically make their own choice of file extension for the data files which they create or use; for example, WordStar 1512 uses the extensions .MLI and .MLD for its mail-merge files, and SuperCalc3 printer files saved to disc are given the extension .PRN. Be sure not to alter these extensions, or the program may be unable to find or use the files again.

# Discs and directories

When you want to load a document file into a word processing program, the program will need to know exactly where to look for the file you want. This involves telling it at least in which drive the appropriate disc has been placed and the file's name and extension; it may also involve telling it in which directory on the disc the file has been saved.

Individual programs often try to simplify this procedure, so the way in which this is done varies a little from one program to another. For example, when WordStar 1512 is set up – **installed** is the technical term – on a two-drive system, it automatically assumes that document files will be on Drive B. The situation is a little trickier with a hard disc system, for the required document may be on either the hard disc (usually Drive C) or on the floppy disc Drive A.

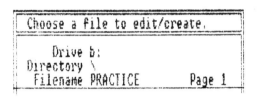

Fig. 1.4 Drive, directory and path information from WordStar 1512

Fig. 1.4 shows how WordStar 1512's Choose/create a file menu displays a list of documents on Drive B. Note the convention that the drive name is shown with a colon after it – this is an important point which beginners often forget. Below the drive name is the word Directory, with a backslash '\' against it. Finally the name of the current file is shown.

A special area of the disc called the **directory** is set aside to hold details of the names of all the files kept on the disc and the places where they are stored; in effect, this is an index to the files on the disc. These files will be of many different types: some will be **executable** files – that is, programs; others will be **non-executable** files, which cannot be run as programs, and which are generally data of one sort or another. Finally, there are files which are neither programs nor data, but **sub-directories**, containing within them the names of other executable and non-executable files, and even of other sub-directories.

**A brief introduction to sub-directories** If you are using a hard disc, or if you use the computer for many things beside word processing, then you may find that you need to understand the use of sub-directories. However, if you are only using floppy discs, and especially if you are using your computer system simply for word processing, you will probably need to make relatively little use of sub-directories. The example which is given here may help to clarify matters a little if you are using WordStar 1512; however, it is important that you should not try to copy the procedure described here until you have first installed the program as described in Chapter Two.

Start the computer with the usual MS-DOS startup disc (*not the WordStar 1512 System Disc), then insert the System Disc into Drive A and enter the command*

*DIR*

*followed by* [ Return ]. You should see a display like that printed as Fig. 1.5.

```
Volume in drive A is 1512 SYSTEM
Directory of  A:\

COMMAND   COM      23612   14-07-86   12:13
RAMDRIVE  SYS       6566   14-07-86   12:13
MOUSE     COM       6984   14-07-86   12:14
KEYBUK    EXE       2985   14-07-86   12:16
SETTINGS  PRF       1994   10-12-86   16:48
1512              <DIR>    29-10-86   17:58
WS1512    EXE      61008   24-06-86   22:29
WS1512    PIF        369   27-06-86    8:20
AUTOEXEC  BAT         79   13-12-86    9:31
CONFIG    SYS         48   28-01-87   17:09
         10 File(s)       29696 bytes free
```

**Fig. 1.5** A Directory of The WordStar 1512 Disc

The DIR command is an MS-DOS command which shows what files are on the disc in Drive A – that is, it *catalogues* the disc. You could find what files were on a disc in Drive B by typing

DIR B:

and pressing [ Return ] – remember the colon after the drive name!

When you catalogue the WordStar 1512 disc, you will find that one of the files appears as '1512 <DIR>'. This file is a sub-directory – hence the <DIR> after the name – and it is one level 'below' the main directory of the disc which appears when you first enter the DIR command. This main directory is usually known as the **root** directory, and is represented by a single backslash, '\', after the drive name.

To find what is in the sub-directory called '1512', enter the command

DIR \1512

and press [ Return ]. When this is shown, you will see that it contains yet another level of sub-directories, shown in Fig. 1.6.

13

```
Volume in drive A is 1512 SYSTEM
Directory of  A:\1512

.                <DIR>       29-10-86   17:58
..               <DIR>       29-10-86   17:58
PROGRAM          <DIR>       29-10-86   17:58
SETTINGS PRF         1994    3-02-87   17:17
        4 File(s)      29696 bytes free
```

**Fig. 1.6** The '1512' Sub-directory

The command 'DIR \1512' gives a **path** from the root directory to the subdirectory 1512. Just as MS-DOS doesn't confuse two files on different discs with the same name, so two files in different directories of the same disc would not be confused, because the path to them would be different.

As far as keeping track of documents in WordStar 1512 is concerned, when you are starting out you will probably want to keep all of them on the root directory of the Text and Data Disc; and the fact that you are in the root directory will be emphasised by the '\' against the word Directory in the Choose/create a file menu. As the number of files on the disc increases, this will become less convenient, and instructions for dealing with this eventuality are given in Chapter Six; however, you don't need to bother about that now.

# The keyboard

IBM-compatible personal computers produced by different manufacturers may have keyboards which vary considerably in the way they are laid out. The features listed here are common, but you may find that certain keys are located in a different area of your keyboard and that key-names may be slightly different. In a few cases, keys described here will completely missing on certain keyboards.

The layout illustrated in Fig. 1.7 is typical. The keys can be broadly divided into four groups. First are the alphabetic and numeric keys, arranged in the familiar QWERTY sequence, together with such related keys as [Tab] (often marked with a blunted right-arrow), a space bar and either a [Caps Lock] or [Shift Lock] key, and sometimes both. [Caps Lock] is sometimes called [Alpha Lock]. [Caps Lock] and [Shift Lock] are often provided with a light to show when they are engaged. There is also a [Return] key, sometimes marked with a bent-arrow symbol and sometimes called [Enter]; this serves the same purpose as the Carriage Return key or lever on a typewriter.

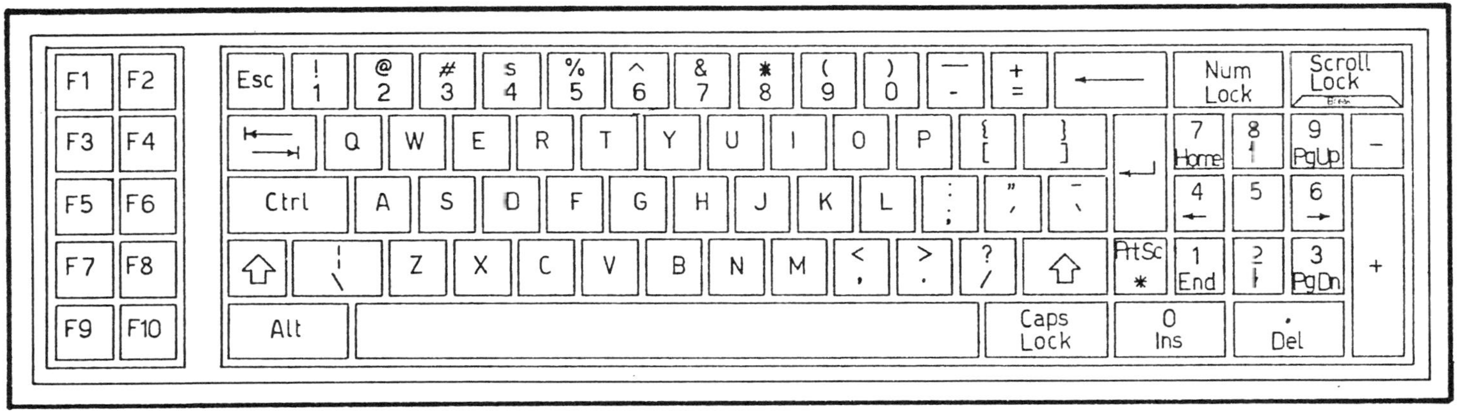

**Fig. 2.7** A typical keyboard layout

15

**The Function keys** Usually to the left of the keyboard, but sometimes arranged in a row on their own above the 'alphanumeric' keys, are ten **function keys**, numbered from F1 to F10. Different programs may use some or all of these for their own purposes, and card keyboard overlays are often provided with these programs as a reminder of how the function keys are used. Unfortunately, the variations in keyboard layout referred to above mean that these overlays cannot be used on some machines.

**The cursor keys** To the right of the alphanumeric keys are the **cursor keys**, a cluster of four keys marked with arrows. These are used to move the **cursor** around on the screen – the cursor is the marker which appears on the monitor screen to show the position at which any new text typed at the keyboard will appear. Closely related to the cursor keys, and usually grouped around them, are [ Home ], [ End ], [ PgUp ] and [ PgDn ], which many word processing programs use to send the cursor to, respectively, the beginning or end of a document or to cause the previous or next screen 'page' of text to be revealed. The [ Scroll Lock ] key is used by some programs to force the cursor to remain in the same position on the screen when the cursor keys are pressed, in effect moving the text rather than the cursor.

**Other keys** The final group of keys comprises [ Ctrl ], [ Alt ], [ Num Lock ], [ Break ], [ Esc ], [ Ins ], [ PrtSc ] and up to three different [ Del ] keys. [ Ctrl ] and [ Alt ] are used to modify the effect of other keys, though exactly how this is organised may vary from program to program; for example, most word processing programs use the ← and → keys to move the cursor one position to the left or right respectively, but if [ Ctrl ] is held down while ← or → are pressed, the cursor will jump one *word's* length in the appropriate direction.

The [ Del ] keys are sometimes marked [ ←Del ] and [ Del→ ]; when pressed, these erase characters from the screen in the direction shown by the arrow. Sometimes the left-delete key is just labelled [ Del ], and sometimes [ Backspace ] or [ Rubout ]. In some programs, the [ ←Del ] key will only cause a backspace without erasing anything.

[ Num Lock ] is a **toggle**; that is, pressing it once enables the cursor keys and the other keys grouped around them to function as a calculator-type number-pad; pressing [ Num Lock ] again will cause these keys to revert to their usual functions.

[ Ins ] is another toggle, used to switch between Insert and Overwrite Modes; pressing it once causes any new characters which are typed in to overwrite what is already on the screen; pressing it a second time makes the new characters shove what is already on the screen further to the right.

[ PrtSc ] is used to produce **screen dumps**, which are representations of the monitor screen on the printer. This is the way in which most of the figures in this book were created. Don't press it unless you have a printer connected to the computer and ready to work, or the computer may 'lock up' and may need to be reset before you can continue working, resulting in the loss of any work which has not been saved to disc.

The effects of pressing [Break] and [Esc] vary widely from program to program; often they will simply have no effect at all. A common use of the [Esc] key is to 'escape' from one particular part of a program to another section; this is the way in which it is usually used in WordStar 1512; in other cases, it is used to abort an operation 'in midstream'. Pressing [Ctrl] and [Break] together will usually abort whatever operation the computer is carrying out.

**Resetting the computer** Pressing down [Alt], [Ctrl] and [Del] in turn, holding down each key and then releasing them simultaneously, is the usual way of resetting an IBM-compatible computer; when this is done, any information which is stored in the memory will be lost.

# Mice

Until very recently, the almost universal way of inputting information into a personal computer was by means of the keyboard, and this will no doubt continue to be the case for many people. Within the last few years, however, the computer mouse has become increasingly common as an adjunct to the keyboard.

A **mouse** is simply a hand-held box with a ball-bearing in the bottom. This box is connected to the computer by a length of cable – the mouse's tail – and when it is dragged around a desk-top, the cursor on the screen – either the normal text cursor or a special mouse-cursor – moves in step with it. A mouse is particularly handy for those applications which involve a great deal of cursor movement, and there are several programs, particularly those which create 'paintings' or other graphic designs on the screen, which make very great use of them.

Even in word processing, which is essentially a keyboard-oriented task, mice can be extremely useful. For example, in most word processing programs, a number of different ways are provided for moving the cursor around a document – to the beginning or end of a line, to the next or previous word, to the start or end of a page or paragraph and so on; and inevitably this means that a large number of key combinations have to be learned.

With a mouse, on the other hand, it is possible to move any distance through a document without needing to learn or type in any special codes; all that is necessary is to move the mouse around on the desk.

Mice have small push-buttons which are clicked to produce particular effects; one, two and three-button mice are all common. Depending on the design of the mouse which you are using and the program which is being run, these buttons may take the place of pressing [Return] or [Shift], or mark out the beginning or end of text blocks, and so on.

# Looking at printers

Probably the most important **peripheral device** which is used in conjunction with a personal computer is a printer, and consequently choosing the appropriate printer for your needs requires careful thought.

Most computer printers are **impact printers**; that is, characters are printed by striking the paper through an ink or carbon ribbon. The advantages of impact printers are that they are capable of generating multiple copies at one pass and that they are available in a wide range of prices, but they do have the disadvantage that they are rather noisy.

**Non-impact printers** use a variety of different techniques, of which the most common are ink-jet printers and laser printers. The former in effect 'draw' individual characters with very small droplets of ink; they are accordingly very quiet, but obviously can only print a single copy of a document at a time. Laser printers have the great advantage of producing extremely high-quality output of all sorts of work, including graphics, at reasonably high speeds – 8 seconds for an A4 page is typical – but they are much more expensive than most other printer types.

## Dot-matrix and formed character printers

The two most common types of impact printer are **dot-matrix printers** and **formed character printers**; most of the latter sort are 'daisy-wheel printers', and this is the term which I have preferred in this book. Thimble-printers and some other types are broadly similar to daisy-wheel printers.

**Daisy-wheel printers** Daisy-wheel printers derive their name from the shape of the print-element; this is circular with a number of spokes, typically about 90 in number, radiating from the hub like the petals of a flower; the characters are located at the tip of each 'petal', and printing takes place by rotating the wheel until the desired character is at the print position and then striking it with a print hammer.

The advantages of this method of printing are that the output is indistinguishable from that of a good typewriter, and that a number of different characters and typestyles can be achieved by interchanging print-elements. The disadvantages are that it is not generally possible to output graphics on a daisy-wheel printer, that it is necessary to stop them in order to replace the wheel whenever the type-face must be changed, and that they are rather slow – typical speeds range from 20-50 cps (characters per second), though higher speeds can be achieved at a price.

**Dot-matrix printers** Dot-matrix printers fire a series of pins through the ribbon onto the paper, so that characters are in effect composed of a series of dots. They have the advantages of being substantially faster than most daisy-wheel printers and of being able to print a virtually unlimited range of characters and type-faces as well as graphics, but the quality of dot-matrix work is not yet quite as good as that of daisy-wheel printers. Early dot-matrix printers in particular were often incapable of producing proper descenders for letters such as 'g' and 'q', which made them totally unsuited for high-quality work.

Most dot-matrix printers, though not all, provide two different modes of operation: **draft mode**, which is a high-speed mode suitable for producing a proof copy of a document, in which the individual dots of which the letters are composed can be clearly distinguished; and **NLQ mode**, or Near Letter Quality, which is typically about one-fifth the speed of draft mode, but in which the letter shapes are much better formed. In draft mode, speeds of 200 cps are fairly common. Printers which can print bi-directionally are naturally faster than those which only print left-to-right; NLQ work is often only done left-to-right.

**Printer speed** All these measures of printer speed are nominal rather than actual; in practice, speeds will usually fall short of those quoted. This is because the advertised printing-speeds do not usually take account of the time which is taken in moving the print-head to the starting-place on the line and in advancing the paper.

Figure 1.8 shows the difference between two good modern impact printers.

```
This is to show the difference in the quality of work produced on a
dot-matrix printer and on a daisy-wheel printer.  This paragraph was
printed on a Micro-Peripherals MP-165, and the individual dots of
which the characters are composed can be clearly seen;  print speed,
howver, is much higher than with a daisy-wheel printer.
```

```
This paragraph was printed on a Juki daisy-wheel printer. The
individual letters are much clearer, and the document as a
whole is easier to read, but the speed of printing is greatly
reduced, and the range of characters is limited to those
available on the printer element.  Graphic work is not
normally possible with a daisy-wheel printer.
```

**Fig. 1.8** Dot-matrix and daisy-wheel printing

# Standards for printers

It would obviously be an impossible situation if different printers were to react in different ways to the signals sent to them by the computers to which they were connected – if one were to print a 'q', say, while another responded to the same signal by printing a 'b'.

**ASCII Codes** All printers designed for use with personal computers understand and accept the same basic code, known as **ASCII**, and pronounced 'Askey'. The initials stand for the 'American Standard Code for Information Interchange', and the ASCII code is in fact one of the most standardised features in computing.

Each character is given a number, ranging from 32 (a space) up to 127 (printing as a blank, but often called Delete). Numbers below 32 are **control codes**, used for such purposes as ringing a bell, sending the carriage to the start of a new line and so on.

For UK users, one major problem of ASCII code is that, as an American code, it makes no provision for the Pound Sterling, '£'. Different manufacturers have got round this problem in different, non-standard ways: some give it the ASCII value 35, which really belongs to the symbol '#', while others give it a value higher than the theoretical top limit of ASCII numbers, often allocating the number 163. The standard number for the Pound Sterling on IBM-compatible personal computers is 156.

**Non-standard character codes** Because all numbers greater than 127 are non-standard, various printer manufacturers and program-writers use them in different ways: sometimes they are used for 'graphics characters', lines, segments of circles and so on with which pictures can be created; sometimes they are used for Greek or Hebrew letters, and so on. However, because these codes are non-standard there is no guarantee that, even if different printers are capable of printing the same non-ASCII characters, they will allocate the same code to them.

Another problem of standardisation arises from the fact that different printers approach the incorporation of different print styles in different ways: features such as underlining, bold type, italics and the like are among those which are handled differently.

On dot-matrix printers, many of these problems can be overcome by using a printer which is 'Epson-compatible'; indeed, many programs assume that an Epson-compatible printer will be available. However, such a printer will not usually correctly reproduce the various graphic symbols available on IBM-compatible personal computers; for this, you will need a printer which is IBM-compatible. Many printers can be changed from Epson-compatibility to IBM-compatibility by moving a switch.

The situation with daisy-wheel printers is not so simple, as the character set varies not only from printer to printer, but from print-element to print-element. The only advice which is always 100% effective is to see a particular printer actually working with a computer of the same kind as your own, and preferably using the same program as you have.

# CHAPTER TWO

# Your first two hours with WordStar 1512

## Preview

When you have finished working through this chapter, you will be able to compose and edit simple documents with WordStar 1512, and print out your work on paper. From start to finish this will probably take you about two hours; about one hour will be taken up in installing the program, including the time you will need to format six discs if this has not yet been done, so if you prefer to work in shorter periods, set aside up to an hour for the installation and another hour later for your first experience of word processing.

Of course, it will take you more than sixty minutes to become an expert at using WordStar 1512; but you will have gained experience of the four essential word processing operations, which you will use time and again in the future. These are: loading a document off a floppy disc; making changes to it and adding new material of your own; saving the finished work back on the disc; and finally making a printed copy of it.

There is, of course, a lot more to word processing than this, and in subsequent chapters we shall look at the many other options which you will soon be using. These include printing text in a variety of different styles; using the program's built-in spelling checker; formatting documents with dot commands; the mail-merge facility and its associated database; and a variety of ways of using WordStar 1512 for even more complex work.

For the moment, though, concentrate on the basics which are outlined in this chapter; a secure understanding of WordStar 1512 can only be built on a firm foundation of practice, and trying to rush ahead to more advanced matters before you are quite at ease with simple document creation and editing will only cause confusion and disappointment at the end of the day.

# Introducing WordStar 1512

Although WordStar 1512 was developed for use on the Amstrad PC1512 computer, it works just as well on any IBM-compatible personal computer. The minimum hardware requirements are a monochrome screen and a single disc drive, but a second drive will greatly reduce the amount of disc swapping which is necessary, and so may be considered virtually essential for serious work; a hard disc can also be used. In this book I have usually assumed that you have two drives, though I have also pointed out some differences which will occur where only one drive is available.

WordStar 1512 is designed for maximum ease of use, both for normal document preparation and mail-merge work. Indeed, the latter is particularly important, as the inbuilt mail-merge facility is in effect a purpose-designed database which can also be used for many other purposes.

**WordStar and WordStar 1512** If you are used to other versions of WordStar, you will find that WordStar 1512 is similar to them in some ways but quite different in many others. Partly this is because it is adapted to make the most of the standard PC keyboard layout, rather than using some of the rather arcane sequences of key-presses typical of other versions of WordStar; and partly because it lacks some of the more powerful – but probably rather infrequently-used – facilities of other versions of WordStar, replacing them with the very useful database already mentioned.

# Installing WordStar 1512

WordStar 1512 is supplied on six 5¼" floppy discs; one of these contains the dictionary for the spelling checker, and another is a tutor disc. These **distribution discs** – a distribution disc is one supplied by the manufacturer – do not correspond one-to-one to the working discs which you will use once the program has been properly installed.

Incidentally, even if you did not have to install the program, it would still be most unwise to use the distribution discs. Instead, you should make **working discs** of your own by copying the distribution discs; in this way, if your working discs become worn or damaged, or if you simply lose them, you can simply make new copies from the distribution discs, which should have been put away in a safe place.

**What you need to have** Before you can install the program, you will need to have six blank floppy discs to hand. Five of these must be formatted for use as data discs, and the sixth should be formatted as a system disc.

On a two-drive system, the procedure for formatting the first five discs is as follows: make sure that your working copy of the MS-DOS master disc supplied with your computer is write-protected by sticking a tab over the write-protect notch – don't ever use the original distribution disc! – then put it into Drive A, close the drive's 'door' and then type

FORMAT B:

and press [Return]. Then follow the instructions on the screen.

When the first disc has been formatted, you will be asked: 'Format another (Y/N)?'– press [y] and then [Return] to format the next disc, and so on until all five have been formatted. If you change your mind about formatting a disc, you can abandon the operation with [Ctrl] / [c] – that is, hold down the [Ctrl] key and tap [c].

On a single-drive system, put the MS-DOS disc into the disc drive and type

FORMAT A:

followed by [Return]; again, the prompts on the screen will then tell you what to do.

To format the sixth disc as a system disc, make sure the MS-DOS disc is in Drive A and type

FORMAT B:/S

or

FORMAT A:/S

as appropriate. This last disc should be labelled '1512 SYSTEM'; it is better not to label the others yet, despite what the manual says.

A **system disc**, in case you are wondering, is one which has a copy of the MS-DOS Operating System on it – the purpose of the operating system was described in Chapter One. A system disc can thus be used to start the computer when it is first turned on – often called 'booting' the computer. (If you have not met the expressions 'booting' or 'bootstrapping' before, they have nothing to do with kicking your computer out of the door; they are merely a jocular reference to the computer lifting 'itself by its own bootstraps' so that it is ready to work.)

**On with the installation!** When you have formatted six discs, you are ready to begin installing the program. Put the distribution disc which is labelled 'Disk 1 Installation Disk' in Drive A – the left-hand drive if you have two; then type

INSTALL

and press [Return], and follow the instructions which will appear on the screen.

If you are a little nervous of the installation procedure, you may be reassured to know that a useful Help facility is available once you have chosen single, double or hard disc installation. You will also be given a chance to back out at this point if you decide not to go ahead for some reason; as it is not possible to stop the installation process in the middle and restart it later, this is the point at which you should abandon the installation procedure if you don't have enough formatted discs ready, or if there is any other reason why you will not be able to complete it in one session.

During installation, you will be offered a choice between using the word processing section of the program alone, or using it in conjunction with mail-merge – mail-merge is used in preparing personalised form letters and other related tasks. Even if you do not intend to use the mail-merge facility as such, it is still well worthwhile selecting the mail-merge option, as you will then be able to use the program's powerful database facility.

**The barometer** While the various sections of the WordStar 1512 program are being copied from the distribution discs onto your working discs, progress will be monitored by a 'barometer' on the screen which will indicate roughly what proportion of the files on a particular disc have been copied.

**Take extra care!** On a two-drive system, you will be prompted as installation proceeds to place your new blank formatted floppy discs one at a time in Drive B and the distribution discs in Drive A. *Be very careful not to get them mixed up*, as if you accidentally insert one of the original discs in Drive B, it may be overwritten and the programs and data on it totally lost. The simplest way of avoiding this is by sticking the little write-protect tabs which are always provided with new floppy discs over the write-protect notches on the distribution discs.

If you have a single-drive machine, even greater care is necessary to avoid confusing the distribution discs with your own newly-formatted ones; keep them separated while you work, double-check every time before you give the installation program the signal to proceed (by pressing the [Return] key), put all discs back in their envelopes as soon as you remove them from the disc drives, and label your installed discs when prompted to do so, remembering to write the labels out *before* you stick them on the discs, in case the pressure of the pen damages the discs.

There is a long-standing custom that if a distribution disc is accidentally damaged in some way by the purchaser, the supplier will replace it free of charge, though there is no compulsion to do so. However, times are changing, and you may find that not all sellers of software are so obliging. It is, after all, not unlike buying a dozen eggs at the supermarket, dropping them on the way home, and then returning to the shop for free replacements. So do take all possible precautions when installing this or any other program!

# Making choices with WordStar 1512

A standard way in which computer programs offer choices to the user is by means of **menus** – in computer terms, a menu is simply a selection of choices displayed on the screen – and during the course of installing WordStar 1512, you will be offered several menus similar to Fig. 2.1. Such menus are particularly important in WordStar 1512, as when the program is finally installed and running, most of the choices you will need to make from time to time are governed by menus which are very similar to these.

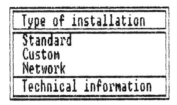

**Fig. 2.1** A WordStar 1512 installation menu

One of the choices on each menu is marked by a highlight bar – blue on a colour monitor – which can be moved up and down the different options either by pressing the ← or ← keys, or, if you are using a mouse, by pulling it towards you to make the bar move down and pushing it away to make it move up. If you try to move the bar either above or below the choices offered, it will simply jump to the other end of the menu.

To select an option, move the bar until the choice you want has been highlighted and then either press the [ Return ] key or click whichever of the mouse buttons corresponds to [ Return ] – usually this is the left-hand button.

**Colour or monochrome?** One important choice which you will be asked to make during the installation of WordStar 1512 concerns the type of screen on which it will be displayed. If you are using the Amstrad PC1512, you should choose the 'Colour' option regardless of whether you are actually using a colour or monochrome screen. This is because the PC1512 treats the monochrome screen as if it were a colour screen, so that it can display shades of grey as well as black and white.

**Non-standard installations** WordStar 1512 can be installed in any of three different ways: Standard, Custom and Network. The first of these will work on almost all computers, but if your computer is non-standard in some way – perhaps it uses high-capacity discs – you may need to choose Custom installation. Network installation is only used where several computers are linked together into a **Local Area Network**, or **LAN**; this is beyond the scope of this book.

Always begin by assuming that a Standard installation will work; if it does not, abort the installation and then start again, this time selecting Custom installation.

For Custom installation on a two-drive machine, choose to have WordStar 1512 copied to Drive B. Then specify the kind of disc drive which is fitted to your computer – the choice is between various sizes and capacities of floppy disc and a hard disc. After this, Custom installation is the same as Standard installation.

**Don't worry about the printer** Another important choice you will eventually have to make concerns the printer. The program is set up to use the Amstrad DMP3000 printer, which is specially designed to complement the computer and which is IBM-compatible. However, nearly all printers will produce satisfactory work, so for most purposes there will be no need to make any immediate changes to the way the program is initially set up.

When you have finished installing the program, put the original discs away in a safe and dust-free place; you will not need them again unless you wish to change some aspect of the installation, or your working discs become faulty. If you feel that you've done enough for now, you should also put your working discs away and then turn the computer off.

# Beginning word processing

To begin a word processing session with WordStar 1512, simply turn the computer on (or reset it if it is already on by holding down [ Ctrl ] and [ Alt ] and tapping the [ Del ] key) and insert the working system disc labelled '1512 System'. When the prompt 'A' is displayed, type

WS1512

and press [ Return ]. The green activity light on the front of Drive A will come on and the WordStar 1512 title page will appear briefly. This will then be replaced by the Opening Menu, shown in Fig. 2.2.

If the computer has already been used in the same session for something else and has not been reset, it is important to reboot it using the correct '1512 System' disc before trying to use WordStar 1512; merely typing 'WS1512; at the ordinary 'A' prompt can result in the program failing to find some files. Specifically, the System Disc must have on it a file called CONFIG.SYS, and CONFIG.SYS must have in it the statement 'Files = 20'. This is because under certain circumstances WordStar 1512 may need to have access to as many as 20 different computer files, and unless 'Files = 20' has been set, it will not be able to do so. The CONFIG.SYS file is stored on the System Disc during the Installation Procedure.

If you have a two-drive system, insert the working disc labelled Text and Data Disc into Drive B; if you only have a single drive, you will be prompted when to put the Text and Data Disc into Drive A.

```
                          F1 = Help
                          Esc = Get out
```

```
┌───────────────────────────────────┐
│ ┌───────────────────────────────┐ │
│ │         Opening Menu          │ │
│ └───────────────────────────────┘ │
│ │Word processing                  │
│ │Printing                         │
│ │Mailing list                     │
│ │List printing                    │
│ │Change settings                  │
│ │File management                  │
│ │Quit                             │
│ │Help                             │
└───────────────────────────────────┘
```

Use ↓ and ↑ cursor keys to move highlight bar to a command.
     Press ↵ to choose highlighted command.

**Fig. 2.2** The WordStar 1512 Opening Menu

At this point, you could immediately select the Word processing option by simply
pressing [Return], as the highlight bar will already be on that option. However,
it is worth taking a slightly longer look at the workings of this menu, as it embodies
features of WordStar 1512 which we shall meet many times as we become more
familiar with the program.

**Looking at the WordStar 1512 screen** First, at the top right-hand corner of
the screen are displayed two key assignments which are used in many different
situations in WordStar 1512: [F1] to call up 'Help' and [Esc] to 'Get out'.

Second, at the foot of the screen are displayed some further instructions, telling
you to move the highlight bar to the desired command with the cursor keys and
then to confirm the choice with [Return].

Although these instructions are accurate as far as they go, they do not tell the whole
story, as there are two other ways in which a selection can be made from most
WordStar 1512 menus.

The first of these is to use the mouse to move the highlight bar instead of the cursor
keys, clicking on the button when the appropriate option has been highlighted.

**Making quick choices** The second approach is even faster. With most
WordStar 1512 menus, it is possible to make your choice by simply pressing the

27

initial letter of the option which you want to select: thus to select Word processing, press [W] (either in capitals or lower case); to choose Help, press [H], and so on. Don't press [Return] when making your choice in this way.

Unless your version of WordStar 1512 has been installed for a hard disc machine, you will now be prompted to remove the 1512 System Disc from Drive A and to replace it with the one labelled '1512 WP'; on a two drive machine this disc will remain in Drive A nearly all the time you are creating or editing a document.

At the same time as you put the '1512 WP' disc in Drive A, place your Text and Data Disc in Drive B – on a single drive machine, you will be prompted to put this in Drive A at the appropriate time. Press [Return] when everything is ready.

**The Main Menu** After a few moments, the Main Menu will appear on the screen. From this menu you can choose to edit the 'current file'– the document which was most recently worked on – or to select a different file from those on the Text and Data Disc.

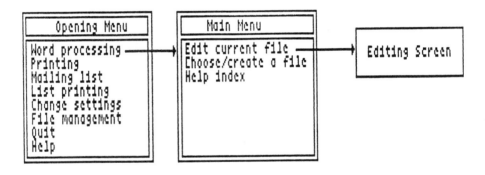

**Fig. 2.3** Getting from the Opening Menu to the Editing Screen

Using WordStar 1512 involves a great deal of movement from one menu to another, and at first, you may worry about becoming lost. Figure 2.3 is a little 'menu map' to show you the route that you should follow. If you *do* ever get lost, you can always get back to the Opening Menu by pressing [Esc] enough times.

## Creating a new document

The Main Menu is shown in Fig. 2.4. In the lower half of this menu are listed details of the 'current' file – that is, the one which was worked on most recently – and above this is an option box from which you can choose, by moving the highlight bar up and down, whether you want to do more work on the 'current file', or choose or create another file, or look at the Help index.

```
┌─────────────────────────────────────┐
│║            Main Menu               ║│
│╠═════════════════════════════════════│
│║Edit current file                   ║│
│║Choose/create a file                ║│
│║Help index                          ║│
└─────────────────────────────────────┘
```

**Fig. 2.4** The Main Menu

**The Help Index** The Help index is a very full listing (occupying 5 screen 'pages') of various topics on which help is available, and you might like to have a quick glance at it. Move the highlight bar to the Help index option and then press [Return], and the first 'page' of the index will appear. You can browse among the pages, moving from one to the other with [PgUp] and [PgDn]; when you come across a topic which interests you, put the highlight bar on it and press [Return] to have more detailed information on that topic displayed. Press [Esc] once to clear this detailed information from the screen and again to leave the Help index.

**Choosing a file** One of the documents which is stored on the Text and Data Disc is called PRACTICE. If PRACTICE appears opposite 'FILENAME' on the Main Menu, then this will be the 'current file', and you can open it by simply pressing [Return]. If PRACTICE is not the current file, then proceed as follows.

From the Main Menu, select Choose/create a file either by moving the highlight bar down with the cursor keys and then pressing [Return], by pulling it down with the mouse (pull the mouse towards you to make the highlight bar move down) and clicking whichever mouse button represents the [Return] key – the left button on the Amstrad PC1512 – or by simply pressing [c], either as a capital or lower case letter.

The screen will clear and you will be offered the Change/create a file menu illustrated in Fig. 2.5. This is the menu which you will use whenever you make revisions to a file which has already been created (other than the 'current file') or create a new one.

The Choose/create a file menu is divided into two parts. The top half shows the name of the current disc drive and directory and the name of the current file (which will normally be the file shown as current in the Main Menu).

In the lower half of the menu are listed all the files stored on the current disc and directory, showing their names, their size in bytes, and the date and time when each file was last changed. If there are more files than can be shown at one time, the display will be broken up into 'pages'; press [PgDn] or [PgUp] to move forwards or backwards to view these other pages.

```
┌─────────────────────────────────────────────────────┐
│ Choose a file to edit/create.                          │
├─────────────────────────────────────────────────────┤
│     Drive b:                                          │
│ Directory \                                           │
│   Filename PRACTICE                    Page 1         │
├─────────────────────────────────────────────────────┤
│ filename           size      date        time         │
│                                                       │
│ SAMPLE.MLD         2318    17-12-86      10.27        │
│ SAMPLE.MLI           66    01-07-86      15.48        │
│ MERGE.LTR           554    03-07-86      14.54        │
│ CHARSET             951    01-07-86      17.13        │
│ COMBINE             327    01-07-86      17.11        │
│ PRACTICE            431    01-12-86      15.42        │
└─────────────────────────────────────────────────────┘
```

**Fig. 2.5** The Choose/create a file menu

We saw earlier that with most WordStar 1512 menus it was possible to make a selection by merely pressing the initial letter of the option being chosen –'W' for Word processing, 'H' for Help and so on. This is only possible because all the options available on these menus begin with different initial letters. There is no guarantee that this will apply to file names, so this short cut is not available from this menu.

The highlight bar can be moved quite freely to any part of the menu, so to change the current disc, directory or file, you need only put the bar over the appropriate item and begin to type in the new details. There is no need to erase the information that is already there, as that will vanish as soon as you begin to enter the new name. name.

**Choosing a file** To select the file named PRACTICE, you could either make sure that the highlight bar is next to 'Filename' at the top of the menu and then type in the name 'PRACTICE', in either capitals or lower-case letters, pressing [ Return ] when you have done, or, more simply, move the highlight bar down until it is resting on PRACTICE in the lower panel of the screen and then press [ Return ]. If you select a file by typing its name, there is always the possibility that you will make a typing error, so it is generally simpler to select an existing file by moving the highlight bar to it and pressing [ Return ] than by typing its name.

**The Typing Screen** The Choose/create a file menu will be replaced by the screen shown in Fig. 2.6. This is known as Editing or Typing Screen, and it is on this screen that all text work with WordStar 1512 is performed.

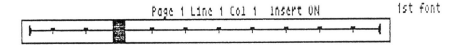

Page 1 Line 1 Col 1  Insert ON          1st font

**Fig. 2.6** The Top of the Typing Screen

At the top right of the screen are reminders of two key-assignments which should be familiar by now: The [Esc] key to 'Get out', that is to finish creating or editing a document and to either save it or abandon it; and function key [F1] to display a Help page. To these is now added function key [F2], which calls up two additional 'Editing Menus' from which bold type, underlines and various other features can be accessed.

**The Status Line** Further down the screen is the Status Line. This is a kind of permanent reminder, showing the number of the current page, line and column, whether you are in Insert or Overwrite Mode, and the current printer Font.

**The Ruler Line** Below this again is the Ruler line, which shows the left and right margins of typed work, with the preset Tab positions marked by small inverted triangles. At the Column 1 position of the ruler line is a rectangular highlight – light blue on a colour screen – which shows the current column position of the text cursor. The cursor itself is in the text space below the Ruler line; it takes either of two forms – a flashing rectangle when WordStar 1512 is in Overwrite Mode and a flashing underline when the program is in Insert Mode.

Beneath the ruler, there may be a little text, perhaps explaining that PRACTICE is there for you to experiment with. To get rid of this, hold down the [Ctrl] key and tap [←Del]. The top line will vanish; go on holding [Ctrl] and tapping [←Del] until the whole screen under the ruler line – the 'text space'– is completely blank.

**Flags** The extreme right-hand edge of the text space is occupied by a column of upwards pointing arrows, ←. These are among a variety of marginal symbols called **flags**, and their meaning is 'Text begins above this point'.

You will encounter many other flags as you become more familiar with WordStar 1512. Perhaps the most common is the paragraph marker ¶, which appears when the [Return] key is pressed at the end of a paragraph. Yet other symbols are used when dot commands are typed in. (Dot commands are special formatting commands; they are introduced in Chapters Five and Eight.) Ordinary lines of text which are not the last line of a paragraph have no symbols associated with them in the right margin.

31

# Starting to type

Entering text with a word processor is quite different from using a typewriter; the differences that strike most people immediately are that it is much quieter and that you can correct your mistakes without recourse to correcting fluid or an eraser. Jump right in by trying to copy the text shown in Fig. 2.7, including the mistakes. Don't worry if you make a few more errors of your own, as they will give you more practice at correcting mistakes later.

```
Try to copy this short text as accurately as you can.  You may
make occasional typing errors like the one in this line, butt
do not let this bother you.  You should not press [Return] at the
end of each line, but only at the end of paragraphs.

        The second paragraph has been set in by using the [Tab] key;
this is used to indent the begining of paragraphs and for other,
related, purposes. You will notice that when the return key is
pressed, a special marker appears on the right-hand edge of the
screen.
```

Fig. 2.7 Some text to input

**The moving cursor writes** If you are unfamiliar with word processors, you may notice a couple of interesting things as you type. First, there is no ribbon slot showing the place where the next character will appear; its place is taken by a highlight on the ruler Line, and by the cursor showing where you are in the text space. As you type, the cursor moves across the screen to indicate the position where the next character will appear, and the highlight marking the column you are in moves along the Ruler Line in step with it. The column counter on the Status Line is also updated continuously.

**Auto-repeat** Second, the keys have a feature called **auto-repeat**; this means that any key which is held down will repeat at quite high speed. The same is true of the delete keys as well, so it pays to develop a light touch or you could find yourself erasing substantial chunks of your work by accident.

**Word wrap** Finally, there is no bell as you approach the right margin. Instead, any word which is too long to fit inside the margins will be automatically removed from the line on which you have typed it and will reappear at the beginning of the following line. This feature is called **word wrap**.

One consequence of this is that it is unnecessary – indeed, it is positively wrong – to press [ Return ] at the end of each line, as you would need to do with a typewriter. The only time when you should press the [ Return ] key is to force a new line at the end of a paragraph.

**Correcting mistakes** When you have finished typing, look back over what you have done. With an ordinary typewriter, correcting the various errors would mean that you would have to get out the eraser or correcting fluid – indeed, you might decide to simply retype a whole page if the corrections which needed doing were very complicated or numerous – but fortunately none of that is necessary with WordStar 1512. Indeed, the whole point of word processors is that they enable you to carry out all your corrections on screen, so that only a perfect copy of your work will actually appear on paper.

To erase a typing error, simply move the cursor (using either the cursor keys or the mouse) until it is resting either immediately on or just after the place where the slip is. Then use the [ ←Del ] to erase a mistyped character to the *left* of the cursor, or the [ Del ] key 'usually in the bottom row under the cursor keys) to erase the character which is lying at the cursor position. For example, to change *butt* into *but*, either put the cursor on the space at the end of the line and then press [ ← Del ], or put the cursor on the second *t* and press [ Del ].

This first piece of word processing is intended primarily as an erasing and replacing exercise, so practise using the cursor keys or mouse and the Delete keys until you feel quite certain that you understand how they work.

## More ways of moving around the screen

In addition to the four cursor keys, WordStar 1512 offers several other keys and key-combinations with which you can move rapidly to the place you want in even a very long document.

The simplest way of moving the cursor doesn't use the keyboard at all; use the mouse, sliding it backwards to move the cursor towards the start of the text or pulling it forwards to move it towards the end of the document. There is no separate mouse cursor in WordStar 1512, but the ordinary text cursor responds to the mouse, and can be taken to any part of the document. If it is taken to the top or bottom of the display, it will cause the text on the screen to scroll rapidly up or down.

Many users find it a little awkward to transfer between the keyboard and the mouse during an editing session. A hint which you may find helpful is to manipulate the mouse with the *left* hand, leaving the right hand free to peck at individual keys.

**Important key combinations** If you are a confirmed keyboard user, or perhaps have no mouse, [ PgUp ] and [ PgDn ] will display respectively the previous and the next screen 'pages' of 18 lines. [Ctrl ] / [ PgUp ] (holding down [ Ctrl ] and tapping [ PgUp ]) will take the cursor to the beginning of the first line of the text, and [ Ctrl ] / [ PgDn ] will take the cursor to the last character in the text. Unlike some word processing programs, these moves are usually virtually instantaneous, though they may not be quite so fast with very long documents.

[ Home ] moves the cursor to the 'home position', at the top left of the text area; text is not scrolled when it is pressed. [ End ] moves the cursor to the beginning of the last line shown on the screen, again without scrolling the text. [ Ctrl ] / [ Home ] takes the cursor to the beginning of the line which it is on, and [ Ctrl ] / [ End ] takes it to the end of the line – that is, to the last character on the line, and not to the right-hand margin.

Finally, [Ctrl]/[←] moves the cursor one word to the left, and [Ctrl]/[→] moves it one word to the right.

**Inserting new material** Of course, correcting mistakes is not just a matter of taking the cursor to the right place and then erasing wrongly-typed characters; it is often necessary to insert new material into what you have already written.

How this is done depends on whether you are in Insert or Overwrite Mode. The former is the usual default with WordStar 1512, although it can be changed, and it simply means that whatever you type in at the cursor position will force whatever else is to the right of the cursor on the same line further to the right to make way for the new material. Overwrite Mode, on the other hand, replaces what is already on the screen with the material which is typed in.

For instance, to insert the word *please* after *but* in the first paragraph, place the cursor on the *d* of *do*, and then type in the new word.

To change from Insert to Overwrite Mode, press [Ins]; press [Ins] again to change back. The Status Line messages 'Insert ON' and 'Insert OFF', and the different shapes taken by the cursor, will help you to remember which mode you are in at any given time.

# Keeping the text tidy

You may have noticed when you were erasing mistakes that if the line on which you were working was shortened sufficiently, then the first word of the next line would be drawn up to the end of it – and if that in turn caused the second line to be sufficiently shortened, then material would be drawn up into *that* line from the the line below, and so on to the end of the paragraph, in a kind of backward cascade action.

This useful feature is called automatic paragraph reforming, or reformatting. It ensures that, no matter how much material you delete from a line, your work will always be laid out as efficiently as possible between the left and right margins. We shall see later that there are some occasions when automatic reformatting is not appropriate; when this is the case, you can turn it off.

Automatic reformatting also keeps your work tidy when new material is being added; if a line becomes too long to fit between the established margins, the last word on the line will be word wrapped onto the line below, and if necessary that line will also be changed, and so on to the end of the paragraph.

# Leaving the typing screen

With some word processors, it is possible to print a document which is in the computer's memory but which has not been saved onto disc. This is not possible with WordStar 1512, so when you are happy with your work on PRACTICE, leave the typing screen by pressing [Esc].

After a brief delay, you will be offered the short menu shown in Fig. 2.8. The Save option will save your new text on disc, while Abandon will cause it to be lost. Choose Save in any of the usual ways; the access light on the drive containing the Text and Data Disc will come on as the new document is saved, and you will then be taken directly back to the Main Menu. Then press [Esc] again, and you will go back to the Opening Menu.

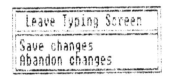

Fig. 2.8 The Save/Abandon menu

# Printing your work

If you have a printer connected to the parallel (Centronics) port of the computer, you can now make a 'hard copy' of the document PRACTICE. Most printers are of this kind. If you aren't sure, check into which socket the printer should be plugged at the back of the computer: if it plugs into a socket marked PARALLEL PRINTER or CENTRONICS or PRN, then it is a parallel printer.

Users of parallel printers should skip the next section, which contains special advice for users with serial printers, and go straight to the section headed 'Getting ready to print'.

## For users of serial printers only!

If you have a parallel printer, *don't follow any of these instructions*, or you will find that you cannot print your work out and that the computer will 'lock up' when you try to do so.

If you are a serial printer user, leave WordStar 1512 by pressing [Esc] until you are at the Opening Menu and then selecting the Quit option. You will be prompted to put the 1512 System Disc into Drive A, and the program will then end.

Put your working copy of the MS-DOS System Disc into Drive A. This disc should have on it a file called MODE.EXE. To redirect all printer output from parallel

35

port 1 (where a parallel printer would normally be connected) to serial port 1 (probably the only serial port on your computer) enter the command

MODE LPT1:=COM1:

(there are no spaces and the colons are essential) and press [Return]. The disc access light will come on and you should see the message:

`LPT1: redirected to COM1:`
`Resident portion of MODE loaded`

If instead you get the message: 'Bad command or file name', check that you have entered the MODE command exactly as shown above, and that the disc in Drive A does have the MODE.EXE file on it.

Assuming that everything has gone well, put the WS1512 System Disc in Drive A and restart the program by typing

WS1512

and pressing [Return]. Don't reset the computer, or it will forget that it should be sending printer output to the serial port. From now until you turn the computer off, all material being sent to the printer will be directed to the serial port.

# Getting ready to print

Prepare for printing by checking that the printer is turned on and that paper has been fed in, and double-check that the cable connections between the computer and the printer are snug; if the connector at the computer end of the cable is equipped with screws, see that they are drawn tight so that the cable cannot slip while printing takes place.

When you are certain that everything is ready, and the Opening Menu is displayed on the screen, choose the Printing option in any of the usual ways. Unless you are using a hard disc equipped machine, you will be prompted to remove the floppy disc labelled '1512WP' from Drive A and to replace it with the disc labelled 'Printing'. On a two-drive machine, the Text and Data disc must not be removed from Drive B; if you have only one drive, you will be prompted when to insert it in Drive A for printing. The route you are following is shown in the menu map in Fig. 2.9.

After you have pressed [Return] to confirm that the 'Printing' disc has been inserted into Drive A, the Print Menu will be displayed; it is shown here as Fig. 2.10. PRACTICE is the 'current file'–the one which has most recently been worked on–so start printing by choosing Begin Printing Current File. (The program assumes that you are using an Amstrad DMP3000 printer, but this shouldn't make any difference to printing your work.)

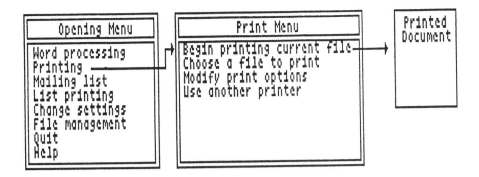

**Fig. 2.9** The route to printing a document

Within a few moments, the Print Menu will be replaced by a barometer showing how much of the document remains to be printed, and almost immediately the printer should begin to work.

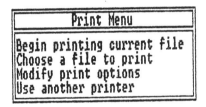

**Fig. 2.10** The Print Menu

**The printer buffer** The barometer doesn't actually illustrate how much of the document has been printed, but rather how much of it has been sent to the printer. Most printers have **buffers**, which are temporary storage areas in which text is held before being printed, and these may hold quite substantial amounts of text before printing it, so what the bar graph really shows is how much of the document has been transferred to this buffer.

When everything has been printed, the printer will feed to the bottom of the current sheet of paper. By then the screen display will again be showing the Print Menu. Press [Esc] once more to return to the Opening Menu, removing the Printing disc when you are prompted, take the printed copy of PRACTICE out of the printer and you have finished.

## Problems with printing

If you are using a serial printer and your work has not printed satisfactorily, and none of the ideas suggested below seem to work, then you may find that you will not get acceptable output until you have adjusted several settings which govern the way in which your computer handles serial output. Typical problems include the loss or garbling of part of your text or even the total refusal of the printer to respond to the computer. Problems such as these are beyond the scope of this chapter, but they are discussed in detail in Chapter Three.

Users of parallel printers should generally find that most printers will produce an acceptable result as long as no special effects such as underlining are required. Assuming that your printer has worked reasonably satisfactorily, you can continue to use it until you are ready to install a new printer file, as described in the next chapter.

However, this compromise route may result in some problems; here we shall take a brief look at the most common ones.

## If the printer does not work at all

If nothing happens at the printer at all, check the printer manual to see that the paper is being fed in correctly; most printers have an 'out of paper' check, and if you have taken the paper through an incorrect path, you may have bypassed this, leading the printer to the false conclusion that it has no paper. If this doesn't work, check to see if there is a switch or button labelled 'On line/Of line' or 'On line/Standby'; if there is one, make sure that it is set for 'On line'.

## Faint printing

If the printer works, but produces only a faint impression, this may be due to low mains voltage, an incorrectly-tapped transformer (look for a voltage-change switch) or just to a worn ribbon; sometimes a similar effect is caused by the ribbon not being properly advanced as the print head travels along. Most dot-matrix printers have a positioning lever with which the print head can be moved nearer or further from the ribbon: the further back it is moved, the stronger will be the impression (and the noisier will be the printer).

## Unwanted blank lines

If your work has been printed with a blank line between each line of text, then you may find that this can be corrected by altering a special switch, called a DIP-switch, on the printer. Such switches are sometimes on the back panel of the printer and sometimes inside it; on some models, they can only be reached by taking off a cover plate.

**DIP Switches** Your printer may have several other switches arranged side-by-side with the line-feed switch; these may control such features as the number of lines per inch (setting to either 6 or 8), the number of lines per page (66 and 72 are typical values) and the number of characters per inch. The most common and useful combination is 6 lines per inch and 66 lines per page.

Your printer manual will tell you exactly what switches there may be; bear in mind that not all countries' products adhere to the European convention that a switch is 'On' when it is down and 'Off' when it is up.

If you cannot find any reference in the printer manual to a line-feed switch, see if there is one labelled Carriage Return; this will have the same function. If there is a switch offering a choice between 0A and 0A + 0D, or between 10 and 10 + 13, this will be the one you need; choose the former setting. Don't worry if none of that makes sense at the moment, as all will be explained later on.

## Paper position

Should the paper be positioned too far to the right or the left, so that some text is printed off the edge on one side or the other, you will probably find that there are margin controls on the printer itself which you can reset, or that the paper-guide (on a single-sheet printer) or sprockets (on a printer using continuous-form stationery) can be slid along to a more suitable position. If you cannot adjust the printer in this way, you will have to alter the settings of WordStar 1512; how to do this is described in the following chapter.

## After printing

Despite everything you have just read, you will probably find that your work will print out without any trouble at all, and even if you *do* have difficulties, they will probably disappear for good once you have made a couple of adjustments.

It may be a good idea to take a break now, and review what you have learned. Don't just turn the computer off – this is a bad habit which can sometimes lead to you losing the file on which you have been working! Instead, select the Quit option, confirm it by pressing [ Return ], and put the 1512 System Disc in when prompted to do so; the computer is now ready for whatever other work you may want to do. If you have finished with the computer for now, remember to take the discs out of the disc drives and put them away safely before disconnecting the power.

## Postscript

This chapter has dealt with creating and printing a simple WordStar 1512 document. It is important before going on that you should be able to find your way between the Opening Menu and the typing screen, and understand how to carry out elementary editing with a document using the cursor keys, the mouse if you have one, and the various [ Del ] keys.

In addition to PRACTICE, there is a second file on the Text and Data Disc which you may find helpful; it is called LETTER. This is a ready-prepared business letter which has a number of errors and omissions in it, and which you can play around with and amend as you wish.

Even the simple word processing which we have done already is so much easier than messing about with a typewriter that you will find it almost impossible to ever go back to those bad old days of correcting fluid and an eraser. But don't feel tempted to rest on your laurels! We have only begun to scratch the surface of what you can do with WordStar 1512, and in the chapters which follow you will learn many more ways in which it can be useful to you.

# *CHAPTER THREE*

# **Adding some style**

## Preview

In the first part of this chapter we shall look at some of the problems that can crop up if you use a serial printer. If you have one and found when you tried to print your work out that it didn't work properly, then read through this section very carefully. If you have a parallel printer then you can skip to the section headed 'The Change Settings Menu', though you may find that some of the material about serial printers may be helpful if you are using another serial device such as a modem with your computer.

Everything beyond the section on the Change Settings Menu is for everyone. As you work through it, we will show you how to make changes to the way WordStar 1512 works, as well as how to match the program to your own printer.

All these changes are only semi-permanent; if you buy a new printer, or for some other reason decide that you would like to alter the way the program has been set up, you can always come back and change things again later.

## More about serial printers

Serial printers must be connected to the computer by means of the serial, or RS232C, interface. In Chapter Two we saw how to redirect printer output to this interface with the MS-DOS MODE command; later in this chapter we shall see that it is also possible to do this directly from inside WordStar 1512.

If your serial printer works properly already then you can consider yourself either very fortunate or particularly well-advised by your supplier, as the serial interface is often a source of difficulty. If things didn't go so smoothly, and you had remembered to use the MODE command as shown in the last chapter, then you will need to spend at least an hour, and maybe much longer, working through the following sections; be prepared to call on expert help if all else fails.

41

# Setting parameters for serial printers

The parameters which must be set before a serial device like a printer will work properly include the rate at which data is sent from the computer (called the **baud rate**), the number of bits per character, the number of stop-bits per character, and whether and how transmitted data is checked for **parity** – a fairly crude way of ensuring that what has been sent by the computer is the same as what the printer has received and that it hasn't been corrupted along the way.

If your serial printer is giving no response at all, or the data is being corrupted, check the printer manual to ensure that the various settings are the same for the printer as they are for the RS232C interface; in particular, check the baud rate and how many bits are being used for data transmission. All the values can be reset with the MODE command; for example, the command

MODE COM1:1200,E,7,1,P

will set output at 1200 baud, even parity, seven bits per character, 1 stop-bit per character. The final 'P' means that the computer will continuously try to send information to the printer as long as it is on-line. For more details of this and similar commands, check your computer manual.

If the baud rate at which the printer works can be adjusted, try using a lower figure; it is usual to choose the fastest rate which still transmits data cleanly; the faster the transmission, the greater the susceptibility to transmission errors arising from electronic 'noise'.

**Problems with pins** If none of this works, your problems may lie in the actual cable connections between the printer and the computer. The biggest problems lie with pins 2 and 3, which are the data wires. Which of these is the Transmitted Data Wire and which is the Received Data Wire depends on whether a particular device is configured as Data Terminal Equipment (DTE) or Data Communication Equipment (DCE). If you have problems with any serial device, this is a reasonable place to start looking for solutions.

The only other essential connection on an RS232C interface is pin 7, which is Signal Ground; that is, it is the return path between the two ends of the transmission. These three wires (2, 3 and 7) are in themselves sufficient for transmitting all data, and all the other wires are only there for control purposes – **handshaking** is the jargon term.

Exactly how this is done differs from system to system. For example, many systems use pin 6 as a Data Set Ready pin, which might be used by a printer to say 'Send me a character'; but on some devices, this pin is unconnected.

You may by now be wondering what is meant when someone advertises a particular printer or other device as RS232C compatible! The answer is that they usually mean that some of the pins conform fully to the standard and none of the others actually violate it, though the device can probably only receive or transmit a small proportion of the total range of signals which a full RS232C can handle.

**Gender problems** A final problem is that some equipment is sold with male connections (DB25P) and some with female connections (DB25S). Special converters, often called 'Gender Benders', are available to convert one type of connection to the other.

Some equipment may have only the 'budget' version of the RS232C port, called RS423, so be very careful to ensure that your cable matches the connections you actually have on your equipment.

Your dealer is the best person to advise you here; as a general rule it is important to make sure that the cable which you buy does actually work with your computer and printer. There are several specialist cable-suppliers who can provide any connections you may need, and these advertise regularly in the various computing magazines.

# The Change Settings Menu

From here on is for everyone! By the time you have worked through to the end of the chapter, your copy of WordStar 1512 will have been changed to suit your own preferences and the kind of printer – or printers – which you have.

There's no need to get through the whole job in one go; if you prefer, you can work on Word processing settings in your first session, Page layout in your second and so on. However, if you are using a serial printer you will have to use the MS-DOS MODE command to redirect output to the RS232C interface whenever you want to print a document until you have completed the Customise printers section; once this is done, you will no longer need to use MODE LPT1:=COM1: before starting WordStar 1512.

Begin the process of configuring your copy of WordStar 1512 by booting the computer with the 1512 System Disc. When the Opening Menu appears, select the Change settings option. The Change Settings Menu will appear on the screen; it is shown here as Fig. 3.1.

For the moment we shall only consider matters concerned with the appearance of ordinary documents, either on the screen or when printed; other options, such as Mailing list settings, will be considered later. You can return to the Change Settings Menu whenever you need, though you will probably not need to do so very often.

```
┌─────────────────────────────────┐
│     Change Settings Menu         │
├─────────────────────────────────┤
│ Word processing settings         │
│ Mailing list settings            │
│ Drive/directory                  │
│ Page layout                      │
│ Set up printers                  │
│ Customise printers               │
└─────────────────────────────────┘
```

**Fig. 3.1** The Change Setting Menu

# Word processing settings

Choose the first option on the Change Settings Menu; the screen will clear, and the display shown in Fig. 3.2 will be shown.

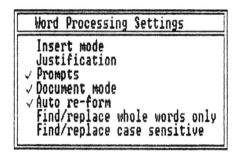

```
┌─────────────────────────────────────┐
│     Word Processing Settings         │
├─────────────────────────────────────┤
│    Insert mode                       │
│    Justification                     │
│  ✓ Prompts                           │
│  ✓ Document mode                     │
│  ✓ Auto re-form                      │
│    Find/replace whole words only     │
│    Find/replace case sensitive       │
└─────────────────────────────────────┘
```

**Fig. 3.2** Choosing start values for word processing

The purpose of this screen is to enable the user to change a number of WordStar 1512's factory-set default values. Each line of the display refers to one option: if there is a tick against it, that option is selected; if there is no tick, the option is deselected. To select any option which has no tick against it, place the cursor against it and press [ + ]; to deselect an option, put the cursor against it and press [Del].

It may be comforting to know that none of the changes you make will take effect until you press [Return]; if you want to get back to the original settings at any time, just press [Esc] and any changes you have already made will be abandoned and you will be returned to the Opening Menu. The usual Help page is also available, accessed as always by pressing Function Key [F1].

**Insert Mode** The program as supplied has a tick against the option 'Insert Mode'; in other words, when you reach the Typing Screen, the default is that new

44

keystrokes are regarded as inserts rather than as overwrites. Most people find that this is the most convenient way to work – if you are in Overwrite Mode, you can too easily type over the top of something you didn't really want to lose.

If you deselect Insert Mode at the Word processing settings menu, you will still be able to reinstate it at the Typing Screen; all that you will have done is to change the default when you first reach the Typing Screen, so that unless you change the setting with [ Ins ] your keystrokes will be treated as Overwrites.

**Justify** The second option available on the screen is Justification; the factory-set option is to have justification turned off.

**Justification** refers to creating an even right margin by inserting extra spaces (called **soft spaces**) when the document is printed. Many people consider that a justified right margin is more professional, and if you share this view you can select Justify with the [ + ] key.

There are, however, certain disadvantages to justification. Some people find the extra spaces which are inserted into the text rather ugly, especially where the lines are comparatively short; text which is being prepared for publication is generally best left 'ragged', as many sub-editors find it hard to gauge the 'extent' of text which has been justified. If your printer can produce proportionally spaced text, you may find it does not lend itself very well to justification.

Regardless of whether Justify is on or off, WordStar 1512 makes no attempt to justify text on screen; rather, this is done automatically during printing. This is partly because there are difficulties in the representation of soft spaces on screen (they cannot be deleted like ordinary spaces, for example) and partly because merging other text into a document file, during a mail merge perhaps, would in any case destroy any resemblance between the image on the screen and the final appearance of the printed work.

**Document mode** We have already mentioned ASCII the American Standard Code for Information Interchange, which allocates a unique code number for every computer character, printable or otherwise – and you may have made the assumption that a document which has been word processed with WordStar 1512 is actually made up of no more than a succession of these codes.

In reality this is only true to a limited extent. Most word processing programs store and handle most text according to ASCII conventions (though there are a few awkward ones which do not), but in addition they use a number of 'control characters' which are inserted into the file to identify the beginning and end of such features as bold or underlined text, superscripts and subscripts, margin settings, the end of the file, etc. These features and the codes which govern them vary from one word processing program to another, though for most purposes the user will never need to be aware of the existence of them.

**Sharing data files** Because different programs use slightly different control codes, you will find that using one word processing program to look at a document created by a different program can cause a few problems. Most of these can be overcome with some judicious editing, and WordStar 1512 can in any case deal with text created by such programs as SuperCalc3, Lotus 1-2-3 and other versions of WordStar without any difficulty.

If you want to see just how different a WordStar 1512 file is from true ASCII, put the Text and Data Disc into Drive A (at some time when WordStar 1512 is not running, of course) and enter the command

TYPE *filename*

giving the name of any fairly short file on the disc, and then press [ Return ]. The file will appear on the screen, clearly revealing the control characters.

## Creating plain ASCII files
You may have occasion to produce a version of a file which has all the control characters stripped out of it. Reasons for doing this include creating pure ASCII batch files for your computer's operating system, and using WordStar 1512 to write programs in Basic, Pascal and other computer languages where for some reason you might not want to use the built-in editor usually supplied with the language. Pure ASCII files are also used for documents which are to be sent through a modem and down the telephone wires.

If none of this makes any sense to you, then you will not need to change WordStar 1512 from Document mode; all the files which it creates will be in WordStar format, which is pretty close to ASCII anyway. If on the other hand you will be using WordStar 1512 to create ASCII files, deselect Document mode by placing the cursor against the Doc Mode prompt and pressing [ Del ].

## Prompts
Though we have not met them yet, there are many places in WordStar 1512 where detailed instructions are placed on the screen in response to some action you have taken. For example, when creating bold or underlined text, a prompt will appear telling you to mark the beginning of the block which is to be changed by taking the text cursor to it and then pressing [ Return ], and then to mark the end of the block in the same way.

After you have become familiar with this procedure, you will find that the on-screen prompts tend to slow you down. When this happens, you can speed up your work by deselecting Prompts; if you change your mind later, or the program is to be used by someone who is less familiar with it than you are, you can always reinstate Prompts.

## Automatic reform

We have already seen that text is constantly reformatted as it is edited: that is, no matter how much material you add or delete, your material will still fit neatly between the set margins.

This automatic reformatting of text can be extremely useful, especially when you are creating documents which have a relatively straightforward layout. If most of your writing involves documents which use only one type-size, use the same margins throughout and have no temporary indents, you should leave automatic reforming selected.

If on the other hand you habitually work with documents which have varying margins or which use a column layout or indents, then you should deselect Automatic reform. When during the editing procedure certain lines become too long to fit within the margins and others become too short, you can reform that paragraph by choosing the Paragraph reform command from one of the two command menus reached by pressing Function Key [F2] as described further on in this chapter.

**Find and replace options** One of the most useful and powerful features of word processors is their ability to scan through a document file to find any word or phrase – indeed, any group of characters – which you have specified. Even more powerfully, this 'search string' can be replaced, either instantly or after you have given confirmation, by another group of characters, the 'replacement string'. (**String** is a common computing term for any group of characters – it can be numbers, letters, a dot command, a mathematical symbol or whatever.)

You can choose from the Word processing settings screen whether your search and search-and-replace operations will find Whole words only; and whether searches will be Case sensitive or not; we shall look at these two choices in order.

When it is searching for a particular group of characters – the 'target string' – the computer behaves in a totally brainless fashion: set to find the sequence 'cat', it would register a 'hit' not only with *cat*, but also with *cat*alogue, *cat*astrophe and even de*cat*hlon.

**Whole words searches** If the Whole words only option is selected, this will not occur, and thus false hits will be avoided. There is, however, the corresponding disadvantage that you might sometimes want to find a word by specifying only part of it. Imagine, for example, that you know that you have used either 'specify' or 'specification' in a long piece of writing, but you cannot remember which – or perhaps you have used the two words, and want to find instances of both. It is convenient to be able to conduct a search for some element that is common to both words: 'specif', say, which will register a hit on both our target words. In this case, you would not want a Whole words only search.

**Case sensitive searches** Case sensitive searches are those which score a hit only when the combination of capitals and lower case letters in the search string is exactly the same as those in the target string. Thus a Case sensitive search would not match 'Cat' with 'cat'.

# Confirming the new settings

When you have finished making your choices from the Word processing settings screen, press [Return] to confirm and save them. The values will be recorded on the 1512 System Disc, and will apply whenever you use the program.

Alternatively, press [Esc] to abandon your work; any settings you have made will be lost, and the next time you use WordStar 1512, it will continue to use the factory-set defaults.

## Page layout

Continue the customising process by selecting Page layout from the Change Settings Menu. This will take you first to the Change Printer Menu, shown in Fig. 3.3, on which the names of up to three different printers can be shown. (The first position is already occupied by the Amstrad DMP3000.) These are the printers which have been named from the Set up printers option, which we shall see later.

Fig. 3.3 The Change Printer Menu

Whether you are using the DMP3000 or not, make sure the highlight bar is at the top of the box and press [Return]; you will then be shown the second, and much more complex screen, reproduced here as Fig. 3.4, from which almost every feature of page layout can be controlled.

The Page Layout Screen can be divided into two halves vertically: on the left is a diagram showing the location on the page of various page layout features, while on the right is a summary box into which you can insert the actual values which you want. To insert a new value, merely position the cursor over the value you wish to change and begin typing; the old value will be removed at once. Should you encounter any difficulty, the familiar Function Key [F1] will call up a Help page; you can in any case abandon your work by pressing [Esc] at any time.

All the values which are set on this screen can be reset from the Typing Screen in one way or another – usually through the use of dot commands, which we shall meet later. Basically, this screen controls the What You See Is What You Get aspect of WordStar 1512, but this can be quite dramatically altered during printout, as we shall see.

## Margins

Margins are those areas of the paper which do not normally contain text. WordStar 1512 has seven different margins: left, right, top, bottom, page offset, header and footer.

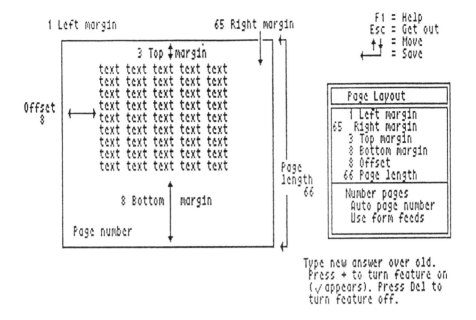

**Fig. 3.4** The Page Layout Screen

**Left and right margins** The left margin of a document can be set to any value between 1 and 238, and the right margin to any value between 3 and 240, provided that the left margin is set at least three columns to the left of the right margin. If you try to select values which do not follow these rules, then an error message will be displayed, the previous values will be reinstated, and you will have to press [Esc] before continuing.

To help you see the effects of your decisions, any new values which are entered in the box on the right-hand side of the screen are also immediately shown in their appropriate place in the diagram on the left of the screen.

The WordStar 1512 default values are for a left margin of 1 and a right margin of 65. These are normal settings for Pica (10 characters per inch, or cps) type on 8½" by 11" continuous-form stationery of the sort most frequently used with dot-matrix printers; for a very neat effect for business correspondence on A4 paper, leave the left margin at 1 and set the right margin at 55.

**Line lengths and character sizes** If you are using a font larger or smaller than Pica, your lines will obviously be of a different length. The formula to calculate the length of a line in a new font is as follows:

$$C2 = C1 \times N1/N2$$

where C2 is the number of characters per line in the new font size, C1 is the number of characters in the old font size, N2 is the new font size and N1 is the old font size.

For example, if you switch from using Pica type (10 cps) to using Elite type (12 cps) then C2 (the number of characters per line in the new size) will be equal to C1 (the number of characters per line in the old size, i.e. 65) multiplied by 12 and divided by 10 (the new and old font sizes respectively). If you work the sum out, you will find that it comes to 78; therefore margins set at 1 and 78 for Elite type will produce a line which occupies the same amount of space on the paper as a line printed with margins set at 1 and 65 with Pica type.

If you find this confusing, read over it a couple of times until it becomes clear. If you anticipate using different type sizes within a document, it is important that you should understand the relationship of line length to font size. This is because the characters on the screen do not change size when you switch from one font size to another; it is therefore tempting to imagine that because the margins for lines in different type sizes line up properly on the screen, they will also do so when a document is printed; in reality they will not.

**Top and bottom margins** Top and bottom margins are the space left between the top edge of the paper and the beginning of the text area, and between the bottom of the text area and the end of the paper respectively. Header and footer texts, which we shall meet when we consider dot commands in Chapters Five and Eight, as well as page numbers, are placed *inside* the top and bottom margins, as appropriate.

The figures for top and bottom margin sizes are notional ones which may be affected by the physical placing of paper in the printer. This is particularly important in the case of continuous stationery, as unless this is correctly aligned with the print-head, the blank area at the bottom of the page may not correspond properly with the perforations. Some printers have markers which show where the top of the first sheet should come; on others, it must be aligned just above the top of the print-head.

There are no restrictions on the depth of the top and bottom margins, except, reasonably enough, that they must not together exceed the chosen length of the page itself.

Some printers, such as the Canon LBP-8 Laser Beam, will not work properly unless the top and bottom margins are set to particular values; details of these special cases are given in the WordStar 1512 manual.

**Offset** The offset is the distance between the extreme left printing position available on a printer and the beginning of the left margin; the purpose of it is to enable printing to avoid the tear-off sprocket strip typical of continuous-form stationery, without needing to change the left margin.

The factory-set default value for the offset is 8; if you find that this is either too large, so that printing appears too far over to the right, or too small, so that printing begins on the tear-off strip, reset it by typing in a new value. Any value between 0 and 255 is acceptable.

**Page length** Page length means the total length of the page, from the physical top of the paper to the bottom, including the top margin, the text area and the bottom margin. The text area can thus be calculated by the following formula:

$$TA = PL-TM-BM$$

where TA is the text area, PL is the page length, and TM and BM are the top and bottom margins respectively.

The standard page length for normal 9½" continuous form stationery is 66 lines, assuming that printing is being carried out at the standard 6 lines per inch; where the top margin is 3 and the bottom margin is 8, this means that the text area will be 55 lines long.

A4 paper is 70 lines long (at 6 lines per inch); given a top margin of 3 and a bottom margin of 8, there will be a text area 59 lines long.

**Getting more on a page** If you need to pack more lines onto a page, you can increase the number of lines which are printed per inch. This figure – the 'line pitch'– can be changed by adjusting the DIP switches on some printers, and also by using dot commands; however, although WordStar 1512 is able to specify five different line pitches, not all printers will be able to use them.

Even when line pitch is changed by means of dot commands, rather than by changing the printer DIP switches, the pitch reverts to 6 lines per inch in header and footer margins. If this were not done, pages of the same document printed in different line-pitches would have different top and bottom margins, which would look very unattractive. The easiest way of making sure that a particular page layout actually looks all right on paper is to experiment with the effects of different values for top and bottom margins until you find an arrangement which is satisfactory for you.

**Number pages** The lower half of the box on the right-hand side of the screen contains three On/Off options similar to those we have already met in the Word processing settings screen. They can be selected or deselected in the same way, using [ + ] to select and the [ Del ] key to deselect; options which are selected – that is, in force – are marked with a tick in the usual way.

All these options can be changed later, both through the Modify print options which are available to you before printing and through dot commands.

The first two options, Number pages and Auto page number, are linked. If you usually want to have pages numbered, with correct page numbers placed in the centre and at the foot of every page, select both Number pages and Auto page number. Page numbers will then be printed at the foot of every page, except that no page number will be placed on a document consisting only of a single sheet.

Should you choose Number pages but not Auto page number, then a single page document will also be numbered. If you select Auto page number but not Number pages, then no pages will be numbered.

Page numbering is another instance of WordStar 1512 providing a simple but rather limited command through the Page layout screen of the Change Settings Menu and a far more sophisticated way of achieving more complex results by other means: for example, from the Page layout screen it is only possible to select or deselect page numbers – their location on the page is fixed. Dot commands, on the other hand, make it possible to adjust where page numbers appear and to insert other text around them if required.

**Use form feeds** Commands to force Form feeds – running paper through the printer until the end of the sheet has been reached – are compulsory on a few printers. Many other printers do not actually *need* Form Feed commands because they keep track of where they are on a page, but will still eject the paper faster or more smoothly if the command is given. If the printer which you intend using with this particular page layout requires or can use a form feed (check both your printer's manual and the section in the WordStar 1512 manual which refers in detail to the needs of different printers) then select this option.

When you are satisfied that all the page layout details are correct, save them on disc by pressing [Return].

# Setting up printers

If the only printer you are using is an Amstrad DMP3000 printer, you can ignore this section, as the program is already configured to use this printer.

Although different makes and models of printers do share certain common standards, such as using ASCII codes, they nonetheless differ in the facilities they offer; these may include a variety of type-faces and styles, NLQ or draft mode, and sometimes the ability to print in more than one colour.

With many word processing programs, configuring the computer to match individual printers can be an extremely difficult and time-consuming task. WordStar 1512 avoids all these difficulties by providing special 'patch files' for over 200 different makes and models of printers, together with facilities for handling other printers which happen not to be included in the list.

We have already seen that up to three different printers can be configured for use with any one installation of WordStar 1512. This means that it is possible to set the program up for the different codes which might be required by a daisy-wheel printer to be used for correspondence work and a dot-matrix printer used for high-speed printing, or even, in some cases, to use the same printer in 'Landscape' and 'Portrait' Mode. Even if you only have one printer, you can prepare a document to use the facilities of a more sophisticated printer which may be available to you elsewhere; in this way, you can prepare a document at home which can then be printed out on a different printer in your office.

**Setting up a printer** Select Set up printers from the Change Settings Menu. On a two-drive machine, you will be prompted to replace the disc in Drive A with your own disc labelled 'Printing', and then to place the original 'Printers' distribution disc into Drive B. On single-drive machines, follow the on-screen prompts regarding disc-swapping.

Fig. 3.5 The Choose a Printer Menu

You will be offered the Choose a Printer Menu, reproduced here as Fig. 3.5. This has room for the names of up to three printers, with the top space already occupied by the Amstrad DMP3000. If you do not intend to use a DMP3000, you can simply leave it highlighted and press [ Return ]; if you want to use both the DMP3000 and another printer, move the highlight bar down to 'Printer 2' and confirm your choice with [ Return ].

**Named printers** You will now be taken to the Set Printers Screen, a part of which is reproduced in Fig. 3.6. On this screen, which comprises altogether 7 'pages' of printer types, are listed over 200 printers in alphabetical order. Moving from 'page' to 'page' using [ PgUp ] and [ PgDn ], find the name of your printer and put the highlight bar on it; then press [ Return ]. There will be a short delay as all the individual details of the printer you have chosen are copied onto your own printer disc from the WordStar 1512 distribution disc, and then the basic job of configuring the printer is complete!

**Un-named printers** Should your printer not be present on the list on the Set Printers Screen, all is not lost; there are two ways in which you will still be able to use your printer.

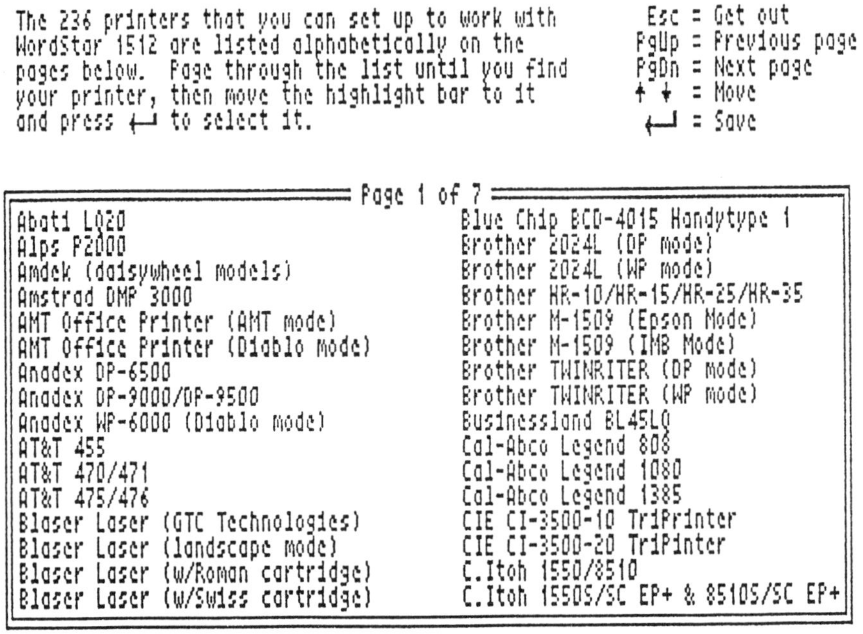
The 236 printers that you can set up to work with WordStar 1512 are listed alphabetically on the pages below. Page through the list until you find your printer, then move the highlight bar to it and press ↵ to select it.
Esc = Get out
PgUp = Previous page
PgDn = Next page
↑ ↓ = Move
↵ = Save
Page 1 of 7
Abati LQ20
Alps P2000
Amdek (daisywheel models)
Amstrad DMP 3000
AMT Office Printer (AMT mode)
AMT Office Printer (Diablo mode)
Anadex DP-6500
Anadex DP-9000/DP-9500
Anadex WP-6000 (Diablo mode)
AT&T 455
AT&T 470/471
AT&T 475/476
Blaser Laser (GTC Technologies)
Blaser Laser (landscape mode)
Blaser Laser (w/Roman cartridge)
Blaser Laser (w/Swiss cartridge)
Blue Chip BCD-4015 Handytype 1
Brother 2024L (DP mode)
Brother 2024L (WP mode)
Brother HR-10/HR-15/HR-25/HR-35
Brother M-1509 (Epson Mode)
Brother M-1509 (IMB Mode)
Brother TWINRITER (DP mode)
Brother TWINRITER (WP mode)
Businessland BL45LQ
Cal-Abco Legend 808
Cal-Abco Legend 1080
Cal-Abco Legend 1385
CIE CI-3500-10 TriPrinter
CIE CI-3500-20 TriPinter
C.Itoh 1550/8510
C.Itoh 1550S/SC EP+ & 8510S/SC EP+

**Fig. 3.6** The Set Printers Screen

The simplest is to use one of the two 'Standard' printer patch files at the very bottom of the second column of the last 'page' of the Set Printers Screen. These are labelled 'Backspacing Standard' and 'Non-backspacing Standard', and which you should use depends simply on whether or not your particular printer is capable of backspacing.

This information should be contained in the printer manual, though sometimes it is rather hard to find it. Even if there is no reference to backspacing in so many words, there may be a chart of the characters which the printer can produce, together with a list of the codes for each: you are looking for the code '08', sometimes called 'BS'.

If this code is implemented, configure your printer as Backspacing Standard; if not, configure it as Non-backspacing Standard.

This approach does have the disadvantage that there may then be certain characters that your printer will not be able to reproduce properly – the most common is the Pound Sterling, £. You can often get around this by using the # symbol instead of £ when you are inputting material from the keyboard, but this does not work on some printers.

Another solution to the un-named printer problem is to configure it as if it were a named printer which you happen to know is similar to what you have. If you don't have this information, it is usually safe to configure a dot-matrix printer as an Epson FX-80 and a daisy-wheel printer as a Diablo; indeed, many manufacturers' daisy-wheel printers use Diablo elements. You will probably miss out on being able to use certain of your printer's facilities, but it is still better than having to buy another printer.

## Customise printers

Once you have configured your system for a particular printer, you must customise the printer in order to make the best use of its facilities. This too is an extremely simple procedure.

Select Customise printers from the Change Settings Menu; as before, on a two-drive system this requires the 'Printers' distribution disc to be placed in Drive B and your own 'Printing' disc in Drive A.

The Choose a Printer Menu will appear once more, allowing you to select which printer you are going to customise. When you have made your selection, you will be given the Customise Printer Screen, printed here as Fig. 3.7.

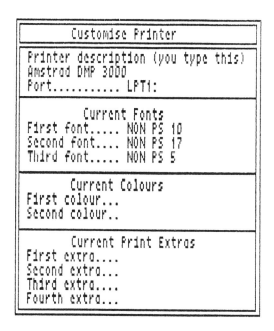
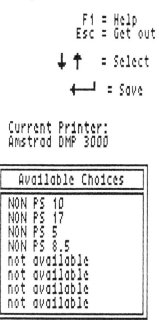

Fig. 3.7 The Customise Printer Screen

This is a rather complex screen, and the selections from it are not made in quite the same way as on the other screens and menus we have used. It can be vertically divided into two sections: on the left is a summary box into which you will have to insert the various choices you wish to make, and on the right is a window showing what the Available Choices are for any particular part of the summary box. A 'Help' page is available from Function Key F1, though this is unfortunately not as friendly as some of the others we have met.

**A simple example** We shall proceed as if we were customising an Epson FX-80 printer; the settings, and available options, for your own printer may be different from those listed here, so be guided where necessary by the manuals for your own computer and printer.

Begin by typing in the name of the printer against the prompt 'Printer description (you type this)'. This does not have to be the actual name of the printer—it could as well be 'Letter-quality work' or some similar descriptive term. It is this name which will henceforth be used to identify this printer on the Choose a Printer Menu and at the foot of the Print Menu.

Next, use the mouse or the [ ← ] key to move the highlight bar to the prompt 'Port' As you do so, you will see that the Available Choices window becomes filled with several different options which you can use; these are shown in Fig. 3.8.

Fig. 3.8 Port Options

**Choosing the printer port** LPT1 is the parallel printer port; your computer's manual may refer to this as PRN; LPT2 and LPT3 are additional parallel ports which may be present on your machine as optional extras.

COM1 is the serial interface; COM2 refers to an additional, optional serial port which may be present on your computer.

If you are using a serial printer, once you have set COM1 as the printer port, you will no longer need to use the MS-DOS MODE command before beginning a session with WordStar 1512.

The Epson FX-80 is a parallel printer. To install it to use the LPT1 port, press the [ → ] key to take the highlight bar from the Port prompt over into the Available Choices window. Any option on which it rests in this window is automatically copied into the space by the Port prompt, and as you use the [ ← ] and [ ← ] keys to move the highlight bar up and down in the window, the different port names will appear in the box on the left of the screen.

When the highlight bar is located on LPT1 in the Available Choices window (and this choice thus also appears by the Port prompt) use the [ ← ] key to move back to the left-hand side of the screen. *Don't* [ Return ], or you will be taken out of the Customise Printer Screen before you have finished.

**Choosing fonts** Fonts – different typefaces – are chosen in the same way, except that here it is not necessary for you to look up your printer's manual to see what fonts are available – as soon as the highlight bar is taken to the Current fonts section of the Customise Printer screen, all the fonts which your printer is capable of reproducing will be displayed in the Available Choices Window; if there are fewer fonts available than would fit the window, the remainder of the space will be filled with the words 'not available'.

Fig. 3.9 shows the fonts which are available for the Epson FX-80 printer. Only three of these can be configured at once, so choose the three which you will find most useful, remembering that Font 1 will always be selected when you begin typing, and thus should probably be either Pica (10 cps) or Elite (12 cps) type.

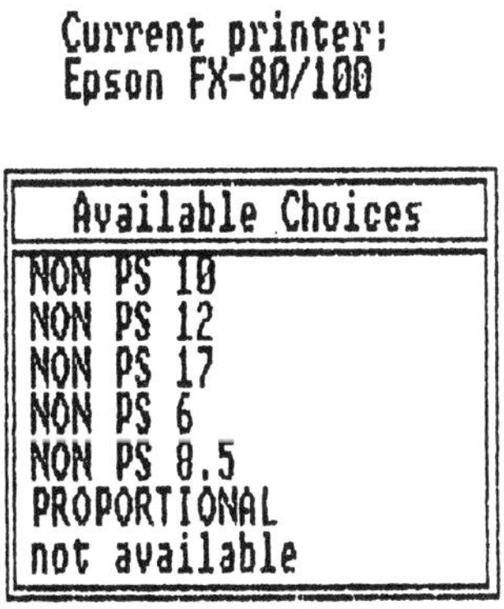

Current printer:
Epson FX-80/100

| Available Choices |
| --- |
| NON PS 10 |
| NON PS 12 |
| NON PS 17 |
| NON PS 6 |
| NON PS 8.5 |
| PROPORTIONAL |
| not available |

Fig. 3.9 Fonts available for the Epson FX-80 printer

Make your choice in the same way as before, moving the highlight bar to First Font on the left of the screen, then using [ → ] to move it to the Available Choices window. Next use [ ← ] and [ → ] to identify the font you want, and then move back to the left of the screen with [ ← ].

**Colours and Print Extras** Neither Colours nor Print Extras are available on the Epson FX-80 printer, so moving the highlight bar into these areas will only generate an Available Choices window full of 'not available' messages. ('Print extras' are special facilities such as italics which your printer may support. The

Epson does actually have a set of italic characters, but they cannot be reached in this way – if you absolutely need to have them, a technique to make them available is shown in Chapter Six).

When you have chosen the options you want, press [ Return ] to confirm them and leave the screen; if things go wrong, you can abandon your work with [ Esc ].

**Printer support material** Each of the printers supported by WordStar 1512 is also listed in the program manual, together with a series of notes about the peculiarities of some individual printers. If you experience any difficulties in getting your printer to work properly, check the entry in the manual for specific advice.

**Testing your printer** When you have customised your printer, it is a good idea to check that it is really working as it should. This process is facilitated by a special document on the Text and Data disc entitled PRINTEST, so get your printer ready to print this out.

You will need to select Printing from the Opening Menu. Then, if the printer you are testing is not shown as the current one on the Print Menu, select it with Use another printer; finally select PRINTEST, using the Choose a file to print option.

The PRINTEST file is a two-page document designed to take your printer through a variety of different print formats, with superscripts, subscripts, bold and underlined text, three different fonts, two colours and four 'print extras'. Where any of these features is not available on your printer, the ordinary print style will apply, thus giving you a complete guide to the range of effects which your printer supports.

# Changing settings at print time

The majority of the values set through the Change Settings Menu can be amended before any document is printed, either by dot commands within the document to be printed or by selecting Modify print options from the Print Menu.

Modify print options will reveal the screen shown here as Fig. 3.10. With this, you can set the number of copies you want to have printed, which pages of the document are to be printed, and the margin offset. Additionally, page numbering can be turned on or off, and you can pause the printer at the end of each page; this is essential if you are using individual sheets which have to be inserted into the printer by hand.

It is not possible with the Print Options Screen to offset the page number itself – that is, to make a document begin at page 40, for example; this can, however, be done with dot commands.

```
┌─────────────────────────────────────────────┐
│                Print Options                  │
╞═══════════════════════════════════════════════╡
│    1  Number of copies to print   (1-9999)   │
│    1  Begin at page (1-9999)                  │
│ 9999  End after page (1-9999)                 │
│    8  Page margin offset (0-255)              │
│       Pause for each new page (on/off)        │
│       Page number (on/off)                    │
│       Auto page number (on/off)               │
└─────────────────────────────────────────────┘
```

**Fig. 3.10** The Modify Print Options Screen

# Postscript

Configuring WordStar 1512 is a relatively straightforward operation which can be divided into four parts: Word processing settings, where you can set the defaults which will apply when you are creating or editing a document; Page layout, where you define your preferred margins and page-numbering; Set up printers, used for telling the program which printer you will be using from the available list; and Customise printers, where you say which of the various facilities which are available on your printer you will actually want to use.

The most important choices you will make are those governing the printer, so when you have finished, test that everything has gone according to plan by trying to make a printed copy of the file called PRINTEST; if this is printed correctly, you will know that your printer is working as it should.

If difficulties arise during printer installation, or PRINTEST does not print out as it ought, go back to the Set up printers operation and begin again, making sure that you configure your system for the correct printer; then repeat the Customise printers operation. If you do not have one of the printers specifically supported by the program, you may have to try several different printer names before you find the one which works best.

# *CHAPTER FOUR*

# Using the F2 Menus

## Preview

This chapter is about some of the more advanced tasks which you can carry out with a word processor. A few of these, like underlining and centering a line of text, can be done both with a word processor and a typewriter, and some others, like bold type and using different sizes of type in a document, can be done with some typewriters, but not with most. But most of the topics which we cover in this chapter are completely impossible without a word processor; they include tasks like copying sections out of one part of a document and inserting them somewhere else, or finding all the occasions when one particular word is used and replacing it with something else, or checking your spelling before printing your work out.

Many of these operations involve working with blocks of text which have been marked out. Once you understand the principles of this, everything else follows very easily.

You will probably not need to add all these features to your repertoire in one fell swoop; begin with the ones which you need most, and then move on to the others as the need appears.

## More advanced text work

Once you have finished configuring your printer, it becomes possible to make use of the full range of styles and type-faces in word processed documents. We shall therefore return to our work with PRACTICE, the document which we first used in Chapter Two. Select Word processing from the Opening Menu, then select PRACTICE from the Main Menu – unless you have used some other file in the meantime, it will probably be the 'current file – if it is not, find it using the Choose/create a file option from the Main Menu.

When PRACTICE is displayed on the Typing Screen, press Function Key [F2] to take a look at one of the two Edit Menus shown together here as Fig. 4.1. After you have glanced over it, move on to the next menu by pressing [F2] again, and the second Edit Menu will replace the first on the screen. Then press the [Esc] key to clear the second menu.

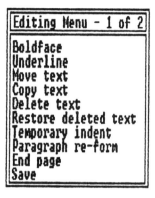

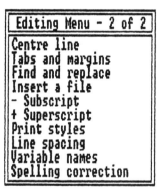

**Fig. 4.1** The F2 Menus

The two menus are arranged so that the first time you press [F2] during a word processing session, Menu 1 will be displayed, with a highlight bar on the first option; however, returning to the menus once they have been used will always result in the menu you last used being displayed first, with the highlight bar placed on the same option as previously.

The options available from these menus belong under four main headings: those concerned with the *appearance* of text, such as Underline and Boldface; those which are used to *manipulate* text, such as Move text and Delete text; **formatting** commands, such as line spacing, margins and tabs; and a few **miscellaneous** options, such as Save and Spelling correction.

# Marking blocks of text

Many of the facilities available through the F2 Menus require 'blocks' of text to be marked to indicate the points at which, for example, boldface or underlined type are to begin and end.

Exactly how this is done depends partly on whether or not you have chosen (from the Change Settings Menu) to have prompts displayed on the screen, and partly on whether the text which you wish to mark has been composed yet. If you are not yet at ease with the program you will find the prompts helpful, but it is faster to dispense with them, and you may find that you will prefer to do this as soon as you are familiar with the way in which the various commands work.

**Using prompts** Assuming that you have not deselected prompts, press Function Key [F2] once or twice to get the particular menu you want, and then select the specific option you want – underlining, for example – either by moving the highlight bar up or down to it and pressing [Return] or by pressing the initial letter of the option's name. There will be a short delay while the disc is accessed, and it is this delay which is avoided by not using prompts.

After about five seconds the menu will disappear, and a prompt will appear at the top of the screen; this will read:

```
Move the cursor to the beginning of the text you want
to underline and press [ ]. (bent arrow)
```

Obey these instructions, moving the text cursor either with the cursor keys or the mouse until it rests on the first character which is to be included in the block; then press [Return].

The start-of-block prompt will now be replaced by the end-of-block prompt reading:

```
Move the cursor to the end of the text you want
to underline and press [ ]. bent arrow
```

Take the text cursor to the last character in the new block and press [Return] again. As the cursor travels through the document, the area of text between the cursor and the start of the block will be highlighted (on a monochrome monitor) or shown against a white background on a colour screen.

When you signal the end of the block with [Return], the text inside the block will be displayed in a different colour. Exactly which colour depends on the precise effect you are marking it out for: text to be emboldened will be coloured brown, while an area which is to be superscripted or subscripted will be purple, and one to be underlined will be a light greyish-blue. Obviously these differences will not be so apparent on a monochrome screen.

**Combining blocks** Different blocks can overlap each other; in this way, you can achieve such combinations as underlined bold type or bold superscript. There is a file called COMBINE on the Text and Data Disc which shows the colours used for all twelve different possibilities, ranging from normal text right down to boldface underlined superscript.

It is possible to mark the beginning of a block which has not yet been written; select the required feature from the F2 Menus, position the text cursor at the point where you are going to start writing, and then press [Enter]. The new text will be highlighted as you write; when you come to the end of the section you wish to enclose in the block, press [Return] in the usual way.

**Marking blocks without prompts** To mark a block when prompts have been deselected, first position the text cursor at the point where the block is to start; you must do this *before* the F2 Menu is displayed. Then move the cursor to the end of the section you are highlighting and press [Return].

To mark a block which has not yet been written, put the cursor at the point where the block is to begin, select the option you want from the menu, and then write the text. Finally, mark the end of the block with [Return].

**Points to watch** There are a couple of extra points about block marking which are worth mentioning. First, although we have talked about marking the beginning of a block first, and then moving the cursor down to the end, there is no especial need to carry out the marking in this order – except, of course, with text which has not yet been written. It is just as effective to begin at the end of the block and to work upwards, so you can use whichever method you prefer.

Second, the [Return] key has a rather ambiguous role in marking blocks. Once you have selected from the F2 Menus any option which involves marking a block, the [Return] key no longer functions to place the text cursor on the next screen line; instead, it only controls the positioning of the block.

This is not actually very confusing, but it does have one rather odd side-effect: it is not possible to mark out in one go a block which extends beyond a Carriage Return *unless it is written first and marked afterwards*.

# A practical example

Although PRACTICE is displayed on the screen, we have not so far made any use of it, except as a background to the F2 Menus. The time has now come to change that; we shall underline a short section in the first paragraph, and then set a part of the second paragraph into bold type.

**Underlining** On most printers, underlined text appears like this.

Press Function Key [F2] to call down one of the menus, and then press it again if the menu which appears does not have the Underline option on it (it is the second option on Menu 1). Then move the highlight bar until it is resting on Underline and press [Return]; alternatively, make the selection by pressing [u].

We shall be underlining the words 'as accurately as you can' in the first line of PRACTICE, so take the cursor to the first letter of 'as' and press [Return]; then take the cursor to the last letter of 'can', and press [Return] again. The text to be underlined will highlight as you do this. Don't worry if you take the cursor too far; you can just retrace your steps until the cursor is at the right spot. The text in the area to be underlined will turn light blue as confirmation that the block to be underlined has been correctly marked. It will not actually appear underlined on-screen.

**Bold text** Although different printers do not all embolden text in the same way, the bold text generally looks **like this**. To embolden the word 'marker' in the second paragraph, repeat the steps you followed when underlining, except that you must select Boldface from Editing Menu 1 – it is the first option on that menu.

On a colour monitor, text to be printed in bold type appears brown.

Assuming that your printer is capable of reproducing both bold type and underlining, you can print your work to check that everything is really working as it should. Leave the Typing Screen by pressing [Esc] and then selecting Save changes; when you are back at the Opening Menu, choose Print. You will be prompted to insert the Printing Disc. Make sure the printer is turned on and that the paper is loaded. Select Begin printing current file from the Print Menu, and after a short delay the document will be printed out with the underline and bold type duly incorporated.

# Abandoning and removing blocks

If you start to define a block but then change your mind about it, you can abandon it either before or after the first marker is in place by simply pressing [Esc]. WordStar 1512 will respond by redisplaying the last [F2] Menu; press [Esc] again and the block will be abandoned; if the first marker is already in place, it will be removed.

Removing blocks which are already fully defined is only a little more work. To see how it is done, carry out the following little experiment with the underline which we have placed in the first line of PRACTICE.

**Finding the block markers** If you have saved the file, call it back onto the screen and put the text cursor on the very first character of the top line; if you haven't left the Typing Screen, you can take the cursor back to the appropriate place by pressing the [Home] key. Then with the cursor keys, move the cursor along the line one position at a time.

As you already know, each press of the [→] key will move the cursor on space along the line. However, this rule is broken at points where blocks begin and end. When the cursor reaches the start of the underlined section, it will require *two* presses of the [ → ] key to move *one* space. Furthermore, at one of those presses of the [ → ] key, the word 'Underline' will be shown at the left of the Status Line just above the Ruler.

The same situation applies at the end of the underlined section; two key-presses are required to get past the end of the block, and once again 'Underline' will be shown on the Status Line.

**Invisible spaces** The rule is that at the start or end of every block, an 'invisible space' is inserted into a line, and an extra press of the cursor key is required to get past it. If two block markers occur at the same place – the beginning of an underlined passage in bold type, for instance – then there will be two 'invisible spaces' inserted at that point; at one of them the word 'Underline' will appear on the Status Line and the word 'Bold' at the other.

Removing a block involves, in effect, the deletion of these 'invisible spaces'. This is done by simply moving the text cursor until it is on the appropriate 'invisible space' – which is confirmed by the appearance of the word 'Underline' or 'Bold' or whatever on the Status Line – and then pressing the [ Del ] (forward delete) key.

Because the block marker has been removed, the immediate effect will be that the coloured characters which characterise the block may 'leak' forward or backward from that point and colour much of the rest of the text. *Don't let this worry you!* Simply move to the 'invisible space' at the other end of the block and delete that in the same way; as you do so, everything will revert to its proper colour.

Experiment with this technique to remove the underline and emboldening from PRACTICE. The only real rules to remember are these: move the cursor until the feature you want to delete is named on the Status Line, and then press [ Del ]; repeat the procedure for the other end of the block; and don't worry about changes to the colour of the text between these steps.

**What your printer can and can't do** A lot of users are confused by the fact that merely because a particular effect is available on a particular word processing program, it does not necessarily follow that the same effect can be obtained on their printer; even more confusingly, some programs are capable of achieving effects with a particular printer which cannot be achieved by a different program using the same printer!

As you read on, you will see that in several places there are notes about particular features which may not be available on all printers. In addition, features which WordStar 1512 expects to control 'through software' – as a part of the program – are sometimes, on some printers, achieved 'through hardware'; for example, on some printers, features such as line spacing and font-size depend on which daisy-wheel is fitted rather than on the commands of the program.

If after printing the PRINTEST file you are still in doubt as to which features your printer can handle, have another close look at your printer handbook and the WordStar 1512 manual; if you are still uncertain after reading them, experiment with different effects to see which ones do work.

**Boldface** Boldface is usually produced by striking a character and then moving the printhead fractionally to the right before restriking it. Sometimes, however, the character is merely restruck in the same position; this is better referred to as double-strike, but the distinction between it and true boldface is not always made.

Not all printers are capable of producing boldface type; those which do sometimes limit the use of it to NLQ mode, and there may be other restrictions such as an inability to embolden superscripts, subscripts and proportionally-spaced work.

**Underline** WordStar 1512 normally underlines all characters and spaces between the beginning and end of the marked block, but a few printers cannot underline the 'pad' or 'soft' spaces which may be inserted while a document is being printed Justified. If this is the case with your printer, you may prefer to use the underscore option explained in the next paragraph or else avoid using Underline and Justification simultaneously. Some printers produce an underline as a series of dashes rather than a continuous line, and some cannot underline bold or proportionally-spaced type.

If you want to underscore individual words but not the spaces between them, turn Underline on at the start of each word and off at the end; however, this gets rather tiresome if you want to underscore a long piece of text.

**Superscript and subscript** Superscripts and subscripts are half-height characters which are printed slightly raised or lowered to ordinary-height characters. They are used in printing expressions such as $H_{2O}$ (subscript) or WordStar$^{512}$ (superscript).

Daisy-wheel printers cannot produce proper superscript and subscript characters, and even dot-matrix printers often restrict the range of styles and type-faces available for them. The printer support documentation in the WordStar 1512 manual will provide fuller details about the implementation of this feature on individual printers.

**Print styles** By Print styles, WordStar 1512 means the various font sizes, colours and 'print extras' which were set in the Customise Printer Menu.

Selecting these differs in two important ways from the block marker commands we have examined so far. First, only a single marker is used, which signals the beginning of the section of text which will be in the new style. Thus if you make a change of font from Pica (10 cps) to Elite (12 cps), for example, all of the rest of the document will be printed in Elite unless you set a new Print style at some later point in the document.

Second, the change of size or colour is not signalled by highlighting or colouring the text on the screen; instead, the words '2nd font', '2nd colour' and the like will appear on the bottom right of the Status Line when the text cursor is in that part of the document where this Print style is in force.

Remember that when you change the font size, the text will no longer line up with the original margin. The easiest way of adjusting the margins to match the different type size is with the Tabs and margins option from the F2 Menu, described later in this chapter; the .lm and .rm dot commands which are introduced in Chapter Five are also useful.

**Deleting changes of print style** Print style changes can be removed by taking the cursor one space at a time along the line in which the change occurs until you reach the 'invisible space' at which a message like '2nd font' or '2nd colour', or whatever else is appropriate, appears towards the *left* of the Status Line; then remove the style change by pressing [ Del ] once.

If you are unsure in which line the change of Print style occurs, take the cursor vertically through the document until the message about the font or colour which is displayed on the *right* of the Status Line is changed; then go through that line from left to right as described in the previous paragraph.

# Text manipulation

So far in this chapter, we have looked at ways in which the *appearance* of the final printed text can be changed. We shall now examine the techniques which are available in WordStar 1512 to enable the user to move, copy, delete and restore blocks of text. Although superficially these operations are different from those described above, they are in practice very similar, as they require blocks of text to be marked out in exactly the way already discussed.

## Scissors and paste

Every writer, whether he or she is creating a memo or a full-length book, is familiar with the unpleasant discovery that material which has been included in one place in the document really belongs somewhere else. With traditional ways of document preparation, the only way to move a portion of text from one place to another is by retyping the relevant section of text; if the passage to be moved is more than a line or two in length, this often throws out the page-numbering, causing either a big retyping job or, more likely, copious applications of correcting-fluid. Sometimes, it's easier to leave things as they are than to fiddle about moving text around.

With a word processor like WordStar 1512, all that is changed; you can 'cut' a section out of one place and 'paste' it somewhere else, without disturbing the page-numbering or needing to retype. More than anything else, it is this 'scissors and paste' facility which sets word processing apart from the old-fashioned typewriter.

## Move text

With the Move text command, a marked block of text can be removed from one location and inserted somewhere else in the same document. For example, you could take a short passage reading

```
Near the village, the railway and the road both
pass through a narrow valley or ravine. The
ancient church of St. Giles is visible in the
distance.
```

Mark out a block containing the second sentence and then put that sentence first. The passage would then read

```
The
ancient church of St. Giles is visible in the
distance.Near the village, the railway and the road
both
pass through a narrow valley or ravine.
```

Obviously the first line here is too short, and some others are too long. If automatic reforming is selected, the text will immediately be reformatted to this:

```
The ancient church of St. Giles is visible
in the distance.Near the village, the
railway and the road both pass through a
narrow valley or ravine.
```

If automatic reformatting is not turned on, you will have to tidy up the paragraph yourself with the Paragraph reform option from the F2 Menus. This is described later in this chapter.

Finally, go back and put a space between the end of the first sentence and the beginning of the second.

Most Move Text operations are like this: first, select a block; then carry out the move; and finally, do any minor tidying up which may be necessary. Obviously this is still much easier than having to retype a complete document.

**An example to try** Try a similar Move operation with PRACTICE. Call down the first F2 Menu and select Move Text. You will be prompted to put the cursor at the beginning of the text you want to move and press [Return]. Put the cursor on the first character of the second sentence and press [Return].

Next, you will be prompted to mark the end of the block in the same way. Put the cursor in the space after the full stop at the end of the same sentence; the highlighting will then cover the whole sentence. Press [Return] again.

Finally, put the cursor at the 'Home' position – Line 1 Column 1 – and press [Return] a third time. The block will be immediately moved to the new position, and the text will be reformatted if Automatic Reform is selected; otherwise select paragraph Reform from the F2 Menu.

**Limitations affecting the Move command** There are a couple of restrictions governing the use of the Move text facility. The first is that there is a limit of a page or so to the amount of text which can be moved at one time; if you wish to move a larger section, it can still be done by moving it in sections.

Second, it is not possible, for obvious reasons, to move a block into the middle of itself; no error message will be given if you try, but the command will be ignored.

A point which is worth watching if you are moving a section of text which has been previously marked for underlining or any other effect is that you must make sure that the 'invisible spaces' are moved as well as the visible text. This can be done by watching the left of the Status Line for the appropriate message, and marking the beginning of the block to be moved one space to the *left* of the opening 'invisible space', and the end of the block one space to the *right* of the closing 'invisible space'.

If the section which you are moving is part of, say, an underlined section but includes neither of the underline markers, then the portion which has been moved will not appear in colour on the screen, nor will it be underlined while printing. Conversely, if a section is moved into a block defined for underlining, etc., it will appear on the monitor in the appropriate colour and will be underlined when printed.

If this seems confusing, try out various combinations on PRACTICE, and it should all become clear.

# Copy text

The Copy text facility is similar to Move text, except that the original section is not deleted at the same time. Once the copying operation is complete, the block markers are removed.

On the face of it, this would appear to mean that making multiple copies of a section of text could only be done by repeatedly marking out the same block and recopying it; there is, however, a simpler way, which is outlined below in the section on restoring deleted text.

As with the Move text command, there is a limit of about a page to the amount which can be copied at one time; it is, however, possible to copy a section of text into itself.

The warnings given above about the inclusion of block markers also apply to the Copy text command.

# Delete text

We have already seen how individual characters can be deleted using the [Del] and [←Del] keys. WordStar 1512 also has two commands which enable larger areas of text to be deleted *en bloc*; one of these is accessed through the F2 Menus, but the other is reached directly through the keyboard.

**Block deletes** The simplest and fastest is the Delete text command on F2 Menu 1. This works in exactly the same way as the Move and Copy commands we have already met, except that once the block has been defined, it is immediately deleted from the document.

When carrying out a block delete, be careful that you don't accidentally remove a formatting command of some kind – a Print style command, maybe, or a dot command – along with everything else, as this may have an unforeseen effect on the appearance of your document.

**Line deletes** In addition to the full Delete text command, it is possible to delete a complete line of text without recourse to the F2 Menus. Locate the text cursor anywhere on the line which you want to delete, hold down [Ctrl] and press [←Del]; the line will be deleted, the text underneath will move up to fill the space, and the cursor will be moved to the extreme left-hand column.

It is possible to delete several successive lines in this way, by placing the cursor in the uppermost line to be deleted and then repeating the [Ctrl]/[←Del] sequence. This has the advantage of being much faster than using the F2 Menus, but the disadvantage that it restricts the amount of text which can be recovered if you later realise that you have deleted more than you intended.

# Restore deleted text

WordStar 1512 is equipped with an **undelete buffer** – sometimes graphically called an 'oops buffer' – in which a copy of the last piece of text to be block-deleted is kept, and which thus enables you to recover any deletions about which you have second thoughts.

To see how this works, use either Delete text or Line delete to delete a single line of PRACTICE. Then select Restore deleted text from the F2 menu, place the cursor at the place on the screen where you wish the deleted text to be reinserted, and it will at once reappear.

The most important restriction on this useful facility is that only the *last* block-delete can be restored. This means, for example, that if you have used [Ctrl]/[←Del] to delete several lines one after the other, only the most recent one can be restored. Text deleted one character at a time with [Del] and [←Del] cannot be recovered, of course.

**Making multiple copies** A useful dodge with the Restore deleted text command is to use it to make multiple copies of a block of text throughout a document; doing it this way is faster than using the ordinary Copy text command, because with that command the block markers are removed as soon as each Copy operation is completed.

To make multiple copies of a passage, block-delete it and then immediately Restore it in the same place (if required). Then move the text cursor to the place where you want the next copy to appear and Restore the deleted text there as well. You can do this as many times as you want, provided that you don't block-delete anything else in the meantime.

# Find and replace

The Find and replace option enables you to find any word or short phrase and, if required, replace it with another, either automatically or after you have confirmed the substitution.

We have already seen how the Change Settings Menu makes it possible to select whether the Find and replace operations will operate only upon whole words, and whether they will only find those instances where the search string and the target string are identical in their use of capitals and lower case letters. Our advice for most purposes is to set the program to find only complete words, but not to be case sensitive.

An important point about the Find and replace command is that it is only effective between the place at which the cursor is located when it is called up and the end of the document. In this way it is possible to restrict a search to only one portion of what might be a very lengthy document. A search can be abandoned at any point by pressing [Esc].

**Using the Find command** To see how this very powerful command works, take the cursor to the beginning of PRACTICE by pressing the [Home] key, then select Find and replace. You will be prompted with: 'Text to find?' Next to this prompt is space for up to 31 characters into which you must type the search string – the word or expression that you want the program to find. Any mistakes you make can be corrected with the [←Del] and [Del] keys in the usual ways, and you can also use the [←] and [→] cursor keys as necessary. You are not limited to the characters which appear on the keyboard: the full character set shown in Chapter Six can be used.

Enter the search string 'second' next to 'Text to find', then press [Return]. The cursor will be taken to the second prompt, which reads 'Replace (+/-)?'. Pressing the [+] key will initiate a Replace operation; we are only carrying out a Search operation, so press [-] and [Return].

As soon as you do this, the word 'second' in the first line of the second paragraph will be highlighted to show that a hit has been scored on it, and the cursor will be placed immediately to the right of the highlight.

If you are satisfied with this one hit and don't wish to continue the search, press [Esc] and the highlight will disappear, leaving the cursor conveniently situated for any alterations you may want to make. If on the other hand you want to repeat the same search, press [Return]. As the word 'second' does not recur in the document, no further hit will be registered, and a message will be displayed to say so; press [Esc] to return to ordinary editing.

The search string is remembered between one Find operation and another, so you won't have to re-enter the same string if you want to carry out a second search with it at some later stage. To remove a complete search string from the 'Text to find' prompt, either use repeated presses of the [Del] key or a single press of [Ctrl]/[←Del].

**The Replace command** If you respond to the 'Replace('+/-)?' prompt by pressing [ + ] and then [ Return ], two additional prompts will appear at the top of the screen. 'Replacement text?' provides room for up to 31 characters which will form the replacement string; type in 'subsequent' here and then press [ Return ]. 'Automatic replacement (+/-)?' asks for a ' – ' or ' + ' depending on whether you want to have all occurrences of the target string replaced automatically by the replacement string or whether you want to be asked for confirmation first.

If, for example, you press [ + ] and then [ Return ], every occurrence of 'second' throughout the document will be automatically replaced by 'subsequent'; and if automatic reforming has been selected (from the Word Processing Settings Screen which derives from the Change Settings Menu) then the text will be automatically reformatted to take account of the greater length of the new word.

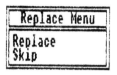

Fig. 4.2 The Replace Menu

If you do not choose automatic replacement, a highlight will be placed on the target string whenever a hit is made, and the little Replace Menu shown in Fig. 4.2 will appear below the Status Line. To confirm a replacement, select 'Replace'; to reject it and move on to the next occurrence of the search string, select 'Skip'. Alternatively, the whole operation can be abandoned in midstream by pressing [ Esc ].

# Insert a file

It is often helpful to be able to insert another file into a document. WordStar 1512 offers two ways of achieving this: the Insert a file command from the F2 Menus and a dot command (.fi) which we shall examine in Chapter Five.

The essential difference between the two commands is that the F2 Menu option physically copies a chosen file into the file on which you are working *while you are editing it*, but the dot command does not bring the new file in until printing is in progress.

When you select the Insert a file option from the second F2 Menu, you will be prompted to take the cursor to the point in the text at which the new file is to be inserted and then to press [ Return ]. The Typing Screen will be replaced by a directory of the files on the Text and Data Disc (on a single-drive machine you will be prompted to change discs), and whatever document you choose from this will

73

be immediately inserted in the original document at the place you have chosen. Alternatively, pressing [Esc] will return you to the Typing Screen.

Newcomers to word processing frequently fail to realise the full potential of the Insert a file option, and limit its use to the occasional joining together of shorter files. In reality, it has many other functions beyond this.

One very powerful and practical idea which you may find useful is to prepare a number of short files each containing some 'module' which might be useful in many different documents. These 'modules' are called **boilerplates**, and their use in conjunction with the dot command .fi is described in Chapter Five. If the idea of building up documents such as contracts from standard blocks appeals to you, you will find several useful suggestions in the next chapter.

## Saving blocks from documents

It is often useful to be able to cut a section out of one document and to save it on disc, later pasting it into another document or just printing it as it stands. WordStar 1512 is not able to do this directly; however, there is a very useful separate accessory program called Sidekick which makes it possible.

Sidekick is an unusual program in that it stays in the computer's memory while you are still running WordStar 1512 – or almost any other MS-DOS program. It is called up by simply pressing [Alt]/[Ctrl] or by holding down both Shift keys simultaneously; once active, it offers a range of desktop accessories including a notepad, a calculator, a calendar and an automatic telephone dialler.

Not only can sections of text be transferred from WordStar 1512 to the Sidekick notepad, but it is also possible to cut – for example – a section out of a spreadsheet and copy it into a letter which is being composed with WordStar 1512.

# Text formatting

Several of the options on the F2 Menus are concerned with changing the format of the text on the screen. Most of the operations will already be familiar to you if you have used a typewriter. However, they are much easier to use with WordStar 1512.

## Tabs and margins

The left and right margins and the tab stops can all be changed at any time while you are working on a document, and the effects will be shown immediately on the screen. For example, if you set the left margin at, say, Column 10, every line which you subsequently type in will start in that column.

Begin by calling down F2 Menu 2, and select the Tabs and margins option; PRACTICE should still be on the screen. You will be prompted as follows:

In many ways, WordStar 1512 treats tabs and margins quite differently from each other. Margins, for example, can be set at the Word processing settings screen, but tabs cannot; furthermore, non-standard margins are not stored with a document on disc, and thus have to be reset when that document is read back (unless the settings are made with dot commands), whereas tab settings *are* remembered from one session to another.

# Margins To change the left and right margins, use the [←] and [→] keys to move the cursor to the required positions and then set the margins with [l] or [r] as required (either in upper or lower case). It is often easier to leave the onscreen left margin setting unaltered and to use the Temporary indent facility (or the .lm dot command described in Chapter Five) if you want to inset a section of text.

The highlighted column marker on the Ruler doesn't move beyond the current right margin, but you will find that the text cursor can be taken as far to the right as you want, and the column counter on the Status Line will continue to record its current position. If you try to take the cursor beyond the right-hand edge of the screen, then the entire display will roll to the left, preventing the cursor from disappearing off the edge. WordStar 1512 documents can thus be wider then the 80 columns shown on the screen.

If you intend to use more than one set of margins in the course of a single document, make sure that Automatic reform is turned off (from the Change Settings Menu); otherwise WordStar 1512 will try to force what you have written according to one set of margins into the format you have chosen for a different part of your document.

# Ordinary tabs Ordinary tabs are marked by little downward-pointing triangles on the Ruler; to insert new tabs into the Ruler, place the cursor in the appropriate column and press [t].

When you are writing or editing a document, pressing the [Tab] key will move the cursor forward to the next tab mark on the same line; if there are no tabs left to the right of the cursor, the cursor will be taken to the first tab on the next line.

The tab effect is produced by writing a series of spaces from the current cursor position to the tab; any tabbed text can be moved either to the right or the left by typing in extra spaces or by deleting those spaces that are already there. If you are in Insert Mode and there is text to the right of the current cursor position, [Tab] will move that text to the right by the number of spaces which have been inserted.

# Decimal tabs Decimal tabs are used to align the decimal points in a column of numbers. A decimal tab is selected by pressing [d] when the Tabs and margins prompt is showing and the cursor is in the appropriate column. Decimal tabs are marked by hash symbols, #, in the ruler line.

Any text (not just numerals) which is entered after the cursor has been tabbed to a decimal tab will be treated in a rather unusual way: as characters are typed in, those which are already at the decimal tab position will be pushed to the left; the cursor will not move across, but will stay under the decimal tab marker. This will continue until either a full-stop or a space is pressed, or until characters entered at the tab have been forced back against the left margin or against previously entered text.

**Clearing tabs** To clear unwanted tab positions, move the column which contains the appropriate tab marker in the Ruler and then press [c]. When the tabs and margins are correctly set, leave the Tabs and margins option by pressing [Return].

# Paragraph reform

The Paragraph reform command is used to adjust any too-short or too-long lines which may have been created in the course of deletions and insertions; normally this job is done by Automatic reform, but there are several reasons why experienced users often prefer to dispense with the Automatic reform facility.

First, Automatic reform is incompatible with two other important features of WordStar 1512, namely Temporary indent and the ability to reset margins in the course of a document; if you expect to use either of these, you must first turn Automatic reform off. There are also several special effects such as hanging paragraphs (so-called 'outdents') which can only be achieved if Automatic reform has been deselected.

Paragraph reform must be selected from the F2 Menus; then place the cursor at the point from which you want the Reform to take place, and press [Return]. The text between this point and the next 'carriage return'–usually the end of the paragraph–will immediately be adjusted to fit correctly between the margins, and the cursor will be taken down to the beginning of the line immediately following the newly reformatted paragraph.

# Temporary indent

Just as the [Tab] key can be used to indent a single line, so the Temporary indent option from the F2 Menus can be used to set a complete paragraph, or a shorter amount of text, in as far as the first tab marker. The procedure varies slightly depending on whether you are indenting text which has not yet been written or going back to adjust the layout of something already committed to the screen, but in both cases you must first make sure that Automatic reform has been deselected.

**Indenting new text** To indent new text, select Temporary indent. You will be prompted to:

```
Move the cursor to the beginning of the text you want
to indent and press [ ].
```

Place the cursor at the point where the new paragraph is to begin and then press [Return]. As you type, the left margin of the new text will be automatically indented level with the first tab, and this will continue until the next time you press the [Return] key.

One disadvantage of this technique is that it is impossible to indent anything less than the whole paragraph; nor is it ever possible to indent text further than the *first* tab marker -- attempts to 'double' an indent simply will not work. Obviously this has implications for the placing of tabs.

**Indenting text which is already written** Indenting previously-entered text is a little more trouble, but makes possible a greater range of text layouts. Select Temporary indent, and while the prompt is on the screen put the text cursor at the head of the area to be indented; this may be the first line of a paragraph or it may be lower, depending on the effect you want. Then press [Return].

This action will have no apparent effect! Now, *without moving the text cursor from its place* select Paragraph reform and again press [Return], and the area between the cursor and the end of the paragraph will be indented and reformatted. Any text *above* the cursor will be unaffected, so make sure that the cursor is in the right place before you start.

To remove a temporary indent, put the text cursor on the first character at the beginning of the indented area, select Paragraph reform and press [Return]. This technique only works on whole paragraphs – you cannot use it to set a portion of a previously indented paragraph back against the left margin, nor will it work at all if the cursor is placed in Column 1 rather than at the the the first character position.

# End page

The End page command is used to force a 'hard' end to the current page as opposed to the 'soft' page break which occurs automatically when you have written enough lines. You might want to do this at the end of a chapter, for example, or after the title-page of a book; another use of it is when mail-merging letters, in order to make sure that every letter is printed on a new page.

End page is an unusual command in some ways: not only does it have a precise dot command equivalent – .pa – but selecting End page from the F2 Menu actually places that dot command into the text, followed by the double underline with which WordStar 1512 always marks page boundaries.

Before using End page, ensure that the cursor is in the first column and that there is no other text on the same line. This is because selecting End page with the cursor in the middle of a line of text will cause the line to be broken at that point; it is a rule of all versions of WordStar that if any text appears on the same line as a .pa command, it will not be printed.

# Centre line

The Centre line command is used, as its name suggests, to move text on a line to a central position between the margins which are in effect at the time the command is selected. If you reset the margins after centering a line, that line will no longer appear properly centered.

When you select the Centre line option, you will be prompted as follows:

```
Move the cursor to anywhere on the line you want to
centre and press [ ].
```

If you wish, you can select the Centre line option even before you have written the line to be centered; when you have written it, press [ Return ] while the cursor is still located anywhere on the line and it will immediately be shifted over.

WordStar 1512 carries out a centering operation by inserting 'pad' spaces at the beginning of the affected line, and these spaces can be freely deleted or added to later. Centered lines are not regarded as finishing with a Carriage Return unless one is specifically included, so it is possible to centre individual lines from the middle of a paragraph if you so wish, though a line centered in this way will be realigned with the rest of the paragraph if you subsequently reformat the paragraph.

# Line spacing

The WordStar 1512 default is for lines to be single-spaced both on the screen and the printer. This can be altered in several ways, some of which cause spacing to be altered on both the printer and the screen, others on the printer only.

The simplest way to change spacing is with the Line spacing option from the F2 Menu. When this is selected you will be offered a Line Spacing Menu, offering the choice between Single, Double and Triple line spacing. New text written after new spacing is chosen will be spaced according to the choice made, but existing text will not be changed to the new format even if automatic formatting is on. New text will appear single, double or triple-spaced on screen as it is written, as will old text which has been reformatted.

This way of choosing double and triple line spacing has the advantage that it permits the screen display to perfectly match the printed appearance of the text, but the corresponding disadvantage that you can't see nearly as much of your work on the screen at one time. Because of this, you may find it convenient to compose all text with single spacing, and to alter this to the final setting only when you have no more editorial changes to make.

**Another way to change line-spacing** A simpler way of altering the line-spacing on the printer while retaining single-spacing on the screen is to change the line pitch with a Line Height dot command (.lh). This is described fully in Chapter Five, but briefly you should know that, for example, the dot command .lh 16 will set most printers to double spacing, and .lh 24 will set triple spacing, and will do so *without altering the line spacing on the monitor*. Page boundaries will still be shown correctly on the screen, and Header and Footer texts (which again are introduced later) will be printed in their proper places. This is therefore probably the best way of achieving double or triple spacing without wasting screen-space. Unfortunately, not all printers support this kind of variable line spacing.

Alternatively, some printers – particularly daisy-wheel printers – have a switch, either on the front panel or hidden away inside, by means of which the line spacing can be changed; if you have one of these you will be able to double-space your work at the printer without changing the program settings. Of course, this means that page boundaries will not fall where expected, so this option is best used only with very short documents.

# Other options

The most important of the remaining options available from the F2 Menus are Saving and Spelling correction. The other option not mentioned so far is Variable names; this refers to mail merge work, and will be considered in its proper place in Chapter Eight.

## Saving

We have already seen that when you are ready to leave the Typing Screen, WordStar 1512 offers two options, namely Save changes and Abandon changes. However, it is as well to get into the habit of saving word processing (and all other sorts of computer work) at regular intervals, rather than only doing it when a particular task is completed; and this can be achieved with the Save command from the F2 Menu. Selecting this will cause the entire text to date to be saved on the appropriate disc, but without leaving the Typing Screen; you can carry on typing from where you were before as soon as your work has been saved on the disc. This is a very important facility which you should use to the full!

WordStar 1512 can deal with files of just about any length which you may need; this may lead you into the habit of working with very long files and only saving your work to disc when you have finished working with a particular file. Imagine that you have spent a complete afternoon revising a long document of this sort, and five minutes before you finish, something goes wrong – a power failure, or a computer breakdown, for example – then you will lose all the work which you have done but not saved to disc. Several hours of work will have been irretrievably lost, and it will be too late to do anything about it.

By regularly Saving your work, you can make sure that there is always a reasonably up-to-date version of your work on disc; any power blackout or computer failure will mean that you can lose no more than the work done between the last Save and the failure, rather than a whole afternoon's work. We were brought up on the principle of saving work once every half hour, but a more practical guide is to ask yourself how much you would be prepared to retype if your work was lost, and to save at that interval.

If, for example, you don't mind retyping six pages, then use the Save option at the end of every sixth page; if you couldn't bear to retype more than a single page, then Save at every page's end.

This is one of those little pieces of good advice that no-one can see the point of until they have lost a couple of hours' work by ignoring it; the universe functions in such a way that you will *always* lose the one thing of which you have no backup copy and which you have been too busy to save at regular intervals while you were creating it.

**Creating .BAK files** Every time you Save your work, the previous version of the file will be given the same filename but with the file extension BAK, for *BAcKup*; if there is a previous .BAK version, it will be erased. For example, by now you probably have two versions of the PRACTICE file saved on the Text and Data Disc – the most recently saved version, called PRACTICE, and the previous version, called PRACTICE.BAK.

An important consequence of this is that you should get into the habit of keeping an eye on the amount of free space on your Text and Data Disc. It is not enough to assume that if there is ample space for a copy of the file you are working on, then everything will be all right, for under certain circumstances the computer may actually need *three* versions of the file – the present one (PRACTICE) the previous one (PRACTICE.BAK) and a working copy of its own, which you will not normally be aware of unless something goes wrong, called PRACTICE. $$$ . If at any time the disc doesn't have enough room for all of these, you could find yourself in trouble, especially if you don't have another disc already formatted to take any overflow.

# Spelling correction

WordStar 1512 is supplied with an extremely effective and rapid spelling checker, which is reached through the F2 Menu Spelling correction option.

Like all spelling checkers, it works by comparing every word in a document against the contents of its own dictionary, and assuming that those words are incorrect which are in the document but not in the dictionary.

This can cause certain problems. In the first place, even a large dictionary will obviously not be able to hold every single word which you might need, especially if you use specialised or foreign words; there will therefore inevitably be a number of occasions when the program will believe words to be incorrect when they are in fact perfectly all right.

Second, the checker works without any examination of the context in which words appear. If you were to write 'Piece finally came to Europe in 1945', the spelling checker would find nothing wrong, as the sentence contains no words which are not present in its dictionary. There *are* special programs called 'context checkers' which can catch errors of this sort, but they are really still at the development stage, and are not yet available for personal computers.

**Checking a passage** To begin checking a passage, make sure that the cursor is at the top of the part of the document that you wish to check, and select Spelling correction from the second F2 Menu. If you have a double-drive machine, you will be prompted to place the disc labelled Dictionary in Drive A; the Text and Data Disc remains in Drive B. On a single-drive machine, follow the prompts regarding disc swapping.

There is always a short delay while the spelling checker is being set up. When everything is ready, the document is scanned, and if any word is found for which the dictionary has no match, the suspect word will be highlighted in the text area and two prompts will appear at the top of the screen.

The first prompt reads 'Suspect word:' and the first suspect word is listed after it. Underneath this is the prompt 'Suggestion:', with space for any correction that the program may suggest to correct the apparent error.

The various suggestions that WordStar 1512 makes are based on some rather complex rules about the kind of mistakes people usually make, such as confusing single and double consonants; if your spelling errors are of a particularly personal kind, there may be occasions when no corrections are suggested at all. If this happens, the message 'Sorry, no suggestions' will appear at the top right of the screen.

**Using the Correction Menu** A Correction Menu will also appear on the screen, placed so as to avoid hiding the highlighted word in the text area. Exactly what this menu contains will depend on whether or not WordStar 1512 has been able to make any suggestions for correcting the apparent error: if at least one suggestion is made, the Correction Menu will look like Fig. 4.3; if no suggestions have been made, then the top four options will be missing. For our current purposes, we will assume that the menu looks as it does in the illustration – as, indeed, it usually will.

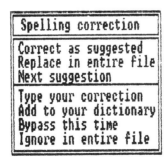

**Fig. 4.3** The Full Correction Menu

The first two options on the Correction Menu will accept the suggested correction as it stands, and replace the error either on this occasion only (the first option) or globally (throughout the current text below the cursor). The third and fourth options enable you to browse back and forth through different suggestions in search of the correct spelling—useful for those insecure spellers who can still recognise the right spelling when they see it.

If WordStar 1512 makes no suggestions, or if the suggestions made do not actually supply the correction you need, you can enter your own correction after selecting the 'Type your correction' option. Your own word will then appear in the 'Suggestion:' line at the top of the screen.

```
┌─────────────────────────────────┐
│ │  Spelling correction        │ │
│ ├─────────────────────────────┤ │
│ │ Correct as typed            │ │
│ │ Replace in entire file      │ │
│ │ Type a new correction       │ │
│ │ Add to your dictionary      │ │
│ │ Bypass this time            │ │
│ │ Ignore in entire file       │ │
│ │ Look for suggestion         │ │
│ └─────────────────────────────┘ │
└─────────────────────────────────┘
```

**Fig. 4.4** The Spelling Checker Second Menu

This correction is itself then checked by WordStar 1512, and the correction process is resumed using the menu illustrated in Fig. 4.4. 'Correct as typed' means that the original error will be replaced by your input once only; 'Replace in entire file' will cause a replacement of the error by your new correction throughout the file 'below the cursor'; 'Type a new correction' will abandon whatever you have already typed, and allow you to try again; 'Add to your dictionary' will store the new correction in your personal dictionary (usually on the Dictionary Disc, as we show below) and simultaneously correct the error globally below the cursor; 'Bypass this time' will accept the new word on this occasion only; 'Ignore in entire file' will cause the correction to be treated as correct as far as this checking operation is concerned; and 'Look for suggestion' will force another search of the dictionary.

Returning to the main Correction Menu, 'Add to your dictionary' will save the suspect word from the original text on your personal dictionary, 'Bypass this time' will cause it to be skipped and 'Ignore in entire file' will cause it to be accepted during this spelling check only.

## The Main Dictionary

The main dictionary supplied with WordStar 1512 contains approximately 85,000 words, and unlike the dictionaries included with many programs, it recognises British spellings, so you won't be constantly irritated by being told that 'centre' and 'colour' are wrong. Nonetheless, you will certainly find that there are a number of words which do not appear in the dictionary; most of these will be personal names and addresses, though there may also be some specialised words belonging to, for example, particular trades, businesses or academic disciplines.

You can include such items in your own personal dictionary, which can hold up to an additional 1,500 words, and when the spelling checker is in operation, the words in this personal dictionary will be treated in exactly the same way as the contents of the main dictionary.

Because there is no easy way to remove an item from the personal dictionary, it is very important to make absolutely certain that any words you add to it are themselves correctly spelt; otherwise, if you make the same mistake again in another document, it will pass unnoticed.

It is also vitally important that you should not attempt to edit either the main dictionary or your personal dictionary using a disc editor, a debugger, or a text editor such as EDLIN. This is because the information in the dictionary files is stored in a special compressed form, and *any* tampering with the dictionary could easily result in the whole file being destroyed. For your own sake, please take this warning seriously – the dictionary files are not a suitable subject for exploration by well-meaning amateurs.

## The Personal Dictionaries

There is already one (empty) personal dictionary file on the WordStar 1512 Dictionary Disc, but there is no reason why you should not add others if you wish, up to, and even beyond, the total capacity of the disc. This is done through the Drive/directory option of the Change Settings Menu.

Figure 4.5 shows how this normally appears; to create a new personal dictionary, simply type in the name of the new dictionary you wish to create over the name which is already there, and then press [ Return ].

Should the disc be too full to allow a new personal dictionary, you can even place it on another disc – on a two-drive system, the Text and Data Disc will probably be the most obvious choice. If you have a hard disc, obviously this will be the most rational place for all your personal dictionaries to be stored.

# Managing without menus

Once you are familiar with WordStar 1512, it is possible to speed up your work to some extent by reducing your reliance on the F2 Menus. For example, if you have already been working with the first menu – the one which has Boldface and Underline on it – you can call up any of the other options on the same menu by pressing Function Key [ F2 ] followed by the initial letter of the option you want to use – there is no need to wait for the menu itself to appear.

```
┌─────────────────────────────────────────────────────┐
│  ┌──────────────────────────────────────────────┐   │
│  │  Drive / directory (path) / filename          │   │
│  ├──────────────────────────────────────────────┤   │
│  │ Text files                                     │   │
│  │ B:\                              PRACTICE       │   │
│  │                                                 │   │
│  │ Personal dictionary                             │   │
│  │ A:\1512\DICTNARY\              PERSONAL.DCT      │   │
│  │                                                 │   │
│  │ Main Dictionary                                 │   │
│  │ A:\1512\DICTNARY\               MAIN.DTY        │   │
│  │                                                 │   │
│  │ Internal Dictionary                             │   │
│  │ A:\1512\DICTNARY\             INTERNAL.DTY       │   │
│  │ Mailing list file                               │   │
│  │ B:\                            SAMPLE.MLD        │   │
│  └──────────────────────────────────────────────┘   │
└─────────────────────────────────────────────────────┘
```

### Type new answer over old.

**Fig. 4.5** Changing the Dictionary Disc Drive

This short cut is not so readily available if the 'wrong' F2 Menu has been most recently used; however, if you happen to remember that the 'wrong' menu is current, you can still speed you work up by pressing Function Key [F2] *twice* before pressing the option letter. At first, this may seem rather an awkward process, but in reality you will find that before long this will come almost automatically.

## Postscript

Once you have become familiar with the information contained in this chapter, you should be able to achieve a wide variety of different effects by the judicious use of the options provided by the F2 Menus. A number of these effects are represented on screen by colour codes, while messages which appear on the Status Line are used to signal the beginning or end of others.

Deleting these special effects involves finding and removing the 'invisible space' which marks their beginning, and often their end. It is worth spending some time familiarising yourself with this technique.

The F2 Menus also provide several ways in which the layout of a document can be changed; these include altering the left and right margins, inserting normal and decimal tabs, centering lines, indenting whole paragraphs and the like.

Finally, WordStar 1512 offers an extremely rapid and sophisticated spelling checker, which not only checks your text for errors but also offers its own suggestions for corrections. You can also build up your own personal dictionary for those items which are not in the main dictionary provided.

# CHAPTER FIVE

# WordStar 1512 Dot Commands

## Preview

In this chapter we shall look at a new kind of WordStar 1512 command: the dot command.

If you have used 'standard' WordStar, or a program which imitates it, you will already be familiar with dot commands. Most of the dot commands which you already know can be used in just the same way in WordStar 1512, and you will probably only need to glance through this chapter to refresh your memory and to check up on the few differences which exist.

If you are new to WordStar-type programs, you will find that dot commands provide several useful ways to format your work while you are printing it. Some of the commands are used to set parameters which will generally apply to the entire document on which you are working, while others can be used to make minor adjustments to keep your work looking tidy when it is printed out.

Dot commands are most important when used in conjunction with mail-merging. This aspect of their use is dealt with in detail in Chapter Eight, but you should try to understand the principles of dot commands as described in this chapter before you begin to tackle mail-merge work.

## About dot commands

As we have seen, most word processing programs fall into one or the other of two fairly clearcut categories: either they present the user with a more-or-less accurate representation on the screen of what will eventually appear on paper – a WYSIWYG format – or they rely on codes incorporated in the text to control formatting, the changing of print styles and other similar features.

WordStar 1512 offers both of these facilities. The fact that so many options can be reached through the F2 Menus makes it possible to achieve quite sophisticated results with great ease, without requiring the user to learn any of the complex key-combinations which form an essential part of many other word processing programs.

More advanced users are often less concerned with a program's absolute ease of use than with achieving complex effects relatively easily. It is these users who will find dot commands most useful.

With these dot commands it is simple to create one part of a document right-justified, and another part with a ragged right margin; to use special header and footer texts; to start a document at a particular page number, printing that number at a chosen location within either the top or bottom margin; to turn page numbering on and off at will; to change margins while a document is being printed; and very many other similar effects.

When work like this is being done, the screen display at times moves away from the WYSIWYG format to which you have probably become accustomed. Provided you are prepared to grasp the additional advantages that the new format offers, this is nothing to worry about.

You will in any case need to become familiar with at least the general principles of dot commands before you can make full use of the very powerful database facility which WordStar 1512 provides for form letters and the like, as most of the mail-merge features are controlled by special, and extremely powerful, dot commands allowing you, for example, to select just which items will be mail-merged according to details which you have already stored in a separate file. We shall see how this is done in Chapter Eight.

Dot commands and the F2 Menu commands which we have already met can be freely mixed in the same document.

Incidentally, dot commands can pose problems for users of electronic mail services, as some of them also use dot commands for their own purposes. To avoid unpleasant surprises, it is a good idea to strip dot commands out of any document which you intend to transmit down a telephone line.

## What are dot commands?

Although in this chapter and others we have talked at some length about dot commands, we have not yet actually defined them. The time has now come to attempt a simple definition: basically, a dot command consists of a 'dot'– a full-stop – followed always by two command letters, and often by a space and a set of letters or numbers which form the 'command tail'. The dot is always placed in column one, and it must be followed immediately by the two command letters. The dot and the associated command letters appear highlighted, and the characters themselves are coloured red on a colour monitor. Dot commands can be entered in either capitals or lower-case letters; in this book, all the commands are shown in lower-case.

If a dot command is incorrectly or incompletely entered, a question mark '?' appears in the flag column on the far right of the screen. Incorrect commands, and anything which occurs after them on the same line, are merely ignored during print out.

**Dot commands and paragraph reformatting** You should be very careful about where in your documents you place dot commands; in particular, don't put them in the middle of paragraphs. This is because if you reformat a paragraph containing a dot command, the command may well be moved away from Column 1, and when this happens it will no longer function as a dot command.

For the same reason, be careful not to centre a line which has a dot command in it; normally you wouldn't want to do this, but you might do it to a line in a Header or Footer without thinking.

# Using dot commands

The WordStar 1512 manual provides an alphabetical list of what it calls 'Page layout commands'. Our approach will be a little different; we shall look at the commands in groups, beginning with those which would normally occur at the very beginning of a document.

If you enter several dot commands at the very beginning of a document, you may be surprised to notice that as far as the Status Line is concerned, you are still on Line 1. This is because dot commands don't count as lines in the same way as ordinary text. In this regard they are a little like the 'invisible spaces' which store the codes for bold and underlined type, etc. This point is particularly important when you are preparing a new page layout; unless the dot commands governing that layout are placed *before* the first line of 'real' text, they will not come into effect until the beginning of the second page.

A sensible way of taking advantage of this is to create a 'template' file containing a large number of these 'top of document' commands. In this way, you can establish headers, page length, margins and many other similar features which you want to keep consistent from one document to another, and then Insert the file containing these commands into the very beginning of each of your new documents, thus ensuring that successive documents will have the same settings without your needing to remember and re-enter them afresh each time.

## Top of document commands

Remember that although these commands are described here as 'Top of document commands', they can be used elsewhere as well; however, as they affect details of page layout, they will not be effective until a *new* page has been started. It follows that their natural place is either at the very beginning of a new document, or else at some point where a document must take on a radically different appearance; in the latter case, they might naturally occur immediately before a hard page break.

**.hm, .fm, .mt, .mb—Header and Footer margins** WordStar 1512 offers four different commands to establish or adjust top and bottom margins. These are .hm, .fm, .mt and .mb.

.hm refers to the amount of space which is to be left between any text which is to appear in a header and the top line of the actual text of the document. The normal form of the command is

.hm *n*

where *n* (the 'command tail') is any suitable value. Note that there must be a space between the second letter of the dot command itself and the beginning of the command tail.

Closely related to the .hm command is .mt, which fixes the size of the margin between the top of the paper and the first line of the actual text; the header appears *within* this margin. Figure 5.1 should help to illustrate the relationship between these two rather similar commands.

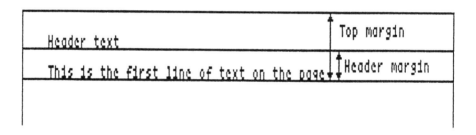

**Fig. 5.1** The relationship between Header Margin and Top Margin

WordStar 1512 normally assigns a default value of 2 to .hm and of 3 to .mt—in other words, the header appears on the very first line of the paper, and there are then two blank lines before actual text begins. If you want a greater separation between the header text and the top of the document, you might use .hm 3 and .mt 4, which would leave four lines between the top of the paper and the top of the text, with the header appearing three lines above the text.

A similar situation applies to margins at the foot of the page; .fm shows how much space is to be left between the end of the text and a footer, and .mb indicates how many lines are to be left between the end of the text and the actual bottom of the paper; the footer is to be printed within this area. The relationship is illustrated in Fig. 5.2.

If no .fm or .mb commands are used, WordStar 1512 will assume a Footer Margin of 2 lines and a Bottom Margin of 8 lines.

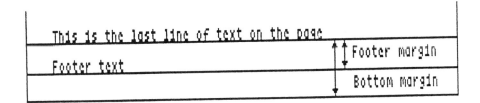

**Fig. 5.2** The relationship between Footer Margin and Bottom Margin

In calculating the details of page layout, it is important to remember that WordStar 1512 always assumes a line-pitch of 6 lines to the inch in both top and bottom margins, regardless of what values may have been set elsewhere.

**Header and Footer texts** Headers and footers are single lines of text which appear respectively at the top and bottom of pages. A report writer might place the page number and the name of the report in the header of each page, and perhaps 'Continued' in the footer; a writer of articles might put the title of the article and his name in the header and 'More' or 'mf' in the footer.

**.he and .fo—Header and Footer texts** Header and footer texts are controlled by the .he and .fo commands respectively; simply type the dot command, leave one space blank and then type in the header or footer text as appropriate.

Text in headers and footers can be manipulated in most of the usual ways with the F2 Menu – it can be underlined or emboldened, for example – and it can be located with the aid of the [Tab] key. However, it cannot be centered by means of the Centre line command, because this will centre the dot command as well, and thus render it ineffective.

To change the text in a header or footer, simply use a new .he or .fo command; to cancel headers or footers, enter .he or .fo and then press [Return]; from that point on, the header or footer line will be blank.

If you want to insert page numbers at some point other than the usual WordStar 1512 position (which is in the centre at the bottom), you can do this by placing a hash, '#', in the place where you want the number to be printed, always provided that page numbering has been previously turned on by the .pn command introduced below.

# Pagination commands

WordStar 1512 has five dot commands which affect pagination; like the margin and header commands which we have already seen, they will most commonly be used at the head of a document, although they can occur elsewhere.

**.pl—Page length** .pl is used to change the length of a page from the WordStar 1512 default of 66 lines, or whatever other value may have been set at the Page Layout Screen. The form of the command is

.pl *n*

where *n* represents the page length in lines.

This command sets the *total* length of the page, from the top of the paper to the bottom; this includes any area set aside for top and bottom margins and for headers and footers.

Although a standard 9½" x 11" continuous-form sheet will accommodate 66 lines of text at the standard line pitch of 6 lines per inch, this can be changed if the line pitch is altered as described immediately below, or if some other setting is applied by, for example, the use of the printer DIP switches as described in Chapter Two.

**.lh—Line height** To alter the line pitch, use the command

.lh *n*

where *n* has one of the values shown in Fig. 5.3.

```
COMMAND                 RESULT

.lh  6        8 lines per inch - close single spacing
.lh  8        6 lines per inch - normal single spacing
.lh 12        4 lines per inch - one-and-a-half spacing
.lh 16        3 lines per inch - double spacing
.lh 24        2 lines per inch - triple spacing
```

Fig. 5.3 Possible values for line height settings

As soon as the number has been entered and the cursor has been taken away from the command line, the on-screen page-break markers will be revised to take account of the new values; these take the form of a double line across the screen with a 'P' in the flag column on the right of the screen.

Actually, many printers will be able to cope with values other than those shown, though sometimes with unpredictable results; try out a few values to see whether your printer can make sensible use of this facility. However, it is best not to try setting the value of *n* to zero, as this can cause difficulties with the page-break markers.

Remember also that the .lh command only affects line pitch in the text area of the screen, and not in the top and bottom margin areas, where lines are always printed at a spacing of 6 per inch.

**.pa—Page break** Hard page breaks are forced by the .pa command; this is identical to the End page command from the first F2 Menu. There is no command tail, and anything which appears on the same line as the command and to the right of it will be ignored during printing. All subsequent soft page breaks will be recalculated when this command is used.

The most obvious use of the command is at the foot of a title page or the end of a chapter, in order to make the next section appear at the head of the following page; it may also be used to force a break so that a lengthy table which follows the break can be displayed on a single page. It *must* be used at the end of a mail-merge letter, to force each new letter onto a different page.

Another command which is very similar to the .pa command is the conditional page break command .cp, which is introduced later.

**.pc, .op and .pn—Page numbering** When a footer text has not been explicitly defined with the .fo command, page numbers will normally default to the centre of each page at the bottom – column 33 when the default margins are in use. This can be altered with the command.

.pc *n*

which forces page numbers to appear in the column specified by the number *n*.

This command should not be used when printing text right justified, as the page number will be forced against the right margin regardless of the column number specified. To avoid this, turn the justification off at the foot of each page and restore it at the beginning of the next page.

Page numbers can be omitted altogether from the printed text with the .op command. If this is done, WordStar 1512 will continue to keep a record of page numbers, assuming that the first page of the file is number 1.

Page numbering can be switched on, and any number chosen as the initial page number, with the command

.pn *n*

where *n* represents the number to be given to the next complete page; subsequent pages will be numbered consecutively.

You can use .pn on its own to turn the default page numbering back on after it has been turned off with the .op command.

# Formatting commands

Five of the WordStar 1512 dot commands are used for formatting; they differ from the commands we have seen already in that they can occur at any point in a document, and are effective immediately. They are used to determine the left and right margins, to set conditional page breaks, to select and deselect right – justified printing, and to vary the offset between the extreme left head position on the printer and the edge of the text area.

It is with these commands that WordStar 1512 moves most strongly away from a WYSIWYG format. The variations in line and page-length which they control are not reflected in any way on the screen, and page boundaries no longer occur predictably. Because of this, you may occasionally find it helpful to print a draft copy of your work to ensure that page boundaries and other features are sensibly located; however, this situation can be avoided by the use of the conditional page-break command discussed later.

**.pf – paragraph formatting** The marginal and justification commands described later in this section do not take effect unless the . pf command have been turned on – 'pf' is sometimes expanded into 'Paragraph Forming' and sometimes into 'Print Formatting'.

The purpose of Paragraph Forming is to force all text which is printed after its selection to lie properly between the *dimensions* of the set margins, rather than according to the number of characters in each line. In effect this means that unless the margins have been changed by the dot commands introduced below, the left margin will be set at zero and the right margin at 65.

For example, if one section of a piece of work is composed in Pica (10 cpi) type and a second section in 17 cpi type, the right margins of the two sections will not match each other unless Paragraph Forming has been selected; with Paragraph Forming turned on, the lines of the section composed in 17 cpi type would occupy the same distance left-to-right on the paper as the lines in 1- cpi type. The point is rather a tricky one to grasp 'cold', but Fig. 5.4 shows how the same passage composed of both 10 cpi and 17 cpi type would appear first with Paragraph Forming turned off and then with it turned on.

WordStar 1512 assumes that Paragraph Forming is normally off except when you are carrying out mail-merging, in which case the default is Paragraph Forming On. This is because the essence of Paragraph Forming is that it forces all material to lie properly between the margins *regardless of the appearance of the document on the screen*.

To select Paragraph Forming, use the command

.pf on

and to turn it off again use

.pf off

94

This paragraph was composed in Pica type between the default
WordStar 1512 margins.  Paragraph Formatting is off.

This paragraph is printed in 17 cpi type with paragraph
formatting off.  The line-breaks are in the same place on the
paper as they are on the screen, but the lines are much shorter.

.pf on
This paragraph is also composed in Pica type.  Paragraph
Formatting is on, but this has no effect on Pica type.

This paragraph is printed in 17 cpi type with Paragraph
Formatting turned on.  The lines are printed to the same length
as those in the previous paragraph, but the line breaks are not
the same on paper as they are on-screen.

(How it looks on the screen)

This paragraph was composed in Pica type between the default
WordStar 1512 margins.  Paragraph Formatting is off.

This paragraph is printed in 17 cpi type with paragraph
formatting off. The line-breaks are in the same place on the
paper as they are on the screen, but the lines are much shorter.

This paragraph is also composed in Pica type.  Paragraph
Formatting is on, but this has no effect on Pica type.

This paragraph is printed in 17 cpi type with Paragraph Formatting turned on.  The lines are printed to the
same length as those in the previous paragraph, but the line breaks are not the same on paper as they are on-
screen.

(How it looks when printed)

**Fig. 5.4** Paragraph Forming

A third option is to make Paragraph Forming discretionary, with the command

.pf dis

Discretionary Paragraph Forming means that provided a paragraph contains no mail-merge variables (which will be introduced in the next chapter), and provided that it is already properly formed (meaning, in effect, that it would not be changed if the Paragraph reform command from the first F2 Menu were applied to it), then it will be printed exactly as it appears on screen, regardless of any font changes and the like which might cause it not to line up properly with other sections of the document.

## .lm and .rm — Left and Right margins
With .pf turned on, it is possible to reset the left and right margins by means of two dot commands, .lm for the left margin and .rm for the right margin. As you will probably have guessed by now, the commands take the form

.lm $n$

and

.rm $n$

where — and this is an important point to remember — $n$ represents the position of the margin not in real characters but in 'Pica-equivalent characters'; in other words, $n$ really measures tenths of an inch rather than actual character widths.

To illustrate this, look at Fig. 5.5. This was printed with the right margin set by .rm 40, and the top paragraph (in 10 cpi type) does indeed have the right margin 40 characters to the right of the left margin. However, the second paragraph, in 17 cpi type, is set within the same margins, although its lines are longer than the nominal 40 characters set by the dot command.

The great advantages of the .lm and .rm commands over changing the margin settings through the F2 Menu are that they apply to all text below them in the document, without any need to manually reform each paragraph if a new ruler is used; and that they permit margins to be altered with only a couple of key-strokes. Their disadvantage is that they make it impossible to identify page breaks on screen.

## .oj — Justification
Even if right justification has not been selected when a document is being composed, it can still be turned on during printing by the command .oj. Like the margin commands described above, this is only effective when Paragraph Forming has been turned on.

```
This paragraph is printed in Pica type
(10 cpi), with the left margin set at 0
and the right margin set at 40. The
line-breaks are not in the same place on
paper as they were on the screen.
```

This paragraph is printed in 17 cpi type; the margins are set in the
same positions as in the previous paragraph, but there are many more
characters to a line. Once again, the on-screen line-breaks do not
correspond with the printed text.

**Fig. 5.5** Constant margin settings with different fonts

The command tail takes three forms – on, off or dis – with the following meanings

.oj on

will turn right justification on,

.oj off

will cause the right margin to be printed ragged – this is the default – and

.oj dis

will cause printed text to be right justified only if it contains mail-merge variables, as described in the next chapter, or if the text would be changed if Paragraph reform were applied to it.

**.cp – Conditional page break** When composing a document using WordStar 1512's WYSIWYG features, you can always be quite certain of where the page breaks will occur, because they are clearly marked on the screen by a double line; and any adjustements which you may want to make to the natural 'soft' breaks can be carried out with the .pa command, to force a hard break at any point you wish.

When you are composing a document which makes use of a number of different margin settings and type-sizes, determining just where page breaks lie becomes very difficult. Most of the time, this probably doesn't really matter too much, as long as hard breaks can be forced at appropriate points such as at the end of each chapter or section.

Sometimes, however, you may want to be certain that a particular group of lines really will all be printed on the same page. This is where the Conditional Page break command comes in. This has the form

.cp *n*

where *n* represents the number of lines occurring *after* the command which must be kept together. Obviously the value of *n* must be less than the number of lines allocated to the text area of a page; otherwise it will not be possible to fit the group onto any page of your document.

Suppose, for example, that you are quoting Ben Jonson's 'Ode'. This is only 12 lines long, and obviously you would not want it split between pages nor, probably, printed with double spacing. You would therefore enter it as follows (the notes on the right of the page would not be in your work – they are here for guidance only.)

.lh 8   *(to force single line spacing; not necessary if already in effect)*
.cp 12 *(to prevent the poem being split between pages)*
.pf on *(to enable new margins to be set)*
.lm 30 *(sets left margin in by 30 Pica characters – 3 – )*

It is not growing like a tree
In bulk, doth make men better be;
Or standing long – an oak, three hundred year –
   To fall at last, dry, bald and sere.
     A lily of a day
     Is fairer far in May,
Although it fall and die that night
It was the plant and flower of light.
   In small proportions we just beauties see,
   And in short measures, life may perfect be.

     Ben Jonson
.lm 5 (resets left margin)

Use the .cp command frequently while you are doing work which cannot be formatted on screen – it will help to keep everything tidy when your documents are printed out.

**.po – Page offset** The last of the formatting commands is used to alter the offset between the extreme left head position on the printer and the actual edge of the text area. The command takes the usual form,

.po *n*

where *n* represents the page offset in nominal character widths of one tenth of an inch.

# Miscellaneous commands

The remainder of the WordStar 1512 dot commands are rather a miscellaneous collection. They are used for inserting comments of some sort into your text, and for enabling you to chain several documents together at printing time.

**.ig – Ignore** The first of the miscellaneous commands is .ig; the letters stand for *ig*nore, and any message which appears on the same line as the .ig command will be ignored during printing.

The same effect can be achieved by using two dots one after the other, '..', or, less officially, by using any combination of letters which WordStar 1512 does not recognise as a command after a dot in the first column. In this case, a question mark will appear in the flag column on the right of the screen to warn you that the command has not been understood.

**.fi – File insertion** Very long documents are frequently built up out of a number of shorter ones. A book, for example, is usually made up of a number of chapters, and a long report may be composed of several sections and subsections. It is often wise to adhere to this same arrangement while word processing a document, assigning each chapter or section to a separate file and then joining them together during printing.

The command which is used for File Insertion takes the form

.fi *path and filename*

where *path and filename* includes all the directory and path information necessary for WordStar 1512 to find the named file. If the file to be inserted is on the root directory of the disc in Drive B, the command tail will take the form

B: \ *filename*

If the file is in a subdirectory called LETTERS in Drive B, the command tail will look like this:

99

Directories, subdirectories and paths are described in more detail towards the end of the next chapter.

If a file named for insertion is not printed with the file which 'calls' it, the probable reason is that WordStar 1512 was not able to find it on the specified disc and directory; check that the name and path are correctly given after the dot command before trying again.

The File Insert command can be used in two different ways, called **nesting** and **chaining**. The distinction between these two modes of operation is an important one to understand.

In nesting, one file is inserted into the middle of another during printing; after the end of that file has been printed, WordStar 1512 resumes the printing of the first document from the point which had been reached when the File Insert command was found. If you want, a third file can be similarly nested within the second document, and so on; in fact, up to eight documents can be nested one inside the other, though few people will ever need to use so many.

Chaining, on the other hand, involves calling a new document from the end of the current document, rather than from the middle of it; once the second document has been printed, WordStar 1512 does not return to print the remainder of the first document; however, the second document may itself chain a third, and so on.

Chaining and nesting can be carried on in any combination, subject only to the maximum of eight files being handled at any one time. This number can be enlarged further, of course, by using the Insert a file option from the second F2 Menu. Unlike the .fi command, the Insert a file option physically puts a copy of the named file into the first file during editing, and this may cause the size of the resultant joint file to become inconveniently large.

With ordinary printing, it is not possible to use the command recursively – that is, you cannot put '.fi PRACTICE' at the foot of the document called PRACTICE so that it will be chained to itself and thus printed repeatedly. You *can* do this with the List printing option, and the file will then be printed twice – once as the original file and once as the 'insert'. This probably isn't very useful!

# The order of commands

In general, the order in which dot commands occur is not very important. There are, however, a few rules which must be observed.

First, all commands which affect the top and bottom margin areas of a page must come higher in the document than any of that page's text. This is most immediately relevant to the first page of a document: top and bottom margins, page numbers, header and footer texts and the like *must* precede the first line of text, or they will not become effective until the second page of the document.

Second, dot commands controlling justification and right and left margin settings will be ignored unless they have been preceded by the command '.pf on'. The same command should also be used before font changes, unless you are content for the right margin to vary as the font changes. If a font change occurs in the middle of a line of text and you have not selected Paragraph Formatting, then the line in which the font change occurs may not match the margins of either previous or following text.

Third, dot commands affect both the document in which they occur and any documents called from it and printed at the same time with the File Insert dot command '.fi'; because of this, if you want an inserted document to have different marginal settings from the document which calls it, suitable dot commands must be included at the head of the inserted file.

# Postscript

With the dot commands described in this chapter, you can create a wide range of special effects, many of which are not available in any other way. Because they move away a little from the easy-to-use WYSIWYG format of most WordStar 1512 work, you will find that you will need to experiment a little with them before you can be sure of getting the best out of them.

Many users find that dot commands are most useful in combination with Word Star 1512's mail-merge facilities. The next chapter describes the use of mail-merge, and introduces the additional necessary dot commands.

# CHAPTER SIX

# Some advanced effects with WordStar 1512

## Preview

In this chapter, we look first at some of the extra facilities which WordStar 1512 offers, such as its expanded character set; next, we see how some simple dodges can be used to supplement the program's features; and finally we shall look at some of the ways in which the MS-DOS utilities supplied with your computer can be used to make your word processing even easier.

## The extended character set

Each of the different keystrokes available from a computer keyboard has its own ASCII code number – we met ASCII briefly in Chapters One and Three. Most of these keystrokes generate characters, such as 'A' or '&' , but others produce 'control codes' , like 'Backspace' and 'Carriage Return' .

Standard ASCII codes only occupy the numbers between 0 and 127 inclusive, leaving the numbers between 128 and 255 inclusive blank. Computers which make use of these 'missing codes' are said to have an 'extended character set', but because the codes are non-standard, different computers – and different programs – use them in quite different ways.

The extended IBM character-set which can be reached through WordStar 1512 includes, in addition to the characters shown on the key-tops, a few Greek characters (unfortunately not the complete alphabet), some graphics characters, and some useful mathematical and other symbols. You can see the full range of characters, and their ASCII numbers, by displaying the file called CHARSET, which is on the Text and Data Disc.

| Denary | Hex | Denary | Hex | Denary | Hex |
|--------|-----|--------|-----|--------|-----|
| 1 | 1 | 2 | 2 | 3 | 3 |
| 4 | 4 | 5 | 5 | 6 | 6 |
| 7 | 7 | 8 | 8 | 9 | 9 |
| 10 | A | 11 | B | 12 | C |
| 13 | D | 14 | E | 15 | F |
| 16 | 10 | 17 | 11 | 18 | 12 |
| 19 | 13 | 20 | 14 | 21 | 15 |
| 22 | 16 | 23 | 17 | 24 | 18 |
| 25 | 19 | 26 | 1A | 27 | 1B |
| 28 | 1C | 29 | 1D | 30 | 1E |
| 31 | 1F | 32 | 20 | 33 | 21 |
| 34 | 22 | 35 | 23 | 36 | 24 |
| 37 | 25 | 38 | 26 | 39 | 27 |
| 40 | 28 | 41 | 29 | 42 | 2A |
| 43 | 2B | 44 | 2C | 45 | 2D |
| 46 | 2E | 47 | 2F | 48 | 30 |
| 49 | 31 | 50 | 32 | 51 | 33 |
| 52 | 34 | 53 | 35 | 54 | 36 |
| 55 | 37 | 56 | 38 | 57 | 39 |
| 58 | 3A | 59 | 3B | 60 | 3C |
| 61 | 3D | 62 | 3E | 63 | 3F |
| 64 | 40 | 65 | 41 | 66 | 42 |
| 67 | 43 | 68 | 44 | 69 | 45 |
| 70 | 46 | 71 | 47 | 72 | 48 |
| 73 | 49 | 74 | 4A | 75 | 4B |
| 76 | 4C | 77 | 4D | 78 | 4E |
| 79 | 4F | 80 | 50 | 81 | 51 |
| 82 | 52 | 83 | 53 | 84 | 54 |
| 85 | 55 | 86 | 56 | 87 | 57 |
| 88 | 58 | 89 | 59 | 90 | 5A |
| 91 | 5B | 92 | 5C | 93 | 5D |
| 94 | 5E | 95 | 5F | 96 | 60 |
| 97 | 61 | 98 | 62 | 99 | 63 |
| 100 | 64 | 101 | 65 | 102 | 66 |
| 103 | 67 | 104 | 68 | 105 | 69 |
| 106 | 6A | 107 | 6B | 108 | 6C |
| 109 | 6D | 110 | 6E | 111 | 6F |
| 112 | 70 | 113 | 71 | 114 | 72 |
| 115 | 73 | 116 | 74 | 117 | 75 |
| 118 | 76 | 119 | 77 | 120 | 78 |
| 121 | 79 | 122 | 7A | 123 | 7B |
| 124 | 7C | 125 | 7D | 126 | 7E |
| 127 | 7F | 128 | 80 | 129 | 81 |
| 130 | 82 | 131 | 83 | 132 | 84 |
| 133 | 85 | 134 | 86 | 135 | 87 |
| 136 | 88 | 137 | 89 | 138 | 8A |
| 139 | 8B | 140 | 8C | 141 | 8D |
| 142 | 8E | 143 | 8F | 144 | 90 |
| 145 | 91 | 146 | 92 | 147 | 93 |
| 148 | 94 | 149 | 95 | 150 | 96 |
| 151 | 97 | 152 | 98 | 153 | 99 |
| 154 | 9A | 155 | 9B | 156 | 9C |
| 157 | 9D | 158 | 9E | 159 | 9F |
| 160 | A0 | 161 | A1 | 162 | A2 |
| 163 | A3 | 164 | A4 | 165 | A5 |
| 166 | A6 | 167 | A7 | 168 | A8 |
| 169 | A9 | 170 | AA | 171 | AB |
| 172 | AC | 173 | AD | 174 | AE |
| 175 | AF | 176 | B0 | 177 | B1 |
| 178 | B2 | 179 | B3 | 180 | B4 |
| 181 | B5 | 182 | B6 | 183 | B7 |
| 184 | B8 | 185 | B9 | 186 | BA |
| 187 | BB | 188 | BC | 189 | BD |
| 190 | BE | 191 | BF | 192 | C0 |
| 193 | C1 | 194 | C2 | 195 | C3 |
| 196 | C4 | 197 | C5 | 198 | C6 |
| 199 | C7 | 200 | C8 | 201 | C9 |
| 202 | CA | 203 | CB | 204 | CC |
| 205 | CD | 206 | CE | 207 | CF |
| 208 | D0 | 209 | D1 | 210 | D2 |
| 211 | D3 | 212 | D4 | 213 | D5 |
| 214 | D6 | 215 | D7 | 216 | D8 |
| 217 | D9 | 218 | DA | 219 | DB |
| 220 | DC | 221 | DD | 222 | DE |
| 223 | DF | 224 | E0 | 225 | E1 |
| 226 | E2 | 227 | E3 | 228 | E4 |
| 229 | E5 | 230 | E6 | 231 | E7 |
| 232 | E8 | 233 | E9 | 234 | EA |
| 235 | EB | 236 | EC | 237 | ED |
| 238 | EE | 239 | EF | 240 | F0 |
| 241 | F1 | 242 | F2 | 243 | F3 |
| 244 | F4 | 245 | F5 | 246 | F6 |
| 247 | F7 | 248 | F8 | 249 | F9 |
| 250 | FA | 251 | FB | 252 | FC |
| 253 | FD | 254 | FE | 255 | FF |

**Fig. 6.1** Conversion table Base 10/Base 16

This file also shows the code for each character in hexadecimal form. (Hexadecimal numbers, often abbreviated to 'hex', are numbers in Base 16 – they use the ordinary number symbols to represent digits between 0 – 9, then A for 10, B for 11 and so on, up to F for 16; they are frequently used in computing work, and a complete list of hex numbers and their Base 10 equivalents between 0 and 255 is shown in Fig. 6.1.) Printer manuals often refer to characters by their hexadecimal codes rather than by the more familiar Base 10 numbers.

# Characters that aren't shown on the keyboard

To use any of the characters from the extended set, hold down [Ctrl] and press keys on the number pad (*not* the numbers on the top row of the ordinary alphabetical part of the keyboard) to make up the ASCII code of the character you want. You do not have to press the [Num Lock] key.

For example, if you want alpha, 'α', which has the code 224, hold down [Alt] and press, one after the other, the [2], [2] and [4] keys; when you release [Alt], the 'α' will appear.

You can use the same technique to select all the WordStar 1512 characters, not just the ones which can't be reached through the keyboard. For example, holding down [Alt] and then selecting [6] and [5] will give you a capital 'A'.

# Printing non-standard characters

One of the problems with the set of non-standard characters – those with ASCII codes greater than 127 – is precisely that because they are non-standard, printers which are not IBM-compatible will refuse to print them, or will print different non-standard characters of their own. If your printer has its own set of non-standard characters, you will probably find that selecting, for example Character 193 (which will appear on the screen as a graphics symbol like an inverted capital 'T') will cause a completely different character to be printed, depending on your own printer's character set. For example, on an Epson FX-80 printer it will print an italic capital 'A'.

In this way you can print any character of which your printer is capable by holding [Alt] and pressing the required code; what appears on the screen will probably bear little resemblance to what is actually printed, but you may regard this as a fairly small price to pay for being able to print out non-standard characters.

This technique is particularly useful if you need to gain access to accented characters, which are supported by most printers but have no standard ASCII numbers and are not represented in the IBM character set – simply enter the code which your printer uses for whatever character you need.

**Backspacing and overprinting** You can also make most printers backspace so that they will overprint one character on top of another. In this way you can produce characters like the Danish 'ø' by pressing first [o], then using [Alt] and an appropriate code number to produce a Backspace character (usually identified in printer manuals as BS, and coded 136 on the Epson FX-80) followed by [/].

The effect of this is to print the 'o' followed by an immediate backspace, then a '/' . Among other characters which can be produced in this way are left and right arrows (produced by printing a hyphen, a backspace, and a '<' or '>') and a Cent symbol, by backspacing and placing a '/' over a 'c'.

# Place markers

It is often helpful to be able to mark particular points in a document to which you wish to return later. For example, you may want to go back to one part of the file, make some alteration, and then go directly back to where you were before.

Especially if you are working on a long file, finding your way back to where you were can be a slow business. Many word processing programs offer 'place markers' of some sort to speed things up, but WordStar 1512 does not. However, it is an easy matter to construct any number of such markers by using fake dot commands.

On the extreme left margin of the point to which you wish to return, insert the line

.pm $n$

where $n$ = 1 or whatever other number you wish.

A question mark flag will appear in the right hand margin to show that you have used an illegal dot command, but don't let this bother you; you can now return to that point very rapidly by using the Find facility from the F2 Menu to look for '.pm 1' or whatever number you used. Of course, there is nothing magic about the letters 'pm' , and you could use any other combination of letters that isn't used in any genuine dot command.

There is no limit to the number of place markers which you can use. Once you have finished with them, try to remember to remove them, as otherwise they may clutter up your text unnecessarily; however, even if you forget to take them out, they will not be printed accidentally, as it is a feature of WordStar 1512 that no dot commands, not even unrecognised ones, are ever printed; nor are they counted when the program works out which line you are on, and thus do not affect pagination.

# Multi-column work

Most word processors are designed to work on documents which go right across the page from one side to the other, and WordStar 1512 is no exception. However, it is possible to produce multi-column work, provided that you don't mind taking a certain amount of trouble over it.

From the F2 Menus, set the page margins to the width of the column that you intend to use, and enter your text as usual. When you reach the foot of the page (which will be marked by the usual double-underline across the screen) head the text on the second page with a page offset dot command large enough to throw the text that follows to the right of the existing column; then, at print-out run the same sheet of paper through the printer twice, once for the left-hand column and once for the right-hand column.

For example, you might set the left margin at 1, the right margin at 30, and then create a document like this:

.op          *omit page numbers, or they will be incorrect*
One of the outstanding puzzles
of Indian archaeology was the
dating of the megalithic tombs
of the South. In many places,
from Mysore to Hyderabad,
there were known enormous
cemeteries marked by mounds
and stone circles; very many
of them had been opened and
plundered. All the graves were
of one type.
.pa          *end first column; put paper back in printer*
.po 35       *set offset to 35 to print second column.*
A hole was dug down in the
soil, and in it was
constructed a cist or chamber

built of huge slabs of stone,
one for each side, one for the
floor and one for the roof;
the chamber would measure
about seven feet by four, and
the slab at one end had, high
up in it, a circular 'port-
hole' through which offerings
could be made.
.pa          *end second column*

# Keeping margin settings between documents

Retaining marginal settings from one document to another is something of a problem with WordStar 1512, as it is with 'standard' WordStar and several other word processing programs. This is because, although it is easy enough to set margins from the F2 Menu, the new settings are not saved along with the text of the document.

In reality, this is not nearly as much of a problem as it appears at first sight, simply because most users settle on a single width of paper for all their work, and non-standard margins for those few documents which need them can in any case be handled in non-WYSIWYG mode by setting the left and right margins with dot-commands.

However, if you are one of those people who does a fair amount of work with non-standard margins, and who prefers to do this in a WYSIWYG format, you may find this aspect of WordStar 1512 something of a nuisance; but, it is possible to ease the difficulty to some extent.

This is done by relying on the fact that margin settings are kept on the System Disc, and are automatically loaded when the system is booted. If you habitually use three or four different margin settings, make several copies of the System Disc; then on each one store a particular page layout, and label the discs according to the setting which are preserved on them.

For example, you might want to set one disc aside for multi-column work of the sort described above, using a right margin of 30 and no top-of-page margin; set these values at the Page Layout Screen, then label that disc 'System Disc – Column Work' . A second disc, called something like 'System Disc – Page' could then be used for the more common settings used for letters and other writing which used the full width of the page.

# Using the RAM drive

When installed on the Amstrad PC1512 computer, WordStar 1512 is designed to expect a 'RAM disc' with a capacity of 200K, and a similar arrangement can be created on other compatible computers by means of the VDISC.SYS parameter of the MS-DOS DEVICE command. This command is outside the scope of this book, but you should find a description of it in your computer's User Guide.

A **RAM disc**, sometimes called a 'silicon disc' or a 'virtual disc' , is merely a portion of the computer's internal memory, or RAM, which is treated as if it were an ordinary disc drive complete with floppy disc. If you don't have a hard disc, the RAM disc is usually treated as Drive C; if you have a hard disc, it is usually Drive D. It is actually possible to have more than one RAM disc in memory at the same time if you wish, but not many people do this.

**Advantages of a RAM disc** The great advantage of a RAM disc over the usual floppy kind is that data can be read from it or saved to it very much faster than is possible with a 'real' drive (which relies on the relatively slow operation of electric motors and other mechanical components). However, any files which are stored on the RAM disc will be lost when the computer is turned off (or if there is a power cut), unless they have been copied to an ordinary floppy or hard disc.

Because WordStar 1512 treats the RAM disc just like an ordinary floppy, it is possible to store text files on it for editing and then save them back there when work on them has been completed. Where only a single 'real' drive is available, storing text files on the RAM disc while you are working on them can mean that you will have a lot less disc-swapping to do.

Of course, if the power supply is interrupted or you turn off the computer without first copying your files from the RAM disc onto a real disc, then your work will be lost; WordStar 1512 displays a warning (in red) about this danger whenever you quit the program.

Of course, *any* work which has not been saved onto a real disc will be lost if there is a power cut or if you trip over the mains cable and pull it from the wall, whether that work is in the ordinary working space of the WordStar 1512 program or 'saved' on a RAM disc. And certainly it is much easier to use the RAM disc than to be for ever swapping discs in and out of a single drive.

# Copying files to the RAM disc

This section is really aimed at the user with a single disc drive, and all the commands are shown with him or her in mind. If you have a twin-drive or hard disc system, then you may still find the RAM disc useful, but you will need to alter the details of some of the command lines.

Copying files from floppies to the RAM disc, and back again when you have finished working with them, can be done in either of two ways. The simpler way is to boot (start up) the computer using the WordStar 1512 System Disc as usual, but then to copy the files you are going to use from the Text and Data Disc onto Drive C before running WordStar 1512.

**Copying files with MS-DOS** To do this, remove the System Disc from Drive A and replace it with the Text and Data Disc. When the 'A>' prompt is showing, enter

COPY *filename.extension* C:

and press [ Return ], and the file you have named will be copied onto the RAM disc. Repeat the command until you have copied all of the files on which you expect to be working; any which you forget can always be copied later if you wish, using the technique described below. Note, incidentally, that in the COPY command there *must* be a space both before and after the file-name, and there *must* be a colon after the final 'C' .

If you want to copy all the files from the floppy disc to Drive C in one go, you can use the COPY command with wildcards, thus:

```
COPY *.* C:
```

though you will run into problems if there are more files on the floppy disc than there is room for on Drive C.

(**Wildcards** are characters which can be used when you specify file names to be erased or copied. There are two wildcard characters: '?' can be used to replace any single character in the filename or extension; and ' * ' replaces one or more characters. Thus TEXT?.LTR would include TEXT1.LTR, TEXT2.LTR and so on, and TEXT.* would include TEXT.LTR, TEXT.DOC, TEXT.BAK and so on. To erase or copy everything use '*.*'; but be sure that you really mean it!

When you have copied the text files onto Drive C, put the System Disc back into Drive A and start WordStar 1512 by typing 'WS1512'. Provided all the files you want are on Drive C, and that you tell the program to look for text files on the RAM disc – this is described below – you will not have to insert the Text and Data Disc again until the end of the word processing session, except to back up the file you are working on from time to time for security purposes.

**Copying files from the RAM disc** When you have finished word processing and left WordStar 1512, you will have to copy everything back from Drive C onto the real Text and Data Disc. The use of wild cards can be helpful here too; if all your documents have the file-extension .TXT, for example, you can simply put the Text and Data Disc into Drive A and then enter

COPY C:*.TXT A:

Notice that there is no space between the first colon and the asterisk, though there *is* a space between 'TXT' and 'A'. If you get this wrong, the command won't work.

This command will cause all those documents on the RAM disc which have the .TXT extension to be copied onto the disc in Drive A, but none of the files with a .BAK extension – i.e. the original versions which have now been edited – will be copied, so you will avoid cluttering up your Text and Data Disc with unnecessary backups.

**Copying files inside WordStar 1512** The alternative way of copying documents to the RAM disc is to start WordStar 1512 in the usual way (or with the automatic start option described below) and then use the File Management option at the Opening Menu to Copy the required files from Drive A to Drive C.

You can use the same option when you quit WordStar 1512, or at any time while you are using it, to copy or move files from the RAM disc to the real Text and Data Disc and *vice versa*.

# Telling WordStar 1512 where to look for files

If you have a two-drive system, WordStar 1512 will usually expect to look for files on Drive B; if you have just one drive, it will expect to find files on Drive A. However, you may decide to change these defaults – to tell it to look for files on the RAM disc, for example.

**Changing the default drive** If you want to change the defaults, so that every time you use the program it will expect to look on Drive C, for instance, then select Choose settings from the Opening Menu, and then Drive/directory from the Change Settings Menu. The Disc/Directory Menu printed here as Fig. 6.2 will appear on the screen.

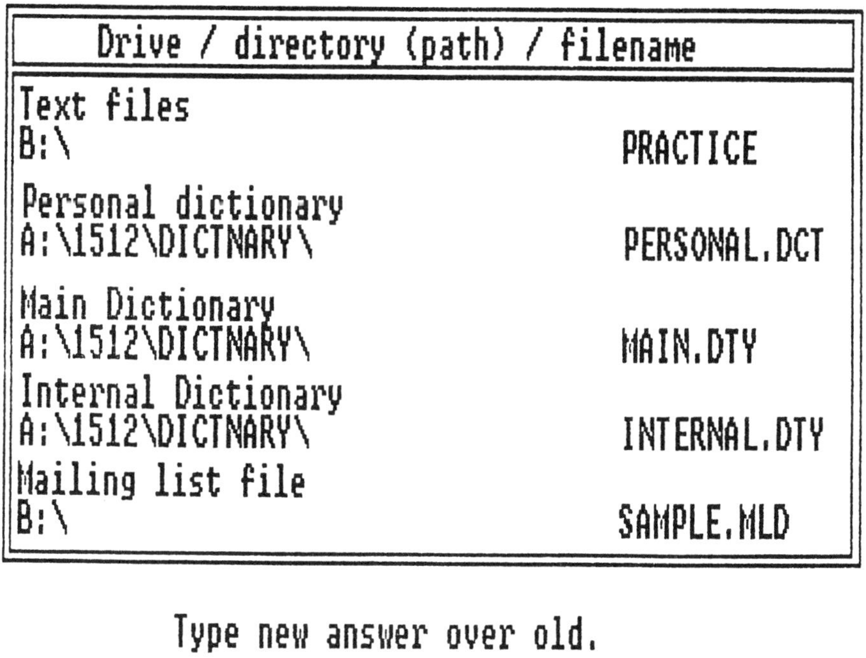

```
┌─────────────────────────────────────────────────┐
│  Drive / directory (path) / filename             │
├─────────────────────────────────────────────────┤
│ Text files                                        │
│ B:\                              PRACTICE         │
│                                                   │
│ Personal dictionary                               │
│ A:\1512\DICTNARY\               PERSONAL.DCT      │
│                                                   │
│ Main Dictionary                                   │
│ A:\1512\DICTNARY\               MAIN.DTY          │
│                                                   │
│ Internal Dictionary                               │
│ A:\1512\DICTNARY\               INTERNAL.DTY      │
│ Mailing list file                                 │
│ B:\                              SAMPLE.MLD        │
└─────────────────────────────────────────────────┘
```

### Type new answer over old.

Fig. 6.2 The Disc/Directory Menu

This menu is used to tell WordStar 1512 the name of the default disc and directory to look for the various files which it uses – this includes both the program files it uses when running and your text and data files. To change the default so that it will look for text files on Drive C, simply type 'C' beneath the prompt 'Text files', so that the whole line reads

C:\

and then save this setting by pressing [Return]. From now on every time you use WordStar 1512, it will automatically expect to find (and save) text files on Drive C.

**Changing drives temporarily** Sometimes you will just want to make a temporary change to the drive on which WordStar 1512 looks for a particular file; for example, the default drive may be Drive B, but you may need to load one particular file from Drive C. Or you may find when at the Choose/create a file option from the Main Menu that the file you want isn't on the Text and Data Disc which is in Drive B but on a different disc.

If this is the case, you will need to remove the current Text and Data Disc and insert the new one, and then tell the program that the disc has been changed; this is called **logging onto** the new disc.

In either case you will need to be at the Choose a file to edit/create screen (the one which appears when you have selected Choose/create a file from the Main Menu).

111

Take the highlight bar up to the very top of the screen and enter the name of the new drive against the prompt 'Drive' ; then with the highlight bar still at the top of the screen, press [ Return ]. The directory of the new current drive will then be shown and you can make your choice from it as usual.

# Making life easier with MS-DOS commands

MS-DOS, the operating system which makes your computer work, has a very large number of commands which can go a long way to making your word processing simpler and your files more secure. In the next few pages, we shall look at some of the most useful MS-DOS commands.

First of all we shall take a look at a special file called AUTOEXEC.BAT, which is on the System Disc from which WordStar 1512 is 'booted' . The .BAT extension means that this is a **batch** file; that is, one which contains a series of instructions which are obeyed one after the other. A file named AUTOEXEC.BAT will be automatically executed if it is on the system disc used when the computer is started up or reset.

We shall be making some very simple alterations to the AUTOEXEC.BAT file; it is important to realise, however, that if you make significant errors while making these changes, you may find that you can no longer get WordStar 1512 to work at all. Don't worry about this; there is absolutely no risk involved as long as you make a security copy of the WordStar 1512 System Disc before going any further; then, if anything does go wrong, you will still have a working copy of the batch file to fall back on.

**Using WordStar 1512 to alter the .BAT file** When you have made that copy and not before, prepare WordStar 1512 to carry out the changes to AUTOEXEC.BAT by going to the Opening Menu and selecting Change settings; then from the Change Settings Menu select Word processing settings. Finally, at the Word Processing Settings Screen, deselect Document Mode by taking the cursor down to the tick opposite that prompt and pressing [ – ]

The effect of this is to avoid inserting any control codes into your text; this makes it possible to create computer control files of the sort we are now going to work with, as well as files which are suitable for transmission down a telecommunications line with a modem.

Confirm your choice with [ Return ], and go back to the Opening Menu. Now select Word processing, and when you insert the 1512 WP disc into Drive A (on a double-floppy disc system) place the System Disc into Drive B at the same time. On a single-drive system, insert the System Disc into Drive A when prompted to insert the Text and Data Disc.

## Automatic running

Because it is necessary to 'boot' the computer using the WordStar 1512 System Disc, rather than merely typing 'WS' after MS-DOS has been started with some other disc, it makes sense to adapt the loading program so that WordStar 1512 can be run automatically as soon as the system disc has been inserted, either from a 'cold start' or after resetting with [Alt]/[Ctrl]/[Del].

If you are using a single-drive system and want to copy files from the Text and Data Disc to Drive C before starting WordStar 1512, then you should not use automatic running as described here; you can, however, still use automatic running if you are prepared to copy files to the RAM disc from the File Management Screen.

With WordStar 1512 running, choose the Word processing option from the Opening Menu, and then at the Main Menu select the Choose/create a file option and select the file named AUTOEXEC.BAT; this file should look like the example shown here, though there may be some differences in detail:

```
Rem WordStar 1512 (MS-DOS 3.2)
Prompt = p = g
Keybuk
Mouse
```

Take the cursor down to the bottom of this short file and insert the following line:

```
ws1512
```

using any combination of capitals and lower-case letters that you wish. Then leave the file with [Esc], Save your work, and Quit the program. The job is now done.

You should now test the new version of the batch file. Put the altered System Disc in Drive A and reboot the computer with [Alt]/[Ctrl]/[Del]; you should see the various command lines appear on the screen as usual, but instead of the usual 'A>' prompt while the computer waits for you to start the program by typing 'WS1512', the program will start automatically.

## Restoring the 'A>' prompt

You have probably noticed that when you leave WordStar 1512, the prompt which appears on the screen does not have its usual 'A>' form. You can restore the prompt to this form either by typing in the command

PROMPT

after you have left the program, or by carrying out another modification to the AUTOEXEC.BAT file. Once again, this is a very simple one: just put the command PROMPT at the very end of the file.

## Configuring the computer for local use

While you are editing the files on the WordStar 1512 System Disc, you will find it worthwhile to display on screen the file called CONFIG.SYS. We have already seen that this file must contain the line 'FILES=20', or WordStar 1512 may not be able to access all the disc files it needs.

Another very useful addition to this file is the line

COUNTRY=*nnn*

where *nnn* is a three-digit code representing a country; the code is the same as the International Telephone Dialling codes. A British user should thus enter 'COUNTRY=044'.

The advantage of this is that the computer will then display time, date and currency according to the appropriate local convention. This is particularly useful when using the Date facility provided by WordStar 1512 and many other programs.

## MS-DOS and file-management
There is a good deal of 'housekeeping' involved in word processing, with files to be copied, erased and backed up. Although a lot of this can be done from inside WordStar 1512 from the File management option of the Opening Menu, many users prefer to use equivalent MS-DOS commands because they are generally more powerful than the WordStar 1512 commands, although they are not quite so easy to use. Once you have mastered these commands, you will be able to use them with other programs as well.

## Protecting important files

It is very easy to erase files by mistake, especially if you use wildcards. For example, you may have a series of letter-files, with names like LETTER1.DOC, LETTER2.DOC and the like. One day you decide to erase one of these, but because you are tired, instead of entering

ERASE LETTER1.*

you type

ERASE *.DOC

Even if you realise your error almost immediately, your precious files (that is, everything which has a .DOC extension) will be erased, and MS-DOS offers no way of getting them back unless you have an up-to-date backup disc from which to restore your missing files. (There are special utility programs which you can buy which will often help in cases like this, but let's assume you don't have one.)

It may be that you don't even notice your error at once, and continue to use the Text and Data Disc to store other documents on. If this happens, then it's a dead certainty that not even the cleverest utility program will get your files back, as they will have been overwritten by other work. This is not a good thing to happen, and will not make you easy to live with when you find what you have done.

Fortunately, MS-DOS offers several ways in which you can keep your files safe; none of them is foolproof, but used together they will go a long way towards making your documents more secure if you use them carefully.

**Physical file security** The most obvious way of protecting your files is to 'write protect' the entire disc by sticking one of the little tabs which are always supplied with new discs over the write-protect notch. When this is done, the contents of a disc can be read freely, but cannot be added to, erased or renamed.

This is obviously inappropriate for the Text and Data Disc, as it would be impossible for you to edit a file and then save the amended version if the disc had been protected in this way; however, it does make sense to protect some of the other WordStar 1512 discs once you have set up the program to suit your own equipment. Specifically, the discs named 1512 WP, Printing, and MailList can all be write protected; the others should be left unprotected.

**File security through software** MS-DOS offers a way by which individual files – or a group of files on a disc or directory – can be made into Read Only files without requiring you to stick a tab over the write-protect notch, and without affecting other files on the same disc.

This is done with the ATTRIB command. To use it, place a disc which has a file with the name ATTRIB.EXE on it in Drive A, and the disc which has files you want to protect in Drive B. (ATTRIB.EXE should be on the original MS-DOS System Disc which was supplied with your computer.)

If you have a single-drive system, you will have to copy ATTRIB.EXE onto the RAM Disc C and then insert the Text and Data Disc into Drive A; then make Drive C into the default drive by typing 'C:', and follow the instructions given below, substituting 'A:' for 'B:' as necessary.

To change a file to Read Only status, enter the command

ATTRIB +R B:*filename.extension*

leaving a space both before and after '+R', but no space after the colon. The file specified will be immediately set to Read Only status. If you wish, you can use wildcards to change the status of a group of files in one go.

Any file which has been changed to Read Only can be edited by WordStar 1512 in the usual way, and the original version will be given a .BAK extension; however, it cannot be deleted, even though renamed to .BAK.

To set a file back to Read/Write status, use the ATTRIB command again thus:

ATTRIB −R B:*filename.extension*

Normally only your most valuable files should be changed to Read Only status; these would probably include the MailList files which are described in the next chapter (they have the extensions .MLD and .MLI), and any other files which are particularly important to you.

Incidentally, it is also possible to hide MS-DOS files completely from a directory search; this can be a useful way of ensuring that confidential documents are not read by those who have no right to access them. Unfortunately, this cannot be done directly from any standard MS-DOS commands; there are, however, utility programs available to do this.

## Security through backups

We have already suggested that making regular security copies of all your documents is a very worthwhile investment of your time. This procedure can be simplified if you use the XCOPY command, one form of which enables you to make copies of only those documents which have been modified since the last backup was made; this is called **archiving**.

The easiest way to carry out archiving is to copy the XCOPY.EXE program from your original MS-DOS system disc supplied with the computer onto your WordStar 1512 Text and Data Disc. When you are ready to archive the disc, place it in Drive A, and put the disc on which you are keeping the backup copies into Drive B. Then type

XCOPY *.* B:/M

The final 'M' in this command is used to put a special 'mark' on all the files that are archived to show that archive copies have been made; the next time that you use XCOPY, the only files which will be archived are the ones which have been altered in the meantime. The 'mark' doesn't affect the text in the files in any way. If the archiving operation is successful, XCOPY displays a Zero to show that no errors were encountered; a '1' would show that no files were found which needed archiving.

If you are using a single disc machine, you can still enter the command in the form shown above; you will be prompted to swap discs and press a key when you have done so.

Should you prefer not to put XCOPY.EXE on the Text and Data Disc, you can instead modify the command to make it possible to use it from the original disc; put the backup disc in Drive B and your MS-DOS disc in Drive A, and enter

XCOPY *.* B:/M/W

The '/W' means that the command will not be carried out until you press a key, thus giving you an opportunity to replace the MS-DOS disc in Drive A with the Text and Data Disc which you want to Archive.

## Organising for security

Real file security depends not on one particular trick or command, but rather on developing an intelligent routine which fits in with the way you personally work. There is no point in devising a complex and potentially foolproof security system if it is so time-consuming and troublesome to use that you sometimes don't bother with it; but equally you will waste far more time trying to reconstruct lost documents after issuing an unwise or ill-thought-out command than if you spent three or four minutes Archiving your files after every word processing or mail merge session.

A typical security routine would use all the ideas described: write protect those discs which *can* be so protected, as this is by far the most stringent way of avoiding errors; convert all files which are not frequently updated but which are vital to your work, such as mail-merge master files, to Read Only status; and Archive your work after *every* session. If you do all this religiously, you will assuredly one day be grateful that you did.

# Keeping an eye on your Text and Data Disc

It is always sensible to keep a weather eye open for possible problems with your Text and Data Disc; files have a nasty knack of growing almost without your noticing it, and quite suddenly you can find yourself running out of room on a disc which you believed had ample space on it. It is also possible for occasional computer malfunctions to cause errors in a disc directory, so that you cannot reach all the files on the disc.

**Using CHKDSK** The MS-DOS command CHKDSK (*CHecK DiSK*) will help you to find these problems, and to correct them when they do occur. If you have a two-drive system, you can use the CHKDSK.EXE program directly from your original MS-DOS disc; if you have only one drive, you will probably find it best to Copy the CHKDSK.EXE program from your original MS-DOS disc onto the Text and Data Disc; the only disadvantage to this procedure is that it will reduce the amount of space which is available for your document files on that disc.

If CHKDSK is on the same disc as the text files, put that disc into Drive A and type

CHKDSK *.*

and press [Return]. If CHKDSK is on a different disc, put that disc into Drive A and the Text and Data Disc into Drive B, and type

CHKDSK B:*.*

and [Return].

CHKDSK will report how much total space is available on the disc, how many files and directories are on it and how much room they occupy and how much disc space is still free for files. It will also let you know about any file or directory errors on the disc. If any such errors are found, you will be told what sort of error has occurred and the name of any affected file(s).

You can put either or both of the following parameters after the command shown above: '/V' causes the name of each file and directory on the disc to be displayed, and '/F' sets the program up to try to correct any errors which it may find.

**Automatic error correction** Because correcting errors is a complex and unpredictable business, CHKDSK will ask if you are willing for a correction to be tried before starting any remedial work. If you accept this by typing [y], an attempt will be made to repair the damage, but this can result in some data being lost; if you have a damaged file, it is best to first try to recover as much of the material in it as you can, if necessary by using one of the many widely available disc utility programs. Incidentally, don't bother trying to fix a program file; it will probably only be a waste of effort. Only data files are worth trying to repair.

Another piece of useful information which CHKDSK will give you is whether or not all the files on the disc are contiguous. Normally, files are stored on adjacent tracks and sectors of the disc, but if you frequently save and later erase documents, the disc can become full of **fragmented** files. This will normally cause you no problems, except that it may take a little longer for such a file to be read into the computer's memory. If you particularly want to make sure that all files are contiguous, you can use the COPY command to transfer the contents of the disc onto a newly formatted blank disc; don't use DISKCOPY, as this merely creates an identical copy of the original disc, complete with its fragmented files.

Hard discs are much more likely to suffer from fragmented files than floppies, simply because of their much greater capacity. Utility programs can be bought which can eliminate this fragmentation, though they often do not greatly improve the speed with which files are accessed.

# Using subdirectories

You will probably be quite surprised at how quickly the number of documents on your Text and Data Disc will increase, especially if you are one of those compulsive hoarders who never likes to throw anything away.

As your collection of files grows, you will find it increasingly awkward to have to flip through several 'pages' of the Choose/create a file Menu before you can find a particular file. When you have filled several Text and Data Discs with documents, just locating the particular letter or report that you are looking for can become quite a daunting task. The solution to this problem is to organise your files into separate disc subdirectories.

We looked very briefly at the idea of directories and subdirectories in Chapter One, and we shall now look at this topic in more detail. If you put the ideas introduced here into practice, you will never find that there are so many file-names that you are not able to locate the document you want quickly and easily.

## The root directory and its subdirectories

To explore the workings of MS-DOS directories, you should have your computer turned on with the 'A>' prompt displayed; put your working copy of the MS-DOS system disc into Drive A and the WordStar 1512 System Disc into Drive B, and then enter the command

TREE B:

The computer will respond with the message:

```
DIRECTORY PATH LISTING FOR VOLUME 1512 SYSTEM

Path: B:/1512

Sub-directories: PROGRAM

Path: B:/1512/PROGRAM

Sub-directories: None
```

This means that there are three directories on the disc in Drive B, each of which contains a number of different files (the names of which are not listed on the screen). At the 'top' is the (unnamed) **root directory** which is always present and which is represented by the backslash ' \ ' after the drive–letter 'B:'. This contains a subdirectory named '1512' which is one level 'below' the root directory; the line reading 'Path: B: \1512' means that you can 'travel' to that subdirectory from the root directory ' \ '.

'Below', subdirectory 1512 is another subdirectory called 'PROGRAM'; the final line shows that there are no more subdirectories below this.

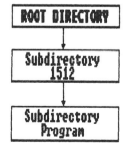

**Fig. 6.3** The structure of the 1512 System Disc

119

In diagrammatic terms, the arrangement is similar to the 'tree' shown in Fig. 6.3. If you are interested in seeing what files are stored in each directory, enter

TREE B:/F

and both the subdirectory structure and the various files held at each 'level' will be shown.

**Devising a structure for your own files** Although the root directory of the 1512 System Disc has only one subdirectory, there is no reason why it could not contain several. Applying this principle to your own files on the Text and Data Disc, you could have one subdirectory to hold, say, letters, one for reports, one for minutes of meetings, and so on. This structure is illustrated in Fig. 6.4.

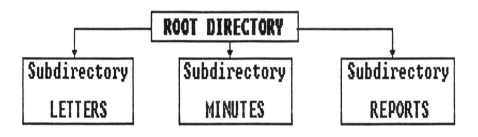

Fig. 6.4 A possible file-structure for the Text and Data Disc

When you have thought out a suitable structure for your own files, put the Text and Data Disc into Drive A and then enter the command

MD \LETTERS

or whatever name you have chosen for the first subdirectory. The new directory will be created immediately, and if you type 'DIR' to catalogue the files on the disc, you will find 'LETTERS <DIR>' duly listed.

The MD command is used to *M*ake a *D*irectory; you can if you wish use the longer form MKDIR. Then create your second directory, using the command 'MD \REPORTS', and repeat the process until you have all the directories you need. All these subdirectories will be one level below the root directory.

**Copying files into the new subdirectories** The new directories will still be empty, but you may very well have some files already on the disc which ought to go into them. You can put them in with the MS-DOS COPY command, which copies items from one directory to another in just the same way as it copies files from one disc to another.

To copy a file called WILSON.LTR from the root directory to the new LETTERS subdirectory, just enter the line

COPY WILSON.LTR \LETTERS

The computer will respond with: '1 File(s) copied'. Notice that we didn't need to specify a new name for the file, as it will have the same name in the subdirectory LETTERS as it did in the root directory.

You can speed things up by using wildcards; for example, if all your letters have the file-extension .LTR, you can use the command 'COPY *.LTR \LETTERS' to copy them into the LETTERS subdirectory in one go.

**Deleting the original files** Although copies of your documents are now placed in the new subdirectory, the original files still exist in the root directory. You should now delete them from the root directory, or you will have two copies of your files instead of one, and your problems of finding files will become harder instead of easier.

If all the files which have been copied into a subdirectory have the same file-extension, you can use wildcards to delete all of them from the root directory at once; for example, the command 'ERASE *.LTR' will delete all the root directory files with the extension .LTR, but leave any subdirectory files with the same extension untouched.

**Accessing subdirectory files** To reach files in a subdirectory, you must tell the computer exactly where they are; in MS-DOS this instruction is called the **path**. A path is merely a list of all the directories and subdirectories through which you must 'descend' to reach the particular subdirectory you need, with all the subdirectory names separated by backslashes.

For example, to specify a file called WILSON.LTR which is in the LETTERS subdirectory one level below the root directory on Drive B, you would specify Drive B followed by a colon, then the subdirectory name and the filename, with each item separated from the others by a backslash thus:

B:\LETTERS\WILSON.LTR

To select this file on the WordStar 1512 Choose/create a file menu you would enter '\LETTERS\' against the prompt 'Directory' at the top of the screen and then press [Return]; all the files in that subdirectory will then be listed in the lower half of the screen, including WILSON.LTR. Of course, only those files which are in this subdirectory will listed, so that choosing the file you want will be much simpler.

To choose a file from a different subdirectory – such as REPORTS – you would simply replace '\LETTERS\' with '\REPORTS\', and then only the files in *that* subdirectory will be shown.

To access a file directly from the MS-DOS 'A' prompt – to TYPE it or ERASE it perhaps – you would enter the full path and name on one line after the command; for example, to erase WILSON.LTR in the LETTERS subdirectory of the disc in Drive B you would enter

ERASE B:\LETTERS\WILSON.LTR

To get a directory listing of all the files in the MINUTES subdirectory of the disc in Drive A you would use

DIR \MINUTES\

# Removing subdirectories

Subdirectories are very useful ways of organising your files, but they need not be permanent features of a particular disc; once a particular subdirectory is no longer required, you can simply get rid of it.

For example, you may have set aside a subdirectory to hold documents connected with a special project – letters, minutes, reports, estimates, recommendations and so on. When the project is finished, you can archive the records onto another disc, or 'stream' them onto tape if you are a hard disc user. Finally, you can reclaim the space which the special subdirectory had occupied.

First of all, you must empty the subdirectory of all the files which it contains, as it is not possible in MS-DOS to remove a subdirectory which still contains any files.

If the subdirectory you want to remove is one level below the root directory on Drive B, you can then remove it with the command

RD B:\*directory name*\

You can if you prefer use the full form of the command, which is RMDIR.

If you get an error message reading: 'Invalid path, not directory, or directory not empty', this will probably be either because you have not removed all the files from the directory or because you have mis-typed the name of the subdirectory. The root directory of the disc cannot be removed.

**A little more about the commands** MD, RD (and their longer forms MKDIR and RMDIR) as well as COPY and DIR are 'internal' MS-DOS commands; that is, they are not loaded off the MS-DOS system disc before they can be obeyed. TREE is an 'external' command, so you must make sure that the program TREE.EXE, which should be on your MS-DOS system disc, is available in the current drive before you try to use it.

In addition to the commands introduced here, there are several others which you may need to use if you develop the subdirectory structure much further. These include CD, or CHDIR, with which you can change the current directory, JOIN, which attaches one disc drive to the directory structure of a different disc, and PATH, which establishes a sequence of directories through which MS-DOS will search for a particular file, starting from the root directory, and continuing either until the file is found or the end of the path is reached.

However, all these commands are really beyond the scope of an introductory book like this. Users of hard disc systems are more likely to use them then others, and if you have only floppy discs you will quite probably find that you hardly ever need to use them.

# Postscript

WordStar 1512 is a tool; how well you get on with it will depend partly on how well you learn about its foibles, and partly on how inventive you are in devising new ways of using it.

In this chapter we have looked at some of the by-ways of the program, and some of the MS-DOS commands that you can use to bulk out its file-handling capabilities. Some of these will prove useful in fields far beyond simple word processing, so we do recommend that as soon as you feel really comfortable with your computer, you should begin to explore them, and then persevere with them until they become second nature.

# CHAPTER SEVEN

# Preparing and Using Mail-Merge Data Files

## Preview

When documents are **merged**, this simply means that text taken out of one document is put into another, different, document. In this way, you can produce 'standard' letters, contracts or whatever and then 'put in the details' as necessary from another file.

This technique is most commonly used to create mail-merged letters – that is, letters which are personalised with details taken automatically from a special data-file so that they look as if they were individually written and addressed. This is done by creating a standard 'form letter', often called a **matrix document** which contains special codes which cause items from a data file to be placed into all the letters when they are printed.

Of course, in our computer-conscious age it is a matter of opinion just how many people actually do believe that these letters really are individually created just for them, but even so it does seem more appropriate to send out personally addressed letters, however they are produced, than to use 'Dear Customer' and similar phrases.

The beginning of a typical matrix document might look something like this:

&Mr__Ms& &Fullname&
&Address__1&
&Address__2&
&Town&
&County&
&Post__code&

&Date&

Dear &Mr__Ms& &Last&,

As a loyal supporter of Otley Town Cricket Club, I
know you will be delighted to hear ....

From this matrix could be produced hundreds, or even thousands, of individually
addressed letters like this:

Mr. John T. Smith,
90 Allhallows Road
West Hambourne
Otley
Hertfordshire
FE6 8JI

15-08-88

Dear Mr. Smith....

You can see that the codes in the matrix document – the sections included between
ampersands, '&'– have been replaced during printout by details taken from another
file, containing the name and address of Mr. J.T. Smith and all the other people to
whom the letter is to be sent.

Two quite different types of document are involved here; one is the matrix
document – the form letter containing the codes enclosed in ampersands – and the
other is the database, or masterfile, which holds the information which will replace
those codes during printing – in our example, this would be the details of Mr. J.T.
Smith and all the other intended recipients of the Cricket Club's letter.

In this chapter we shall learn how to make a masterfile, and see ways in which it can
be used for many other things beside form letters; then, in the next chapter, we shall
tie this in to different types of matrix documents.

The masterfile described in this chapter is crucial to mail-merging with WordStar
1512; this is one of those areas where this program differs quite substantially from
'standard' WordStar, so even if you are used to the way in which 'ordinary'
WordStar and similar programs handle the production of form-letters and the like,
you should still read through this chapter and try out the examples given.

# About databases

WordStar 1512 data files are called 'Masterfiles', but they are actually a special kind of **database**, such as you may have met with already in other applications, particularly those which involve the storage and manipulation of name, address and other related personal data.

At its simplest, a database is no more than a collection of data so ordered that items in it can be easily found when needed. In this sense, databases are not necessarily limited to computers. One database which is familiar to everyone is a telephone directory. Like every other database, it contains information arranged according to a set of predetermined rules – in this case, by alphabetical order of the subscribers' names.

Information can be found – **retrieved** is the usual computer term – by **searching** through the database. How easy it will be to carry out any particular search will depend both on what you need to know and on how the database itself is organised.

**A simple example** For example, the only way in which it is usually practical to search for information in an ordinary telephone directory is by looking under the name of the subscriber. This is because, although the directory contains many different sorts of information, its design makes it very hard to extract some of it. It would be awkward, for example, to have to go through the entire book looking for all the plumbers, or to find the name of the subscriber who had a particular telephone number.

To get round this problem, other directories are available which contain essentially the same information, but which arrange it differently – Yellow Pages, for example, or the various trade directories.

## Some important concepts

At this point, it will be useful to glance at some of the concepts associated with database work; the terms involved are widely used in program manuals and the like, often with little or no explanation, and a firm grasp of them will be very useful in understanding the operation and use of the mail-merge aspects of WordStar 1512 as well as other databases which you may encounter later.

**Files** A collection of related items of the sort handled by a database is usually called a **file**, though WordStar 1512 uses the term **master list**. In this sense, a computer file is not unlike an ordinary physical file of the sort which belongs in an office filing cabinet, with various items of related information contained within it.

WordStar 1512 master lists are primarily designed to hold name-and-address information (though they can be used for much more, as we shall see); a single master list can contain details of *all* your name-and-address records, whether they are those of business associates, companies you do business with, individual customers, or friends.

**Records** Inside a physical file-folder there will usually be a number of separate **records**. A name-and-address file would usually allocate one record (card) per individual, and every one of these records would look pretty much like every other record, in the sense that they would all hold the same *kind* of information.

**Fields** Just as a file is made up of a number of records, so each record is made up of one or more **fields**. A typical field in a WordStar 1512 file would be a person's first name, or his telephone number, or his credit limit, or some other single item of information.

When using a database, you almost always want to find out the details of individual records, and you look for them by searching for the contents of a particular field.

Using the telephone directory as an example again, the search for an individual telephone number would go something like this: first, choose the right telephone directory (the right file or master list); next, find the correct record (by searching the name field, which is how the records are organised); finally, from within the correct record, find the field which contains the telephone number.

**Keys and key fields** In order to ensure that different records don't become confused with each other, it is necessary to make sure that the contents of at least one field of each record are different from the contents of the same field of every other record. This field is called the **key field**, and it typically holds a membership or account number, a car registration number, a social security number or some other piece of unique data.

WordStar 1512 provides an automatic key field by assigning an individual number between 00001 and 99999 to each record. This number can then be used to help you to locate an individual record very rapidly.

In addition to looking for records by their key, it is possible to carry out some very sophisticated searches on the contents of one or more non-key fields. In this way it would be possible, for example, to find all the customers who have *London* in their address and who are doctors.

# Settings for working on master lists

There are four default settings which control the use of master lists, and these can be altered through the Mailing List Settings Menu, shown in Fig. 7.1.

This menu is reached from the Opening Menu by selecting first Change settings and then selecting Mailing list settings from the Change Settings Menu. As you will see from Fig. 7.1, the Mailing List Settings Menu offers four options, each of which can be selected with [ + ] or deselected with [ Del ] in the usual way.

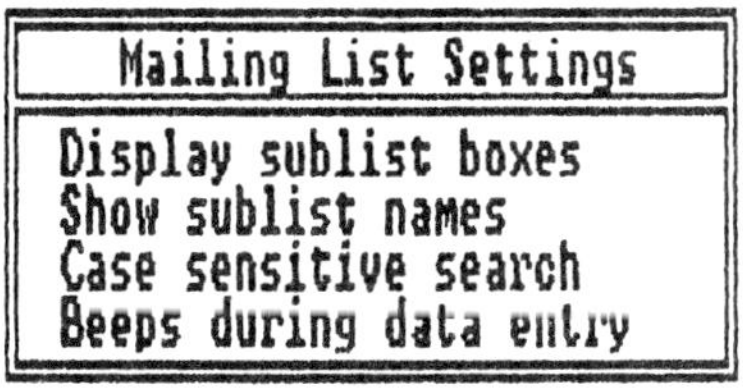

```
┌─────────────────────────────────┐
│   Mailing List Settings         │
├─────────────────────────────────┤
│ Display sublist boxes           │
│ Show sublist names              │
│ Case sensitive search           │
│ Beeps during data entry         │
└─────────────────────────────────┘
```

**Fig. 7.1** The Mailing List Settings Menu

The first two options on the menu – Display sublist boxes and Show sublist names – are used when it is necessary to place individual records together in subdivisions of the master list; we shall be showing how to use these sublists later, but you do not need to understand them at the moment. If you decide, after reading the relevant sections, that you will not need to use sublists, then you can come back to this screen and deselect both options; but for the moment it is best to leave them selected.

The third option, Case sensitive search, refers to the way in which WordStar 1512 looks for individual records; this is done by a process of matching details of every record against a template which you enter; a case sensitive search will only record a 'hit' if the combination of capitals and lower case letters in a particular record is identical to that in the template. For example, if Case sensitive search is selected, searching for 'smith' will not find 'Smith'.

Finally, Beeps during data entry enables you to turn off the bleeping sound which the computer makes whenever a new or altered record is saved (assuming that the volume control on your speaker is turned up). I have a deep-seated and irrational dislike of computers that go beep whenever they have done anything, and so usually deselect such options whenever possible; but some people feel differently about these things.

When you have made any adjustments to the Mailing List Settings, leave the menu by pressing [Return], and the new settings will take effect. To abandon any changes you have made, press [Esc]. In both cases, you will be taken back to the Change Settings Menu, and a further [Esc] will take you to the Opening Menu ready to begin entering your first master list.

# Preparing a master list

The easiest way to learn about creating a WordStar 1512 mail-merge master list is to go right ahead and do it. Boot WordStar 1512, put the Text and Data Disc into Drive B if you have a two-drive system, and choose Mailing list from the Opening Menu. You will be prompted to place the disc labelled Mailing List in Drive A; when you have done this, the MailList Main Menu shown in Fig. 7.2 will appear on the screen.

129

```
┌─────────────────────────────────┐
│║   MailList Main Menu           ║│
╞═════════════════════════════════╡
│║ Begin data entry               ║│
│║ Choose/create a master list    ║│
│║ Sort master list               ║│
│║ Manage master lists            ║│
│║ Help index                     ║│
└─────────────────────────────────┘
```

**Fig. 7.2** The MailList Main Menu

We are going to create a new file called MAILLIST, so from the MailList Main Menu choose the Change/create a master list option in any of the usual ways. You will be offered the familiar directory screen, but this time it will be headed 'Choose a list to edit/create'.

# Creating a new file

At the List prompt, type in the name chosen for the new file; we have used MAILLIST.MLD, but any file-name which obeys the usual rules will do as well. However, whatever name you choose, the file-extension .MLD is compulsory, and you will be prompted to use it if you forget.

This is because WordStar 1512 actually uses two files which share the same file-name but which are distinguished from each other by having different extensions – in addition to the data file which you will make, and which will have the extension .MLD (for *M*ail *L*ist *D*ata), WordStar 1512 creates a file with the extension .MLI (for *M*ail *L*ist *I*ndex). This is an important point to bear in mind when you rename files, or copy them from one disc to another – you *must* move or rename both the .MLD and the .MLI files.

WordStar 1512 will ask:

Do you want to create a new master list?

Confirm that you really want a new file by pressing [ Return ], and the form shown in Fig. 7.3 will be drawn on the screen.

# Entering data

In the top right corner of the data entry screen are the words 'Record number', with the number 00001 displayed in the highlight bar by it; the rest of the screen contains a number of prompts next to which you will enter your data. You can move the highlight bar down the screen from one prompt to another by pressing either [ Return ] or the [ ↓ ] key, or go back to one you have left with [ ↑ ]; [ Home ] and [ End ] are used to move directly to the first and last fields on the screen, and [ ← ] and [ → ] move the cursor left and right within the highlight bar. The [ Del ] and [ ←Del ] keys are used to correct errors in the usual way.

```
┌─────────────────────────────────────────────────────┐
│ADD RECORDS:  Begin typing.  Press PgDn to save a record and│
│              display a new data entry form.           │
└─────────────────────────────────────────────────────┘
```

```
                                    Record number 00000
        Date                                              1
       Mr/Ms                                              2
       First      MI       Last           Honours
       Title                                              3

     Company                                              4
    Address-1
    Address-2                                             5
        Town      County            Post Code
     Country                                              6
     Phone-1      Phone-2
                                                          7
   Keyword-1    Note-1
   Keyword-2    Note-2                                    8
   Keyword-3    Note-3
        Flag
```

Fig. 7.3 A blank data form

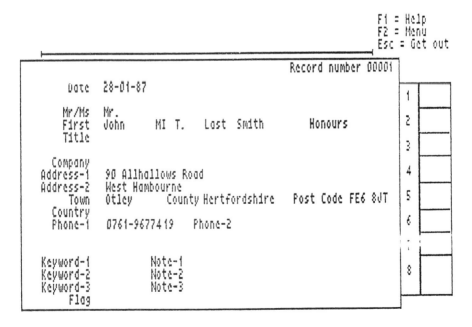

```
                                    Record number 00001
        Date   28-01-87                                   1
       Mr/Ms   Mr.                                        2
       First   John    MI T.   Last Smith      Honours
       Title                                              3

     Company                                              4
    Address-1  90 Allhallows Road
    Address-2  West Hambourne                             5
        Town   Otley      County Hertfordshire  Post Code FE6 8JT
     Country                                              6
     Phone-1   0761-9677419    Phone-2
                                                          8
   Keyword-1    Note-1
   Keyword-2    Note-2
   Keyword-3    Note-3
        Flag
```

Fig. 7.4 A typical form with data entered

131

Try to copy the form shown in Fig. 7.4; the various details shown here form the basis for the Otley Town Cricket Club database which we met at the beginning of the chapter.

**Record number** WordStar 1512 keeps a permanent record of every entry in strict numeric order; once a number has been assigned to a particular record, it cannot be changed. The fact that record numbers cannot be reassigned means that if you delete records from the file, the number which they had occupied will henceforth be left blank.

There is no need to always keep records in the order in which they have been entered; they can, for example, be reordered by name, by company or even by postcode.

To begin entering data, take the highlight bar out of the Record number field either with [Return] or [↓]; there are advantages to using [Return], as we shall see when we customise the data entry form later in this chapter, but if it is pressed when the highlight bar is in the last field, the record will be saved whether there are any corrections to be made or not, whereas [↓] will merely take the cursor back up to the Record number field. [PgDn] will save a record at any time, regardless of the position of the highlight bar. You can always return to any record at any time to make further alterations to it just by typing the number of the record you want when the highlight bar is at Record number.

**Correcting mistakes** When correcting errors which you may have made in entering data, anything which you type in will be regarded as an Overtype, rather than as an Insert. The [Ins] key does not toggle between the two modes as it does when composing ordinary text with WordStar 1512.

However, pressing [Ins] does have the effect of moving any text which is to the right of the cursor and in the same field one space to the right; this can be used to create more room in the middle of the field if you have accidentally left one or more characters out as you type.

**Date** WordStar 1512 allows the date to be entered according to any format you want, provided that two numbers each are allocated for the day, the month and the year, and that the different elements are separated by either a dash, a full-stop or a slash, '/'.

Today's date (assuming that it has previously been set or is kept permanently in battery-backed RAM as on the Amstrad PC1512) can be entered directly in the format fixed by CONFIG.SYS by just pressing the asterisk, '*'.

Unless the computer has been configured for non-American use, as described in Chapter Six, dates entered in this way will be treated according to the American MM-DD-YY, which is unfamiliar to most European users. British users who want to use the DD-MM-YY format will need to insert the line 'COUNTRY=044' in the CONFIG.SYS file; refer back to Chapter Six for more details.

Entries can be sorted according to the date field. This can be very useful, particularly if you use the date field for something other than the date on which a particular record was entered. For example, later in this chapter we shall see that it is possible to use the WordStar 1512 database for keeping details of your record or slide collection or some other similar purpose; you might then use the date field to record the date on which a particular record was made or a photograph taken.

Enter the date number you have chosen, or press '*' to use the automatic date feature, and then leave the date field with [ ↓ ].

**Mr/Ms** The Mr/Ms field is used for a title, such as Mr., Mrs., Dr. and the like. Any title up to 12 characters in length can be inserted.

**First, MI and Last** These three fields are for the first name, middle initial(s) and surname of the individual held on the record. The first name can be up to 11 characters long, the MI field holds up to 3 characters, and the surname can be up to 14 characters in length.

It is possible to sort on the name fields, in order to put all the records in alphabetical order of surname; should two or more surnames be identical, then the first names will be taken into account. Thus an alphabetical sort of all the Smiths would put J. Smith ahead of R. Smith. However, the sort will only be accurate if all the names have been entered using the same combination of capitals and lower case letters; this is because WordStar 1512, like many other programs, puts capital letters before lower case letters in a sort.

As long as you enter items consistently, this will do no harm, but if you enter some surnames in capitals and others in lower-case letters, you will find that names entered entirely in capitals will precede names entered in small letters, whether or not they really do come before them in the alphabet. It is therefore wise to get into the habit of using the same format for all entries.

Incidentally, one disadvantage of the 'ready-made' format of the WordStar 1512 data file may now be apparent to you: it is not possible, because only three spaces are allowed for the Middle Initial, to enter a name like 'J. Alfred Prufrock' into the file. This probably won't cause you any problems, but it does illustrate the difficulty of designing any system to meet every eventuality.

**Honours** The Honours field is for those elements which might be included after a surname, such as B.A., Esq., and so on. Up to 5 characters can be accommodated; the field is not used in sorts.

**Title** The Title field is meant for 'Branch Manager', 'Headmaster' and similar titles. We shall see later that it can be used for other things as well. Up to 30 characters can be fitted into this field.

**Company** In the Company field you can enter the name of a company or other organisation, such as 'Hawley's Nursery', 'Thomas Tompion High School', and the like. Up to 30 characters can be included. This too is a field on which sorts can be carried out, so once again do try to be consistent in your use of capitals and lower-case letters.

## The Address fields—Address-1 and Address-2, Town, County, Post Code and Country The first two fields are set aside for the street address, and there is one each for the Town, County, Post Code and Country; any lines which are not needed should be left blank by pressing [Return].

The Address and Country lines are not used in sorts, but all the others can be. A sort on the County field works a little like the sort on names, in that the primary sort is by alphabetical order of counties, but towns in the same county are then listed in alphabetical order within the county.

**Phone** Space is left for two phone numbers of up to 16 characters each – normally one of the fields would be used for an office telephone number and the other for a home number, but only Phone-1 can be used for sorting.

Although you can put any characters you like in the phone field, it is a good idea to include brackets or a dash as part of every number. This is because programs like Sidekick which offer an automatic-dialling facility use these characters to recognise telephone numbers, and will dial them automatically provided they are displayed on the screen. This only works if you have suitable hardware, of course – you will need a Hayes-compatible modem – but even if you don't have this equipment yet it is still a good idea to set your files up in such a way that they are ready to use such hardware in case you acquire it in the future.

## Keywords, Notes and Flags These three fields, together with Sublists, which we shall meet later, are very useful for 'grouping' records in different ways. For the moment, read the brief descriptions which follow, but don't actually use any of the fields.

**Keywords** The Keyword fields, each up to 12 characters in length, can be used for any words which are meaningful to you when it comes to sorting or searching for records or groups of records. For example, you might want to mark all records of people in the medical profession; one way to do this would be to place the keyword 'Medical' in one of the Keyword files.

**Notes** The three Notes fields are for any additional information which you would like to be able to record, providing enough space for up to 40 characters to be stored in each. The most important difference between Notes and Keywords is that you cannot sort on Note fields.

**Flag** In computer terms, a **flag** is simply a marker used to identify a particular item in some way.

The WordStar 1512 Flag field holds one character which you can insert to identify one or more records. For instance, returning to the example we gave above, you could Flag people in the medical profession by putting, say, an 'M' in the Flag field.

134

There is no limit to the number of different flag characters you can use in a file, but only one can be used in each record. Any WordStar 1512 printable character can be used as a flag, including those which can only be reached by holding down [ Alt ] and pressing keys on the number pad.

# Moving on

When your first entry is complete, check it over carefully to ensure that everything is correct, moving the highlight bar up (with [ ↑ ]) to correct any errors. If you do discover mistakes later, it is still quite easy to come back and correct them, but obviously it is better to catch them now. When you are satisfied that everything is all right, press [ PgDn ] and the complete record will be saved on the Text and Data Disc (and the computer will beep at you if you have not deselected this feature). Then the record number will change to 00002, the other fields will be emptied, and you can enter the details of the next record.

# Customising the form

Entering data into a database file often involves a good deal of repetitive work; for example, the Otley Town Cricket Club, which we met earlier in this chapter, will certainly have most, if not all, of their supporters within the town of Otley, and very few will live outside the county; typing in both the town and county names afresh for every record is obviously a nuisance which it would be better to avoid if possible.

WordStar 1512 offers a rather clever way of avoiding all this unnecessary effort. Press Function Key [ F2 ], and the Data Entry Menu shown in Fig. 7.5 will appear on the right of the screen.

Fig. 7.5 The Data Entry Menu

The option we will be using from this is Customise Data Entry, so select it in any of the usual ways. The Data Entry Screen will then be replaced by the Customise Data Entry Screen, shown in Fig. 7.6.

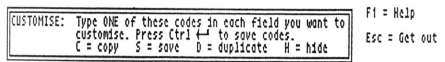

```
┌──────────────────────────────────────────────┐
│CUSTOMISE:  Type ONE of these codes in each field you want to│     F1 = Help
│            customise. Press Ctrl ←┘ to save codes.          │
│            C = copy    S = save    D = duplicate    H = hide │     Esc = Get out
└──────────────────────────────────────────────┘
```

```
                                    Record number 00000

        Date
                                                            │ 1 │   │
        Mr/Ms
        First       MI      Last            Honours         │ 2 │   │
        Title
                                                            │ 3 │   │
        Company
        Address-1                                           │ 4 │   │
        Address-2
           Town     County          Post Code               │ 5 │   │
        Country
        Phone-1     Phone-2                                 │ 6 │   │

                                                            │ 7 │   │
        Keyword-1   Note-1
        Keyword-2   Note-2                                  │ 8 │   │
        Keyword-3   Note-3
           Flag
```

Fig. 7.6 The Customise Data Entry Screen

With this screen, you can modify the default data entry form to avoid having to enter the same item into every record, or most records, and thus speed up the input of data. Using the [Return] key to move from one field to another, enter a 'C', an 'S', a 'D' or an 'H' into each field, or bypass it, leaving it blank; only one of these letters can be used in each field. The effects of each of the letters is as follows:

'H' is the most drastic choice, as it *H*ides an individual field so that data cannot be entered into it. (Actually, 'hides' is something of a misnomer, as the field prompt remains on the screen, but it is not possible to take the cursor to that field while you are entering data). You might well want to Hide the Country field, for example.

'S' causes a field to be *S*kipped when the data entry cursor is moved *down* the form with the [Return] key, though if you use the [Tab], [↑] or [↓] keys the cursor can be taken into the field in the usual way. You would probably want to Skip those fields which you would not often use, such as Honours and perhaps Title; obviously this would depend on the sort of data you are entering.

'C' *C*opies the contents of a field from the same field in the previous record. For example, if most of the addresses you were entering into the file were in the same town or county, you might mark the Town and County fields with 'C' in order to save yourself the trouble of entering the same county name afresh in every record.

136

When you are entering data, the cursor will pause at a field marked with a 'C' in case you do want to make a change – either press [Return] or [↓] to leave the contents unaltered, or type in a suitable new entry. Any new value which you type in will itself then be Copied into the following record.

'D' enables a field to be *Duplicated* from the same field in the previous record. A Duplicated field is completely missed by the cursor when you are entering data, provided you are using [Return] to move from one field to the next. You can still, however, use [↑] to move back to the field if you wish, and if you do so, the new entry will itself be Duplicated in the next record.

For the particular data which we are entering, arrange to Copy the County field and to Hide Country, Post Code and Phone-2.

When you have finished Customising the data entry form, press [Ctrl]/[Return] to save details of the form on disc (or [Esc] to abandon your work). All future entries into the file will be created using the newly customised form, though you can always return to the Customise Data Entry Screen to make any further emendations that become necessary.

**Opening new records** To start entering data into new records at any time, place the highlight bar on the Record number field of any record and enter a zero; a new blank data form will appear on the screen ready for the next entry.

**Using a customised form** Practise entering some data into the customised form; some sample new data for you to try is provided in Fig. 7.7. You will need this many different entries to make the next part of the exercise worth-while, as we are now going to sort the various entries according to different criteria; later, we shall conduct searches for individual records. When you have finished entering all the data, leave the Data Entry Form by pressing [Esc]. You will be returned to the MailList Main Menu.

# Sorting records

Sorting is one of the most important activities which can be carried out on the contents of a database. For example, a sort based on staff surnames can be used to produce a company's telephone directory. At a slightly more complex level, a sort by County would enable a large organisation with members grouped in County branches to send out mailing labels for all their own local members to the various Branch Secretaries, so that they could then use them in their local organisation.

To begin sorting, choose the Sort Master List option from the MailList Main Menu; the screen will clear, and the Sort Menu (Fig. 7.8) will be shown.

```
                                               Record number 00001
        Date 28-01-87

     Mr/Ms  Mr.
     First  John         MI T.  Last Smith          Honours
     Title

     Company
     Address-1 90 Allhallows Road
     Address-2 West Hambourne
        Town Otley           County  Hertfordshire   Post Code FE6 8JT
     Country
     Phone-1 0761-9766419      Phone-2

  -----------------------------------------------------------------

                                               Record number 00002
        Date 08-15-88

     Mr/Ms  Mr.
     First  Allan        MI P.  Last Heywood         Honours
     Title

     Company
     Address-1 42 The Rise
     Address-2 Hartley
        Town Otley           County  Hertfordshire   Post Code FE6 5DW
     Country
     Phone-1 0761-422124       Phone-2


  -----------------------------------------------------------------

                                               Record number 00003
        Date 08-15-88

     Mr/Ms  Mrs.
     First  Alison       MI     Last Smith           Honours
     Title

     Company
     Address-1 15 Station Street
     Address-2 Horton Wood
        Town Otley           County  Hertfordshire   Post Code FE6 6QV
     Country
     Phone-1 0761-964077       Phone-2

  -----------------------------------------------------------------

                                               Record number 00004
        Date 08-15-88

     Mr/Ms  Dr.
     First  Harvey       MI M.  Last Jackson         Honours
     Title

     Company
     Address-1 Cedar Lodge, The Avenue
     Address-2 West Hambourne
        Town Otley           County  Hertfordshire   Post Code FE6 8JG

  -----------------------------------------------------------------

                                               Record number 00005
        Date 08-15-88

     Mr/Ms  Mr.
     First  John         MI     Last Jenkins         Honours
     Title

     Company
     Address-1 15A, Water Street
     Address-2 Barnhill
        Town Otley           County  Hertfordshire   Post Code FE6 8OK
     Country
     Phone-1 0761-867335       Phone-2
```

**Fig. 7.7** Sample File Entries

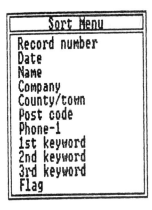

┌─────────────────────────┐
│ **Sort Menu** │
├─────────────────────────┤
│ Record number │
│ Date │
│ Name │
│ Company │
│ County/town │
│ Post code │
│ Phone-1 │
│ 1st keyword │
│ 2nd keyword │
│ 3rd keyword │
│ Flag │
└─────────────────────────┘

**Fig. 7.8** The Sort Menu

All WordStar 1512 sorts are carried out in the same direction, that is from the lowest number to the highest or from the beginning of the alphabet to the end.

WordStar 1512 will attempt to make a sort even if you specify a sort by a field which is blank on all records; if the field is blank for some records but not for others, the blank records will be placed first.

To see how a sort works, at the Sort Menu select Name and press [Return], and the process of sorting all the records into alphabetical order of surname will begin at once. A message will be displayed on the screen while it is carried out. How long this takes depends on several factors, but the most important is the number of records in the file.

When the sort is finished, the MailList Main Menu will be displayed again; choose Begin Data Entry, and then browse from one record to another using [PgDn], seeing how the various entries are now in true alphabetical order. Notice especially how the Smiths have been sorted – because they share a surname, they have been additionally sorted by the alphabetical order of their first names, with Alison Smith coming before John Smith.

To return records to their original sequence, go back to the Sort Menu and select a sort by Record number; when this has been done, the entries will be back in the order in which you entered them. Do this now.

# Searching

The second important operation which can be performed on a database is finding one or more individual records from the file. On our sample database, for example, you might need to find the record of Mr. Jenkins; on a larger file, you might need to retrieve all the records relating to individuals living in a particular county.

**Searching by the key field** The easiest way of finding an individual record is by the contents of the key field, if you happen to know it.

To do this, simply place the cursor on the Record number field when any record is displayed on the screen, type in the number of the record you want to find and press [Return]. If the record exists, it will be immediately displayed; if it does not, you will be told 'Record not found'.

Mr. John Jenkins occupies Record number 5, so enter '5' in the Record number field and press [Return], and that record will be shown on the screen.

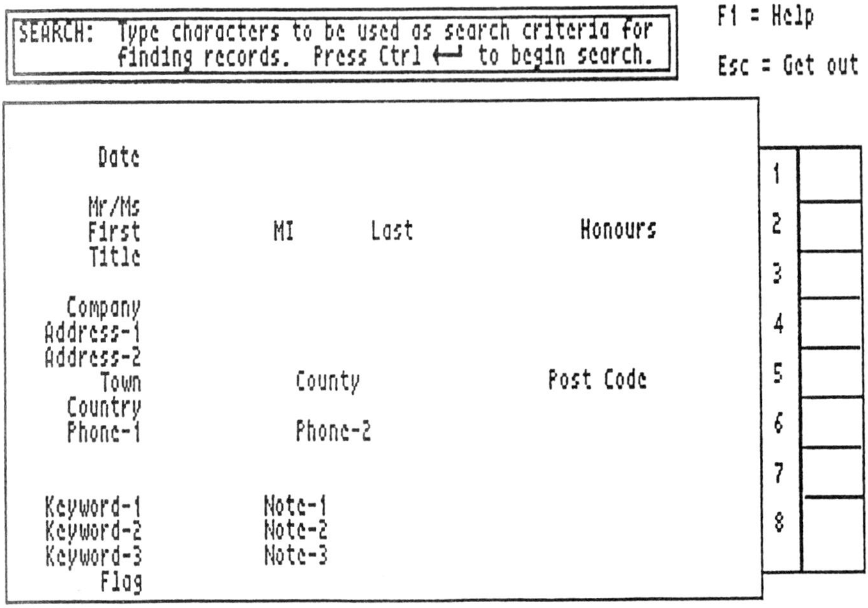

```
┌──────────────────────────────────────────────┐   F1 = Help
│SEARCH:  Type characters to be used as search criteria for│
│         finding records.  Press Ctrl ←┘ to begin search.│   Esc = Get out
└──────────────────────────────────────────────┘

        Date                                              1

    Mr/Ms                                                 2
    First      MI       Last          Honours
    Title                                                 3

    Company                                               4
    Address-1
    Address-2                                             5
        Town       County          Post Code
    Country                                               6
    Phone-1        Phone-2
                                                          7
    Keyword-1   Note-1                                    8
    Keyword-2   Note-2
    Keyword-3   Note-3
        Flag
```

Fig. 7.9 The Search Screen

More sophisticated searches are possible using Begin search from the Data Entry Menu (the F2 Menu). When this is selected, the screen will clear and the special form shown in Fig. 7.9 is offered.

Use this as a template to enter whatever data is sufficient to identify the particular record or records you want to find, bearing in mind that if you have chosen a case sensitive search you will only get a 'hit' if the template matches a record's combination of capitals and lower-case letters precisely.

Usually you can save time by entering only a bare minimum of information: for example, if you want to find an individual by his or her surname, you need only enter the name you are looking for into the Last field; if you know that there are several people who share the same name, but you only want to find one of them, you can narrow the search down by entering any additional data which may be helpful, such as the town where they live, their telephone number, or their post code if you know it.

For example, to find out which individuals have West Hambourne in Address-2, just type in 'West Hambourne' against Address-2 of the Begin search form and then press [Ctrl]/[Return]. Record 1 will be displayed (Mr. John T. Smith).

If this is the record you want, select End search from the F2 Menu; if not, press [PgDn] to see if there are any more records which match the same criterion, and you should find Record 4 displayed (Dr. Harvey M. Jackson). There are no more records which match, so pressing [PgDn] again will result in the message 'No more records found that match that search criteria' being displayed; at the same time you will hear a rather unpleasant sound from the loudspeaker – possibly to express the computer's disgust at the grammar of the on-screen message.

Until you end a search (with End search from the F2 Menu) you can use [PgDn] and [PgUp] to browse from one match to the other as you wish.

A mail-list search is always carried out through the complete file, regardless of which record is displayed on screen when the search begins; even if record number 5 is displayed, the records numbered 1, 2, 3 and 4 will also be checked to see if they match.

**Searching by subsets** Sometimes you may not know all the relevant details of a record for which you are searching; for example, you may be looking for someone named Smith, but be uncertain of whether his address is in Suffolk or Sussex. WordStar 1512 allows a search by subsets; for example, if you enter 'Su' in the County field and 'Smith' as the surname, all the Smiths in your list with a county name starting with 'Su' will be found.

This can be a very powerful tool if used imaginatively For example, many people who live in the Greater London area do not actually have 'London' as a part of their address, but they *do* have telephone numbers beginning in '01'; a search which specifies '01' at the beginning of the Phone-1 field will match all of these, where a search for 'London' under Town would not.

# Notes, Flags, Keywords and Sublists

So far, we have used the masterfile almost exactly as we might use an ordinary physical file made up out of individual cards in a file-box; that is, we have entered data onto the 'cards', reordered the cards, and finally searched for the individual cards which we wanted to look at. Used in this way, the advantages of the computer are hardly apparent (although it is much faster to sort two or three hundred 'card images' inside the computer's memory than to try to reorder the same number of actual file cards).

What the computer is really best at is classifying information, and this is what the Keyword, Flag, Note and Sublist facilities are really for. (We describe Sublists in

141

more detail in a moment – for now you only need to know that they involve the use of the eight 'boxes' which appear on the right of the data form on the screen.)

How you will use Flags, Sublists and the rest will vary, depending on what kind of data you are using, how large the file is, and what subgroupings you will want to have. Probably you will never need to use Notes, Flags, Keywords and Sublists all at the same time.

Use Keywords where a record cannot simultaneously belong to more than one category. For example, you could classify all married individuals as 'Married', widows and widowers as 'Widowed', and unmarried people as 'Unmarried', because it is not possible for one individual to belong to more than one of these classifications at a time. Use Keywords also when records are to be sorted according to some criterion which is not otherwise available. For example, a club may have different categories of membership: Regular, Sustaining, Junior, Retired and the like, and may wish to draw up membership registers for each group.

Use Sublists when records can properly belong to more than one group at a time. For example, the Otley Town Cricket Club might classify its members according to the different sub-committees they belong to; but any member might belong to more than one sub-committee at a time, and several members may well belong to none.

Use Notes for any extra information which it would be valuable to have.

Use Flags sparingly; they can be used for the same purpose as Keywords, but use Keywords first. This is because Flags are best reserved for other purposes, as we shall see later.

# Using sublists

Before even beginning to work with sublists at the computer, spend some time devising intelligent subgroups into which your data can be divided. Think very carefully about this, as there is a direct relationship between the care with which you choose the subgroups and the ease of use of the completed file.

We shall assume that the Otley Town Cricket Club divides its members into subgroups according to their membership of subcommittees. There are four such subcommittees: in order, they are Management, Fixtures, Grounds and Refreshment.

Our first task is to give these names to the first four of the eight sublists available. From the MailList Main Menu, choose Manage master lists; then from the Manage Master Lists Menu, choose Name/update sublists.

```
┌─────────────────────────────────────────────────────┐
│              Name/Rename Sublists                     │
│ ┌───────────────────────────────────────────────────┐│
│ │1                                                   ││
│ │                                                    ││
│ │2                                                   ││
│ │                                                    ││
│ │3                                                   ││
│ │                                                    ││
│ │4                                                   ││
│ │                                                    ││
│ │5                                                   ││
│ │                                                    ││
│ │6                                                   ││
│ │                                                    ││
│ │7                                                   ││
│ │                                                    ││
│ │8                                                   ││
│ └───────────────────────────────────────────────────┘│
└─────────────────────────────────────────────────────┘
```

Type name or new name over old.

Fig. 7.10 Naming Sublists

The screen shown in Fig. 7.10 will then appear. Enter 'Management' against '1', then use [ ↓ ] to move to '2' and enter 'Fixtures'. Use [ ↓ ] to move down again, entering 'Grounds' against '3' and 'Refreshment' against '4'. Pressing [ Return ] will save the names you have already entered, and then take you back to the Manage Master Lists Menu.

When you have entered all the names and checked that they are correct, press [ Return ] to go back to the Manage Master Lists Menu, and then [ Esc ] to return to the MailList Main Menu. Next, return to the data entry forms by choosing Begin Data Entry, and the first record will be displayed.

**Assigning records to subgroups** To assign the first record to one or more subgroups, press [ Ctrl ] / [ → ], and the sublist names will be shown by the side of the boxes on the right of the screen, as in Fig. 7.11. To put the current record into any one or more subgroups, take the highlight bar to the relevant box (with [ ↑ ] and [ ↓ ]) and then press [ + ] to make the assignment; a tick will appear in the box. To remove an assignment, delete a tick by using [ Del ].

When you have finished the assignments for a particular record, press [ Ctrl ] / [ ← ] to leave the sublist boxes, and then use [ PgDn ] to move on to the next record; repeat the procedure for every record in the file.

143

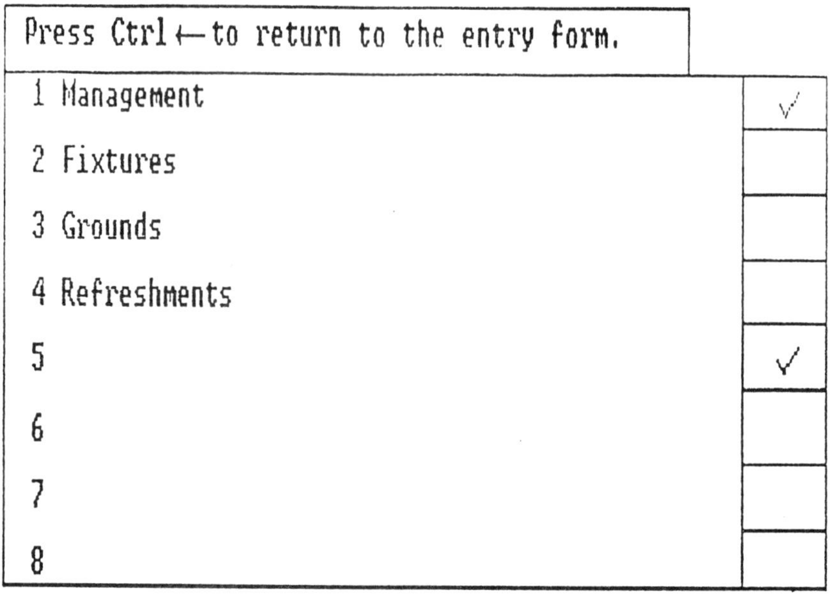

Fig. 7.11 Sublists shown on the Data Entry Form

For now, put Record 1 into Management, Record 2 into Fixtures, Record 3 into Grounds, Record 4 into Refreshments and Record 5 into both Management and Grounds. No doubt you have been to Annual General Meetings where such matters were decided with little more careful consideration than this!

**Updating sublists** Assigning individual records or groups of records to sublists can also be done automatically, and the same automatic procedure can be used to remove records from sublists *en bloc*.

Suppose, for example, that an *ad hoc* subcommittee had been formed to co-ordinate some fund-raising activity, and that you wanted every club member living in West Hambourne to be invited to join that subcommittee. The most convenient way of doing this is by assigning all of these individuals to a sublist named something like 'West Hambourne'.

First, select Manage master lists from the MailList Main Menu, and from the Manage Master Lists Menu choose the Name/rename sublists option; when the sublist screen appears, with 'Management' against '1' and so on, take the highlight bar down to '5' and enter the name 'West Hambourne'. Then press [Return] to confirm the new name, and [Esc] to return to the MailList Main Menu.

Select Begin data entry once more, then press Function Key [F2] and from the Menu select Update sublists. The Update Sublist Screen shown in Fig. 7.12 will appear.

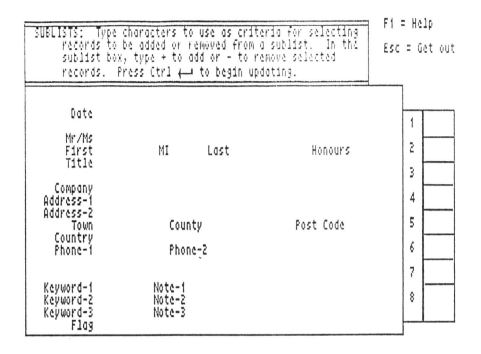

Fig. 7.12 The Update Sublist Screen

Whatever criteria you enter here will be used to assign every record to which those criteria apply into whichever sublist or sublists you mark with a tick at the Update Sublist Screen.

In our case, we simply want to assign all those records with West Hambourne in the Address-2 field into Sublist 5, 'West Hambourne'. Type 'West Hambourne' into the Address-2 field of the Update Sublist Screen, then press [Ctrl] / [→] to put a tick against Sublist 5. Then press [Ctrl] / [Return] – there is no need to use [Ctrl] / [←] first. Every record which has 'West Hambourne' in the Address-2 field will automatically be placed in the 'West Hambourne' sublist.

In our case, there are only two records which will be placed in this new sublist, and the message 'Finished updating sublists. 2 records' will appear to confirm that the updating has taken place.

Removing assignments to sublists is done in the same way, except that ticks in the sublist boxes are removed with [ – ] (the minus key) rather than with [Del]. In this way, once all the letters have gone out to the West Hambourne members, their names can be removed from the sublist, leaving it ready for the next time you need to use it.

You probably won't have been able to follow any of this if you don't have the program 'up and running' in front of you; it really is much easier to do than it is to describe, so try it out and all should become abundantly clear.

# More about flags

Batches of records can be given flags in almost exactly the same way records are assigned to sublists. Select the Flag records option from the Data Entry Menu (the F2 Menu), and from the screen which appears choose the criteria which you wish to be used in the assignment of a particular flag character.

Because flags are inherently rather limited – only one flag character can be assigned to each record at a time – it makes sense to use them mainly in this way, particularly when selecting records for printing. For instance, you could automatically flag all the records which shared certain criteria and then print out the flagged records only.

Another useful idea is to *always* flag every new record which you type in with a particular character – say 'n', for *new*. When you have done this, you can simply print out all the flagged records, so that you have a 'hard copy' of all the new records; when you have done this, you can automatically remove the flag character.

**Searching by sublists** One important use of sublists and flagged records is to enable you to search for all the records which belong to one or more sublists. This is done with the Begin Search option from the Data Entry Menu (the F2 Menu); when the Search Screen appears, use [Ctrl]/[→] to move the cursor into the sublist boxes, and then use [+] to put a tick into the box or boxes you will be using as search parameters. Finally, begin the search with [Ctrl/[Return].

# Deleting records

From time to time, it will become necessary to delete records from your file. With WordStar 1512, before you can delete a record from the database, it is first necessary to display it on the screen; this is a useful precaution against the accidental deletion of a record which you really want to keep.

Select Delete record from the Data Entry Menu reached by pressing Function Key [F2], then confirm that you really do want to delete the current record by pressing [Return]; alternatively, press [Esc] to back out.

An odd feature of this is that although you have deleted the record (and cannot get it back), it will remain 'real' to WordStar 1512. You can prove this by returning to the MailList Main Menu, where you will see that the number of Records in File has not been changed. To correct this anomaly, select Purge deleted records from the MailList Main Menu; this is necessary to complete the deletion process, and should be carried out whenever one or more records have been deleted.

146

Remember that the record numbers of deleted records are never reassigned; this is to avoid the confusion that might otherwise result from having two records sharing the same record number, even though one of them is no longer current.

# Other uses for the master list

Although the main use of the WordStar 1512 master lists is to organise name-and-address data for mail-merge, there is no rule that says that it has to be confined to that. You could, for example, make a perfectly good catalogue of all your records or slides using it.

In this case, you would probably want the Date field to represent something like the date a record was cut. Note-1 could be used for a title, Note-2 for a subtitle, the Keywords for the names of artistes, and the sublists to gather the various items in your collection into appropriate groups; for records, the groups might be Jazz, Classical, Dance and so on.

## Backing up data files

Because a master file may have taken a substantial amount of time and effort to create, it is particularly important to make sure that it is not accidentally lost or damaged; even more seriously, U.K. data users are bound by law to take precautions against accidental loss of personal files; see the Appendix for more details.

If you have a hard disc system, you can make a backup copy of your master file by selecting Back up a master list from the Manage Master Lists Menu; if you subsequently need to use such a backed-up list, select Restore a master list, from the same menu.

Floppy disc users will have to copy files with the MS-DOS Copy command in the ordinary way, remembering that they must copy *two* files – that is, the files with the .MLD and .MLI file extensions. The easiest way to do this on a two-drive system is to put the Text and Data Disc into Drive A, the backup disc into Drive B, and then to type

COPY *filename*.ML? B:*filename*.ML?

## Printing from the file

Returning now to the Otley Town Cricket Club database, this can be used in a very large variety of ways, of which producing actual mail-merged letters is only the most complex and sophisticated. Before we move on to that in the next chapter, there are a variety of other ways in which the file, or parts of it, can be used, and we shall now glance at these.

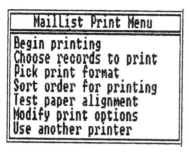

```
║ MailList Print Menu ║
╟────────────────────────────╢
║Begin printing
║Choose records to print
║Pick print format
║Sort order for printing
║Test paper alignment
║Modify print options
║Use another printer
```

**Fig. 7.13** The MailList Print Menu

Return to the WordStar 1512 Main Menu by pressing [ Esc ]; depending on exactly where you are in mail-merge, you may need to press it two or three times before the Main Menu appears. Then select List printing; if you have a floppy disc system, you will be prompted to insert the disc labelled 'printing', and when you have done this, the MailList Print Menu shown in Fig. 7.13 will be presented.

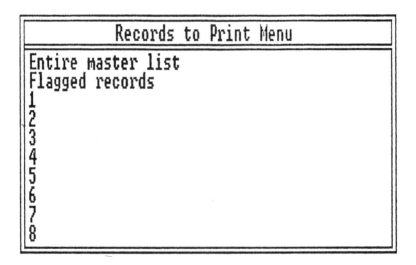

```
║          Records to Print Menu          ║
╟─────────────────────────────────────────╢
║Entire master list
║Flagged records
║1
║2
║3
║4
║5
║6
║7
║8
```

**Fig. 7.14** The Records to Print Menu

Select the second option from this menu, Choose records to print, and the Records to Print Menu (Fig. 7.14) will be shown. This offers a choice of printing either the entire file, only those records which have a particular flag, or only those which belong to one particular sublist; you can, of course, print those which belong to more than one sublist or flag by simply returning to this menu and selecting new flags or sublists, but it is much easier to assign a special sublist or flag (like the 'West Hambourne' sublist suggested above) for this specific purpose.

**Fig. 7.15** The Pick Print Format Menu

Since we are dealing with only a short file, select Entire master list; the MailList Print Menu will reappear. Move to the third option, Pick print format, and the Pick Print Format Menu, reproduced as Fig. 7.15, will appear on the screen.

The top option on this menu, Letters, refers to full mail-merge work, and we shall look at it in detail later; the other options – Envelopes, Telephone directory, Proof report, Rotary cards and Mail labels – all refer to preset options designed for printing specified and fixed fields onto standard stationery types, and we shall try these now.

**Envelopes** The Envelopes option assumes the use of standard business envelopes ('Foolscap' envelopes or a metric equivalent). There are available in both continuous form and individual feed types; if you are using the latter, you should first select the Pause at each new page option from the Change Settings Menu. If you are using continuous form envelopes, you must set the length of the envelopes (in lines) at the Page Layout Screen; remember that the normal line pitch is 6 lines per inch, so that, for example, standard envelopes 3½" tall would need a nominal page length of 21.

The fields printed on envelopes are the Mr/Ms, name, and honour fields, Title and Company, and full address (including Country, unless this field is blank). Any fields which are blank are ignored and any remaining fields are drawn up to avoid leaving blanks. Envelopes are printed in the order in which the file was most recently sorted. Typical envelope printings are shown in Fig. 7.16.

**Telephone directory** The telephone directory format is shown in Fig. 7.17. It includes the contents of Phone-1, the name (surname first), or the company if no name is shown, and Phone-2 if the field is not blank.

```
                    John T. Smith
                    90 Allhallows Road
                    West Hambourne
                    Otley Hertfordshire FE6 8JT




                    Allan P. Heywood
                    42 The Rise
                    Hartley
                    Otley Hertfordshire FE6 5DW
```

**Fig. 7.16** Envelope printings


<pre>
              TELEPHONE  DIRECTORY


00002   Heywood, Allan P.              0761-422124
00004   Jackson, Harvey M.             0761-114094
00005   Jenkins, John                  0761-867335
00003   Smith, Alison                  0761-964077
00001   Smith, John T.                 0761-9766419
</pre>

**Fig. 7.17** A telephone directory

Before this format can be used to make up a useful directory, it is important to sort the records according to alphabetical order of names.

**Proof report** It is a curious fact that errors which are completely unnoticed on a computer screen often leap to the eye when they are printed out. This problem can be avoided to some extent when preparing ordinary word processed documents by the regular use of WordStar 1512 spelling checker option, but this does not apply to the production of data files; even if it did, it would be of limited value because personal names and addresses represent precisely the kind of data which it is almost impossible to check automatically. Avoid this problem by using the Proof report format, which prints as shown in Fig. 7.18. This is the only format which prints *everything*, including the prompts, from the Data Entry Screen.

**Rotary cards** Rotary cards are continuous-form cards of the sort used for library and personnel records. The information which will be printed on them is the same as that printed on envelopes, with the addition of the Record number, Phone-1 and Date.

As the cards are a standard size (4″ x 2⅛″), it is not necessary to set the page length at the Page Layout Screen before printing them.

**Labels** Selecting Mailing labels from the Print Format Menu will enable you to choose from a variety of standard label formats and sizes.

Different sizes and formats of labels allow a variety of different fields to be printed. Specifically, where individual labels are 1″ deep, only five lines will be printed on each label; Title will normally be omitted unless the name fields are blank, and County will only be printed on labels arranged in a four-across pattern.

Deeper labels have room for seven lines of information, including Name, Title and Country (except where any of these fields are blank).

**Testing paper alignment** Once you have picked the records you want to print and the print format, you may find it useful to use the Test paper alignment from the MailList Print Menu before beginning actual printing. This is particularly important when printing sticky labels, as they are not big enough to allow much of a margin for error in aligning them in the printer.

The Test paper alignment option prints a test pattern which matches the print format you have chosen. Once the text pattern has finished printing, make any necessary adjustments to the paper and then select Test paper alignment again to make sure that everything is aligned correctly.

# Postscript

You should by now be able to create your own database file in which you can store any name-and-address information you wish, whether for sales prospects, suppliers, a club, a church or social group or almost anything else.

```
      Record: 00001                              Flag:
        Name: John T. Smith
       Title:                                     Date: 28-01-87
     Company:                                    Mr/Ms: Mr.
   Address-1: 90 Allhallows Road               Phone-1: 0761-9766419
   Address-2: West Hambourne                   Phone-2:
 Town/county: Otley Hertfordshire FE6 8JT
     Country:
   Keyword-1:                     Note-1:
   Keyword-2:                     Note-2:
   Keyword-3:                     Note-3:


      Record: 00002                              Flag:
        Name: Allan P. Heywood
       Title:                                     Date: 08-15-88
     Company:                                    Mr/Ms: Mr.
   Address-1: 42 The Rise                      Phone-1: 0761-422124
   Address-2: Hartley                          Phone-2:
 Town/county: Otley Hertfordshire FE6 5DW
     Country:
   Keyword-1:                     Note-1:
   Keyword-2:                     Note-2:
   Keyword-3:                     Note-3:


      Record: 00003                              Flag:
        Name: Alison Smith
       Title:                                     Date: 08-15-88
     Company:                                    Mr/Ms: Mrs.
   Address-1: 15 Station Street                Phone-1: 0761-964077
   Address-2: Horton Wood                      Phone-2:
 Town/county: Otley Hertfordshire FE6 6QV
     Country:
   Keyword-1:                     Note-1:
   Keyword-2:                     Note-2:
   Keyword-3:                     Note-3:


      Record: 00004                              Flag:
        Name: Harvey M. Jackson
       Title:                                     Date: 08-15-88
     Company:                                    Mr/Ms: Dr.
   Address-1: Cedar Lodge, The Avenue          Phone-1: 0761-114094
   Address-2: West Hambourne                  ,Phone-2:
 Town/county: Otley Hertfordshire FE6 8JG
     Country:
   Keyword-1:                     Note-1:
   Keyword-2:                     Note-2:
   Keyword-3:                     Note-3:


      Record: 00005                              Flag:
        Name: John Jenkins
       Title:                                     Date: 08-15-88
     Company:                                    Mr/Ms: Mr.
   Address-1: 15A, Water Street                Phone-1: 0761-867335
   Address-2: Barnhill                         Phone-2:
 Town/county: Otley Hertfordshire FE6 8OK
     Country:
   Keyword-1:                     Note-1:
   Keyword-2:                     Note-2:
   Keyword-3:                     Note-3:
```

Fig. 7.18 A proof report

Before actually getting down to entering your own information, it is a good idea to think very carefully about what categories you will need to break your file into, as this will affect the way that flags and keywords are used. It is a good idea to start small, entering no more than a couple of dozen records at first, and experimenting with the best ways of grouping these, and then filling in the rest of the file when you are confident that you have got a workable system.

# CHAPTER EIGHT

# Mail-Merging Files

## Preview

The most important use for the database file which we introduced in the previous chapter is the creation of mail-merged letters and other documents. In this chapter we shall begin with the simplest type of mail-merge operation, in which details taken from the database file are incorporated into other documents, and then move on to the use of 'boilerplates'– standard texts which are 'bolted together' to build up longer documents such as contracts, sales letters and the like. Finally, we shall look at conditional mail-merging.

Users who are familiar with 'standard' WordStar will find that boilerplating and conditional mail-merging are handled in the same way in WordStar 1512 as in regular WordStar.

You may experience some problems when you put what you have learned in this chapter into effect—especially the section dealing with conditional mail-merging—if you do not first sit down and work out clearly just what you want to do before you begin working at the keyboard. Thorough planning is particularly important if you are setting up a run of, perhaps, several hundred personalised letters, as mistakes are often not noticed before the letters go out.

## Mail-merging—Preparing a form letter

Mail-merged letters are not difficult to produce, and it is a pity that the WordStar 1512 manual is so coy when describing them. The whole procedure is so important that it is dealt with here in some detail.

In the last chapter, we produced a master list, or database, containing details of some of the members of the Otley Town Cricket Club. Every record contained details of one club member, with the information in each record being subdivided into named 'fields' each of which contained a member's first name, or a line of his address, or his telephone number, and so on.

To use this information in a mail-merged letter, it is only necessary to put a field-name from the master list into a 'matrix' document, enclosing the name between ampersands, '&'. Such field-names are called **variables**, because they vary from one letter to the next.

The easiest way to see how this works is to try it out, using the information already entered into the master list.

# A simple letter

Using WordStar 1512 as a word processor in the usual way, create a document called TEST.LTR, and into it copy the following, being particularly careful to reproduce the variable names (between the '&' symbols) exactly as they are here; the underlines are particularly important, as are the two dot commands at the very beginning and end of the document:
.op
&Mr__Ms& &Fullname&
&Address__1&
&Address__2&
&Town&
&County&
&Post__code&

&Date&

Dear &Mr__Ms& &Last&,

As a loyal supporter of Otley Town Cricket Club, I know you will be delighted to hear of our new raffle. Ten books of tickets are enclosed, and I know that we can count on you to sell all of these.

Best wishes,

J. Pargetter, Club Chairman
.pa

When you have finished entering this letter, Save it and return to the Opening Menu; we shall now print personalised copies of the letter to every member of the club.

# Printing the letters

To start printing the letters, choose List printing from the WordStar 1512 Opening Menu; this will take you to the MailList Print Menu shown in Fig. 8.1.

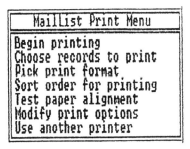

**Fig. 8.1** The MailList Print Menu

Select Pick print format to tell the program that we are printing letters, rather than envelopes or sticky labels. The Pick Print Format Menu shown in Fig. 8.2 will be shown; from this, select Letters. You will then be shown a directory of the files on the Text and Data Disc, and from this you must select the actual letter file (TEST.LTR) into which the data will be mail-merged.

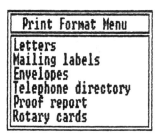

**Fig. 8.2** The Pick Print Format Menu

You will be automatically returned to the MailList Print Menu as soon as you have chosen the letter file. You could now select individual records which you want to print, as well as carry out a final sort on the records which are going to be printed with the Sort order for printing option; however, just to get the flavour of the thing, we are going to print one letter for every record.

**Beginning printing** Check that your printer is on and ready to go, and then select Begin printing. If all goes well, personalised letters will be printed out for all the members of the Otley Town Cricket Club; if you wish, you can abandon printing at any time by pressing [Esc].

If things go wrong, it is most likely that this will be either because you have forgotten to put a .pa command at the foot of the form letter, so that the program attempts to print one letter immediately below another; or you might have used a dash instead of an underline character in the variable name; if so, the variable

157

names will be repeated in each letter instead of the contents of those variables; you might get '&address-1&' instead of the first line of each individual's address, for example.

If page numbers are printed on the letters, you have forgotten to put the .op command at the beginning of the letter.

We are now going to look in more detail at ways of using variables in the matrix document, so when all five letters have been printed, press [Esc] to go back to the Opening menu and then select Word processing; then put TEST.LTR back on the screen.

# More about variables

It may have struck you that the variable names which we entered between the ampersands were not all quite the same as the field names in the master list. This can cause considerable confusion.

The rule is that if the variable name has a dash, '-', in it on the Data Entry Screen (like Address-1 and Address-2, for example) then the dash *must* be replaced by an underline in the form letter, '_'. Address-1 would therefore appear in the form letter as **&Address_1&**.

In the same way, both the slash in 'Mr/Ms' and the space in 'Record number' must be replaced by an underline, thus becoming: **&mr_ms&** and **&record_number&**.

**The &fullname& variable** You may have noticed that we used a new variable, '&fullname&', which does not appear as a field on the Data Entry Form. This makes it possible to include a full name in a letter without needing to specify all the individual components. **&fullname&** can thus be used as a synonym for **&first& &mi& &last&**.

**Empty variables** The details which you entered into the master list in Chapter Seven were carefully chosen to ensure that there were no blank fields for any record. When entering real data, you will sometimes find that blank fields will occur in some records.

For example, not everybody has five lines in their address representing Address-1, Address-2, Town, County, Postcode. This can occasionally cause problems at print-out, because if, for example, a particular record has no entry in the Address-2 field, then when it is printed out, a blank line will be left between the Address-1 field and the Town field.

This can easily be avoided by adding the characters /o at the end of the variable and before the ampersand; the Address-1 field would thus look like this: **&address_1/o&**. (That's a lower-case letter 'o', not a zero; a capital 'O' would do as well – it stands for *O*mit). When '/o' is used, no blank lines appear, and the text below that point is simply printed one line higher. Many users simply make a habit of using '/o' at the end of all their variable names.

Blank lines only happen if an empty variable is the only item on a line; if there is any other text on the same line, then it will simply move back to occupy the blank, and if this makes the line come out too short, it will normally be filled-in from the next line – a sort of reverse word-wrap – under the default which makes Paragraph Formatting apply during mail-merge work.

## Making things simpler

To make life a little easier when inserting variables, an option called Variable names is available on the second F2 Menu. If you select this, you will be shown the Variable Names Menu printed as Fig. 8.3. To use this menu, select the variable name you want from the menu by moving the highlight bar with ↑ and ↓, or by pressing the code-letter which corresponds to each variable name; you will be prompted to position the cursor at the point at which the variable name is to be located in your document, and when you have done so and pressed [Return], the correct form of the name will be inserted into your document. Variable names inserted in this way automatically include the '/o' suffix.

```
┌─────────────────────────────────────┐
│      Variable Names Menu            │
├─────────────────────┬───────────────┤
│ a  Record #         │ n  County     │
│ b  Date             │ o  Post code  │
│ c  Mr/Ms            │ p  Country    │
│ d  Fullname         │ q  Phone-1    │
│ e  First            │ r  Phone-2    │
│ f  MI               │ s  Keyword-1  │
│ g  Last             │ t  Keyword-2  │
│ h  Honour           │ u  Keyword-3  │
│ i  Title            │ v  Note-1     │
│ j  Company          │ w  Note-2     │
│ k  Address-1        │ x  Note 3     │
│ l  Address-2        │ y  Flag       │
│ m  Town             │               │
└─────────────────────┴───────────────┘
```

Fig. 8.3 The Variable Names Menu

**Ampersands that don't enclose variables** Although variable names are always enclosed in ampersands, you can still use ampersands in the ordinary way whenever you need to. Unless pairs of ampersands enclose a variable name that WordStar 1512 recognises, the ampersands will just be printed out as usual.

## Multiple copies

Sometimes it is helpful to be able to run off multiple copies of form letters. WordStar makes this possible with the dot command .rp (Repeat) the format of which is as follows:

.rp *n*

where *n* represents the number of times each letter is to be printed. This command must be placed before any printable text in the form letter.

The .rp command results in a complete set of form letters being produced at print time in the usual way, starting with the first letter which meets the print criteria and ending with the last; a second, similar, set is then printed, and so on for as many sets as are stipulated in the .rp command tail. Printing can be interrupted at any time by pressing the [Esc] key if required.

**Formatting commands** In the Cricket Club letter, all the items being merged into the form letter were in the salutation and the inside address, and so had very little effect on the shape of the body of the letter, and if you look over your printed letters, you will see that the actual text of all of them is identically laid out. However, there is nothing at all to prevent you from using variables at any point in a document, and when this is done, line length ceases to be so predictable.

You have probably received promotional letters which are derived from something like this: 'Imagine the astonishment on your neighbours' faces when you drive up to &address__1/o& in your new car'. Depending on the length of the text inserted by '&address__lo/&', different copies of the document below that point may be laid out in different ways.

Generally, this variation should cause few problems in mail-merged letters; this is because it is assumed that Paragraph Formatting is automatically turned on when you are printing a mail-merge document, unless you have specifically turned it off with '.pf off'. Under certain circumstances, it is possible that a document which occupied nearly a complete page might be tripped onto part of the next page if an unduly long variable were to be merged in, but this is hardly likely to be an everyday problem.

# Choosing records to print

Often, it will only be necessary to print documents for a small proportion of the records on the master list. For example, you may only need to send letters to customers living in a certain area, or to print out a proof list of the most recent entries to the file in order to check that they are accurate.

To do this, it is first necessary to find some way of marking the records which you wish to print, either with a flag character or by assigning them to a sublist; as we have already seen, both of these operations can be done automatically.

Then at the MailList Print Menu select Choose records to print; the Records to Print Menu shown in Fig. 8.4 will appear.

To select records flagged with one particular character, position the highlight bar on Flagged records and press [Return]; you will then be asked which flag character you wish to use.

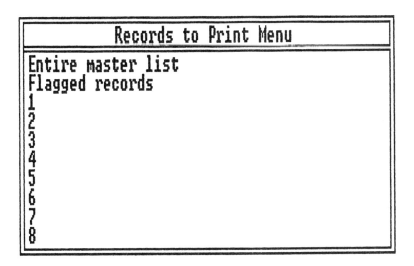

**Fig. 8.4** The Records to Print Menu

To select records belonging to one of the sublists, take the highlight bar down to the sublist you want and press [ Return ]; all records belonging to that sublist will then be printed.

## Asking for information

A very powerful feature of WordStar 1512 enables it to ask the user for information at print time. There are four related commands which can be incorporated in documents and which are used for the combined purposes of inputting information and of controlling the screen which is displayed during printing; they are .cs, .dm, .av and .sv.

**.cs – Clear screen** Used on its own, '.cs' simply clears the message window which appears at the bottom of the screen during printing; it can also take the form

.cs *message*

where *message* is any text which you wish to use – there is no need to put inverted commas round the message. The message will be redisplayed anew in the message window as each succeeding form letter is printed. A message can either be a line of text or the contents of a variable; an example of this is given below.

**.dm—Display message** A very similar command is .dm; this has the form

.dm *message*

and is used to *D*isplay a *M*essage in the message window during printing without first clearing the window. Again, no inverted commas are needed, and the message may include a variable.

There are many ways of using these facilities, some of which we shall meet later. For the moment, consider the situation where a very large number of form letters are being printed. While the print-run is proceeding, it would obviously be useful to be able to get some reliable indication of the number of letters which have already been printed. This can be easily done by incorporating the command line

.dm Now printing the letter to &fullname&

in the matrix document; this will cause the the name of the addressee to be displayed on the screen. The only point to watch is that such a command must occur in the matrix document *after* the first 'real' printed variable such as &Mr__ms& rather than just under the '.op' command. If the letters are being printed in ascending order of record numbers, you could use the line

.dm Now printing letter number &Record&

to show on screen the record number of the letter currently being printed. Once again, this must come *after* the first 'real' variable.

Try these commands on the Otley Town Cricket Club file; use both .dm and .cs to see how they differ from one another.

**.av—Ask for value** Sometimes it is useful to be able to insert new information while a mail-merge document is being printed. For example, the Date field of each record may well not hold the actual date on which the letters are being printed, and it would be convenient to be able to input that date while the letters are being printed.

The command to do this takes the form

.av *variable*

You can also use the alternative form

.av "Message", *variable*

where the message must be in quotation marks, and must be separated from the variable name by a comma.

This command pauses the printer while it *A*sks for a *V*alue (or a Variable, according to the WordStar 1512 manual); if the variable named in the command occurs in the document, it will be replaced at printout by whatever you type in.

162

You can either use variables which correspond to field names in the master list, like Date, or make up variable names of your own. If you use master list names, the command must be placed *after* the first reference has been made to 'real' variables in the file, or whatever data you input at the keyboard will be 'overwritten' by the data from the file; if you use variable names which are not also used in the master list, you can put the .av command at the very top of the document.

For example, if you insert

.av Today

at the top of the Otley Cricket Club letter, and instead of '&Date&' use &Today&, the printer will pause when the .av command is found and the prompt 'Today?' will appear on the screen. Type in the date in any format you like, and this will then be printed when the variable '&Today&' is found.

It is important to note that when the variable name is used in the .av command, no ampersands are used; when the value of the variable is to be printed, the ampersands appear as usual.

**.sv — Set variable** The .sv command is similar to .av, but instead of asking for a variable to be input at the keyboard during printing, it enables you to substitute the value of one variable for another. The format of the command is

.sv *variable name,value*

For example

.sv Date, January 16 1988

would insert the text 'January 16 1988' wherever '&Date&' is found in the remainder of the matrix document.

The syntax of the command should be clear from the above example, but there are some points which may need clarification: as always, there *must* be a space between the dot command and the tail — in this case, the value given to the variable; the variable name (which is not enclosed by ampersands in the .sv command) *must* be followed by a comma; and the comma *may* be followed by a space before the substitute text begins; if there is more than one space, the extras will be ignored.

As with the .av command, you can use either your own variable names or those which are used as field names in the master list, but if you use master list names, the .sv command must come after the first 'real' reference to the master list in the matrix document.

**Boilerplating** The most important use for the .sv command is not for mail-merging, but for boilerplating. A **boilerplate** is a section of standard text which can be used under many different circumstances, often with slight changes or additions

163

made to it. Contracts are an example of documents which are often assembled from standard boilerplate paragraphs, with suitable variations and insertions built in as required.

Imagine that four parties are involved in a particular contract, and that the contract is built up out of four or five different paragraphs each of which is held in its own disc file. This in itself is straightforward enough with WordStar 1512, as each of the paragraphs can be chained to the others with the .fi command, but difficulties appear when it is necessary to actually insert the names of the parties into one or more of the paragraphs. Obviously it would be possible to go through each document file and edit the names of the parties into it, but this procedure would be both tedious and error prone.

Instead, when the original boilerplates are created, use variables like &name1&, &name2&, etc., in them. These are not the sort of variables which exist in the master file which we have been looking at so far; rather, they are variables which are created for this document alone.

Then, at the head of the first document, and before the first printable line, place a series of .sv commands, like this:

.sv name1, John Peters
.sv name2, Alan Rogers
.sv name3, Alastair Beauchamp
.sv name4, Josie Cunningham

The effect of this will be that wherever &name1& occurs, in any one of the paragraphs which have been chained together, 'John Peters' will be substituted for it; the same obviously applies to the other variable names as well.

## Command files

It is also possible to create a special document file, called a **merge command file**, to hold the .sv commands. Imagine that the first section of your actual document is called CONTRACT.ONE; the command file might then look something like this:

.sv name1, John Peters
.sv name2, Alan Rogers
.sv name3, Alastair Beauchamp
.sv name4, Josie Cunningham
.fi b:\contract.one

When this command file is List printed, it will automatically chain CONTRACT.ONE, (which in turn will chain other sections) and the variable names created by the .sv commands in the command file will be passed to the following boilerplate paragraphs.

Two points to bear in mind here are that the .fi command must be the last command in the command file, and that the number of copies which are printed will depend on how many records are selected from the named master file – even if no variables are used from that master file.

One final problem is that WordStar 1512 List printing always assumes that a command file uses .fi as a nesting, rather than a chaining, command, and thus always returns to it at the end of printing the last boilerplate; you will consequently be asked for the names a second time, when everything is already printed. Press [ Return ] twice to get out of this.

# Conditional mail-merging

The final aspect of WordStar 1512 which we shall examine in this chapter is the use of the conditional statements. These are very powerful commands which can be used in order to print certain parts of a document while leaving others unprinted, and once again the manual does not really show either how to use them or how powerful they are.

Conditional statements can take either of two forms, as follows:

.if *condition* goto *label*
*text to be bypassed if the condition is true*
.ef *label*

or

.ex *condition* goto *label*
*text to be bypassed if the condition is false*
.ef *label*

**Rules for conditions** All conditions must be enclosed either between an .if and an .ef command or between an .ex and an .ef command; it may help you to remember this if you know that .ex is an abbreviation for *EX*cept, and .ef is short for *E*nd i*F*.

A complete .if command line can take either of the following two forms, depending on whether you are comparing numeric quantities or just strings of characters:

.if &record__number& = 6 goto

or

.if &last& = "Patterson" goto

165

In other words, string variables which are the subject of a comparison *must* be enclosed in double quotation marks, while numeric variables which are being compared must *not* be enclosed in quotes.

**Multiple conditions** Conditions do not have to be as simple as those listed above. Multiple conditions are possible with .and. and .or. (note the full-stops before and after these words when used in WordStar 1512 condition statements), so that you can devise statements like the following:

.if &record__number& < 100 .and. &county& = "Berkshire" goto *label*

which will divert the printing of the document to the appropriate label provided that *both* conditions are true; if only one of the conditions is true, no diversion will take place.

**An example of conditional mail-merging** Bringing all this down to earth, look at the following example of conditional mail-merging; it is designed to send one letter to all the men on the master list – that is, all those with 'Mr.' in the 'Mr/Ms' field – and a different letter to all the women – all the other records.

.op
&Mr__ms& &Mi& &Last&
&Address__1/o&
&Address__2/o&
&Town/o&
&County/o&

&Date&

Dear &Mr__ms& &last&,

.if &Mr__ms& = "Mr." goto men
Please find enclosed our latest catalogue of fine ladies'
cosmetics. We are sure you will agree that for value and
quality they are unequalled.
.ef men

.ex &Mr__ms& = "Mr." goto finish
Please find enclosed our latest catalogue of fine mens'
watches. We are sure you will agree that for value and
quality they are unequalled.
.ef finish

Yours sincerely,

Direct Home Sales plc
.pa

If you type this is and use it with the Otley Town Cricket Club master list, you will see how it works. You will also find that there is – quite deliberately – a 'bug', or unexpected error in it, in that Dr. Jackson will be sent a letter referring to ladies' cosmetics; he has been wrongly chosen because his title is not 'Mr'. This could be corrected by changing the conditional command lines to read something like

.if &Mr__ms& = "Mr." .or. &Mr__ms& = "Dr." goto men

which would work correctly except when dealing with female doctors!

How you would solve such a situation would depend on other factors – you might well have some other variable you could bring in to settle things one way or the other; here, I merely point out the difficulties in order to convince you that it is possible to make some quite unfortunate errors while mail-merging if you do not stop to think very carefully about what you are doing.

**Different comparison characters** So far, our conditional statements have only tested for equality; there are actually six different comparisons which you can make, as follows

= Equal
<> Not equal
< Less than (or earlier in alphabetical order)
> Greater than (or later in alphabetical order)
<= Less than or equal to
>= Greater than or equal to

# File merging with conditions

Because condition statements divert the printing of a document away from the section between the .if and the .ef when the specified condition is true, you can enclose .fi chaining commands which will be acted upon if the condition is false but not if it is true. For example, the cosmetics/watches letter illustrated above could have used two boilerplate files (COSMETIC and WATCHES let us say) which would have been called up by .fi B: \COSMETIC and .fi B: \WATCHES instead of inserting the actual paragraphs shown above into the letter itself.

The flexibility which this can give is increased even further when you realise that you can also use conditions in conjunction with .sv and .av commands. This, however, is going well beyond the level of an introductory book on WordStar 1512, though it may help you to see just how sophisticated the program is.

Incidentally, in the above examples we have always used goto and a label in the tail of the .if and .ex command lines. This can be abbreviated to G, or even left out altogether, without affecting the operation of a line. If there is only one conditional statement in the document, the label can also be omitted, though for clarity it is probably best to use it anyway.

# Postscript

WordStar 1512 mail-merge can be used at several different levels; at the very simplest level, you can use it to create individualised letters, reading the details off the master list prepared for that purpose.

At a slightly more advanced level, you can choose which records will be used for printing mail-merge documents, and you can use boilerplate texts which you can chain and nest into your main letter, and send the resultant documents out to either every individual represented on the file or to selected individuals chosen by flags or sublists.

Finally, you can build in a series of conditions, either in the matrix document itself or in another document which functions as a controller, and use these conditions to decide whether or not particular files are to be merged and which portions of a document are to be printed for which records.

It is important here not to try to run before you can walk; mail-merge is not really very difficult to use once you are familiar with it, but there is quite a lot that can go wrong, we have seen with the deliberate 'bug' in our own work with conditional statements.

# CHAPTER NINE

# Simple Word Processing with WordStar

## Preview

This chapter is an introduction to what we might call 'standard' WordStar and various other programs which work in a broadly similar way. We use the expression 'standard WordStar' to differentiate it from WordStar 1512, referring particularly to versions 3.3 and later; version 3.2, which was the first version to be released for IBM and IBM-compatible personal computers, differs from later versions in various minor ways.

Topics covered in this chapter include running the program, the creation, editing, saving and printing of a simple document, and some aspects of file handling.

Chapter Ten deals with more advanced editing techniques, progressing through the various options which control such features as underscoring and emboldening, line spacing, rulers and printing. Chapter Eleven introduces WordStar mail-merge, together with the new dot commands which are available in that program.

If you have come to this section after reading the material about WordStar 1512, then you will probably find that you will progress very quickly even though the command structure of the two programs is quite different.

If your main interest is in the use of 'standard' WordStar and you have not looked at the earlier chapters, you may occasionally need to refer back to them if you come across terms which you do not understand and which are not fully explained here.

# Beyond WordStar 1512

The first part of this book has dealt with WordStar 1512, which is an updated version of WordStar designed to be implemented on IBM-compatible computers, and to take advantage of the facilities which those computers offer. It is a particularly easy program to use, so that even complete beginners can get to grips with it very easily, helped by the fact that commands are selected through menus instead of through sequences of key-presses.

Inevitably, WordStar 1512 will not meet everyone's needs; some users may already be familiar with previous versions of WordStar, and thus may find the changes which have been implemented in WordStar 1512 rather distracting; others may have specialised requirements which go beyond what WordStar 1512 can easily perform.

The great advantage of WordStar is that it offers a standard format which has been implicitly recognised in other programs. Consequently, a very large number of programs use key-sequences which are very similar to those of WordStar; these sequences are used, for example, to move the cursor and to manipulate files in the Sidekick notepad mentioned earlier. Understanding something about 'standard' WordStar can therefore be very useful even if you don't actually use it.

There are also on the market several WordStar 'workalikes' or 'clones' which imitate not only WordStar key-sequences but even aspects of the screen layout. (A workalike is a program which produces a similar effect to a different program, using similar key presses; an analogy might be made with different kinds of car, which are powered by either petrol or diesel engines, have either front or rear-wheel drive, and are manufactured by different companies all over the world, but which, despite all these differences, still use similar pedal and dashboard layouts and are driven in the same way).

Most of the material in these chapters is equally applicable to both 'standard' WordStar and to these workalikes.

One of the principles which underlies all these programs is that, as far as possible, they should be capable of working on a very large number of different types of computer. An important consequence of this is that they concentrate on using only those keys which can be guaranteed to be present on *every* computer, namely the alphanumeric keys which correspond to printable ASCII characters together with [Esc], [Shift] and [Ctrl]. Although other keys, such as the cursor keys, are so common as to be virtually universal, WordStar and its clones do not assume their presence.

One consequence of this is that the standard way of carrying out even such simple operations as moving the cursor involves holding down [Ctrl] while pressing one or two other keys, though it is also possible to use the ordinary cursor keys. In any case, most regular users very quickly adapt to these idiosyncratic key-combinations; many users actually regard them as positively advantageous, because once you have learned the necessary commands, you can use them on any keyboard, regardless of how it is configured. You can also leave the [Num Lock] key engaged all the time, which makes it easier to use the number-pad.

A second consequence of the universality of WordStar and its workalikes is that they are capable of working with almost any printer you might name. This gives them even greater flexibility than WordStar 1512, but at the expense of a fairly complex installation routine if you want to get the best out of the printer.

Finally, any kind of screen can be used, provided that it can handle 80 columns of text. For various reasons, including the different character sets which are available on different machines, it is not possible for WordStar to duplicate the graphics of WordStar 1512.

# Before using WordStar

Versions of WordStar intended for the Amstrad PC1512 and other IBM compatibles are generally provided in ready-installed versions (as far as the keyboard and screen are concerned, though not the printer) and thus you will not need to carry out any installation procedure before running the program; any references in the manual to installing the program before running it should therefore be ignored.

WordStar users may find a program called WSU.COM on the distribution disc; this is an uninstalled version of the program, and this will have to be installed with WINSTALL.COM before it can be used. Most users of the program will find that they have bought a ready-installed version, and will only need to use WINSTALL.COM if they need to alter some detail of the way the program works.

Assuming that you have an installed version of the program, getting it running for the first time therefore involves only making a working copy of the original program disc. *You must do this* – it is very unwise to use the distribution disc for your daily work with a program.

Before you start making a working copy, be sure to stick a write-protect tab over the notch in the distribution disc, to avoid any accidental damage to the program. This is vital, as otherwise you could obliterate the program on the distribution disc by making a mistake in the MS-DOS COPY command.

WordStar is not 'copy protected', so you can make working copies without difficulty. This has led to the program being extremely widely pirated. Probably, most people who do this are unthinking rather than wicked, but the point does need to be made that it is not only illegal to make unauthorised copies of programs, but also ultimately suicidal: if the producers of software gain no benefit from copies of their products being distributed, they will not be able to update their programs or develop new ones.

Alternatively, software producers will turn to techniques which make it difficult to duplicate programs, so that even legitimate users will no longer be able to make their own working copies. Taking this to its logical conclusion, some people now argue that when the original distribution disc wears out, the customer should expect to buy a new one, on the analogy that if a book became too worn or battered to be used, a reasonable man would expect to go shopping for another.

In an attempt to combat copyright piracy, some workalikes are sold in both 'locked' and 'unlocked' versions; before you can use a locked version, you will have to telephone the manufacturers to find the individual code number of your disc. However, most distributors will unlock your copy for you.

Before starting to use your program, you will also need another formatted blank disc on which to store your document files. Label this as your Text and Data Disc.

To make a copy of your program on a twin drive system, put the blank formatted disc which will hold your working copy of the program in Drive B and the distribution disc in Drive A, and then enter

COPY WS.COM B: *(for WordStar)*

and press [Return]. The copy will be made automatically. On single drive systems, you will be prompted to swap discs as necessary. When you have made a working copy of your program, put the original distribution disc away in a safe place.

## Getting started

To run the program, put the working disc in Drive A, the Text and Data Disc in Drive B (if you have one) and enter the command

WS *(for WordStar)*

followed by [Return]. A copyright notice will be displayed, and after this the Opening Menu will appear. Below this will be shown a directory of the currently active disc.

```
             < < <  O P E N I N G   M E N U  > > >
   ---Preliminary  Commands---   !  --File  Commands--  !  -System  Commands-
L   Change logged disk drive     !                      !   R  Run a program
F   File directory      now ON   !   P  PRINT a file     !   X  EXIT to system
H   Set help level               !                      !
   ---Commands to open a file--- !   E  RENAME a file    !  -WordStar Options-
    D  Open  a  document  file    !   O  COPY   a file    !   M  Run MailMerge
    N  Open a non-document file   !   Y  DELETE a file    !   S  Run SpellStar
```

**Fig. 9.1** The WordStar Opening Menu

Figure 9.1 shows the WordStar Opening Menu; workalike programs generally offer substantially the same options, but you may find a few slight differences in layout.

In its natural state, WordStar expects to store and read text files on the disc in Drive A. There is not, however, a great deal of room on the program disc for document files – especially long ones – and it is better to keep them on another disc.

If you are using a two-drive system, press [l] (the letter 'L' in either upper or lower case) to change the 'logged' (current) disc drive; select Drive B from the possibilities offered. When you have done so, the program will henceforth expect to find and store any text files on that drive, and the Directory on the screen will display the names of any files which may already be on the disc in Drive B.

If you are using a single-drive machine, it is easiest to create and edit documents on the RAM Disc C, and then copy them from there onto a real disc before turning the computer off. This can be a little risky, inasmuch as a computer failure or power cut while you are editing will wipe out all your work, so you should make backups of anything on the RAM Disc at regular intervals, thus greatly reducing the amount of text you might lose.

# Features of WordStar

Among the features of regular WordStar which are also found in its clones, but which differ from WordStar 1512, are the basic screen displays, the key combinations which are used to initiate most actions, the use of ruler lines, and the way in which different Help levels can be selected.

To see how these work, we shall create a short test document which we shall then experiment with. Do this by pressing [d] at the Opening Menu – this book always uses lower-case letters for these commands, but you can use either capitals or small letters as you prefer. There is no need to press [Return]. The screen will clear and you will be prompted for a name for the document; type in the name of the document we shall be using, which is TEST.DOC, and press [Return].

**'While entering' messages** While waiting for you to respond to prompts such as WordStar's 'Name of File to edit?' a 'While entering' message is always displayed; this shows, among other things, how to correct any errors you may make in entering a file-name.

WordStar then checks whether a file already exists with the same name as you have entered; if it does, that file is loaded ready for editing; if it does not, the message 'NEW FILE' is shown. Some workalikes double-check that you really do intend to open a new file before allowing you to start entering text, and Sidekick's notepad and a few other programs allow you to start typing before you have given a name to your document.

**The Editing Screen** While a document is being edited or created, the upper portion of the screen is occupied by a Status Line, at the very top of the screen, and a brief guide to command sequences below this; depending on which Help level is currently selected, this display can be curtailed or even removed altogether, but usually the default is for all menus and other information to be shown in as much detail as possible. We shall see shortly you can reduce the amount of information on the screen, thus making room for more of the text on which you are working.

173

**Fig. 9.2** The WordStar Status Line

The WordStar Status Line is shown in Fig. 9.2. At the extreme left is a space in which any key pressed in conjunction with [Ctrl] is displayed while the appropriate command is being carried out; to the right of this the current disc drive and the name of the file being worked on are shown, followed by the Page, Line and Column numbers at which the text cursor is currently located; next is a warning of whether you are in Insert or Overwrite Mode.

On the far right of the Status Line, some programs show a 'Fullness Gauge', which is a kind of barometer to show how much of the computer's memory is occupied by the current file–the more hyphens have been replaced by equals signs, the greater the proportion of the total available memory which is in use.

```
                    < < <     M A I N   M E N U    > > >
     --Cursor Movement--    : -Delete- :  -Miscellaneous-  : -Other  Menus-
^S char left ^D char right :^G  char  : ^I Tab    ^B Reform : (from Main only)
^A word left ^F word right :DEL chr lf: ^V INSERT ON/OFF   :^J Help  ^K Block
^E line  up  ^X line down  :^T word rt:^L Find/Replce again:^Q Quick ^P Print
     --Scrolling--         :^Y  line  :RETURN End paragraph:^O Onscreen
^Z line down ^W line up    :          : ^N Insert a RETURN :
^C screen up ^R screen down:          : ^U Stop a command  :
```

**Fig. 9.3** The WordStar Main menu

Beneath the Status Line is displayed the Main Menu, reprinted here as Fig. 9.3; this gives a quick on-screen guide to the use of WordStar under five headings: Cursor Movement, Scrolling, Delete, Miscellaneous and Other Menus. Each option is selected by holding down [Ctrl] and pressing the required key–the caret, (^) which is displayed in front of each letter name is a conventional abbreviation for the [Ctrl] key; this abbreviation is used very frequently in WordStar.

**Cursor Movement** The Cursor Movement section of the menu shows the keys which can be used, in conjunction with [Ctrl], to move the cursor around the screen; these keys are grouped in a rough diamond shape on the keyboard, and this should help you remember which keys do what. If you prefer, you can still use the normal cursor keys in the number pad cluster on the right of the keyboard.

**Scrolling** Scrolling leaves the cursor in the same place but shifts the text around it–up or down either a single line or a complete screenful at a time.

174

**Delete** The use of the Delete commands is largely self-evident. Some workalikes have a useful Unerase command which is reached through [Ctrl]/[u].

This restores the most recent erasure, whether of a block or a single character. The unerased text will always reappear at the current position of the text cursor, so that it is possible to use it to move small blocks of text around.

In WordStar, [Ctrl]/[u] is used slightly differently: it interrupts a command which has not yet taken effect. If, for example, you mark out a block for deletion and actually give the block delete command, you can cancel it with [Ctrl]/[u] provided that you give that command before the deletion has taken place; there isn't much time for hanging about, though.

**Miscellaneous** Under Miscellaneous are displayed the keys which control a variety of unrelated commands. [Ctrl]/[j] is used to alter the Help level; [Ctrl]/[i] duplicates the [Tab] key; [Ctrl]/[v] toggles between Insert and Overwrite Mode, and thus duplicates the [Ins] key; [Ctrl]/[b] reformats text between the cursor position and the end of the paragraph; and [Ctrl]/[l] is used to repeat a search and replace operation which was initiated from the Quick Functions Menu.

[Ctrl]/[n] breaks a line at the cursor, sending the section of text to the right of the cursor to a new line and inserting a Carriage Return. The most important difference between [Ctrl]/[n] and pressing the [Return] key is that [Return] always takes the cursor down a line, whereas with [Ctrl]/[n] the cursor stays on the same line. Also, if you are using multiple line-spacing, [Return] will always send the cursor down more than one line – two lines if you are using double-spacing, three lines for triple-spacing and so on – whereas [Ctrl]/[n] always creates a single Carriage Return.

This feature may not work in quite the same way on all WordStar-like programs, so it is worth checking it out before using it on a workalike.

**Help levels** Pressing [Ctrl]/[j] at the Main Menu opens the door on a whole series of different explanations on the workings of WordStar. Some of the explanations which are available in this way are quite lengthy – up to half-a-dozen screen 'pages' on a single topic – and you will find it well worth your while to explore them.

The help 'pages' can be called up whenever you need helpful advice and instructions on particular topics, but a certain amount of information will in any case be displayed on the screen while you are working. Exactly how much information will appear varies, depending on the Help Level which is currently selected; the Help Level can be altered by pressing [Ctrl]/[j]/[Ctrl]/[j].

The default is Help Level 3, which shows all menus and prompts and the full Status Line at all times. This takes up about a third of the screen, which can be inconvenient at times; you can reduce the amount of this space, which is not available for the display of text, by changing the Help level.

Help Level 2 removes the Edit Menu, but the various sub-menus will still be displayed if you pause after pressing the first key in any control sequence. Help Level 1 does not display any menus while editing, and the page, line, column (and fullness gauge if there is one) are removed from the Status Line; finally, Help Level 0 displays no menus during editing, removes the Status Line, and displays no prompts at all – not even the 'Are you sure?' warning which normally appears to warn you that you are about to take some potentially destructive action like quitting a document before saving it.

Until you become reasonably familiar with whichever program you are using, it is best to keep the Help level set at 3; when you can find your way round the most common key-sequences, setting the Help level at 2 will free the top third of the screen, and thus increase the amount of your document which is displayed at any one time. As you become more proficient, you can then move to even lower Help levels, secure in the knowledge that if you do get stuck, you can always get back to higher Help levels whenever you need to.

**Other Menus** The most complicated of the various options offered from the Editing Menu is Other Menus. This is in effect a series of sub-menus, each of which can be called to the screen by holding down [Ctrl] and tapping the appropriate key. However, users who become familiar with WordStar quickly find that they do not need to wait for these sub-menus to appear; the program is set up to wait for a brief period after the first key is pressed before displaying the appropriate sub-menu, and suppressing it if a second key-press is made during the delay; it is not necessary to continue to hold down [Ctrl] while pressing the second key.

You will probably find that the key-sequences that you will use most often are [Ctrl]/[k]/[d], which saves the document on which you are working to the logged-on disc, [Ctrl]/[k]/[q], which abandons the current document, and the various options from the [Ctrl]/[q] 'quick functions' menu which control the Find and Replace operations as well as providing speeded-up versions of several Edit Menu commands.

Sidekick has a [Ctrl]/[k]/[p] option which allows a block of text – or the complete document if no block has been defined – to be printed directly, without first saving it to disc. This can be a great time-saver if you only want to print out a memo or some other very short document.

**The ruler line** Immediately below the Main Menu is a Ruler Line which shows the location of margins and tabs. The left margin is marked with an 'L' and the right margin with 'R'; tab stops are shown as ' ! ' and decimal tabs by ' # '; all other positions are occupied by hyphens.

**Overlays** In order to reduce the amount of the program which is held in the computer's memory and thus leave more room for your text, WordStar and its workalikes make use of **overlays**. These are sections of the program which are held on disc until they are required – when you call up a sub-menu, for example. Substantially the same situation occurs with WordStar 1512 when you press Function Key [F1] to display a help page.

There will inevitably be short pauses while the overlays are loaded from floppy discs; hard disc users will find that these delays are much less noticeable. An important consequence of the use of overlays is that you must leave the program disc in the disc drive all the time you are using the program, except for users with a single disc system while they are backing up the RAM Disc C onto a real floppy disc.

# A simple document

You should be ready now to begin entering material for our first WordStar document, TEST.DOC. Copy the text laid out in Fig. 9.4, remembering not to press [Return] at the end of each line but only at the end of each paragraph; words which overlap the right margin are automatically word-wrapped – that is, they are taken to the beginning of the following line. As each line is completed and the cursor moves on to the next line, the line which you have just left will be automatically right-justified.

```
A: TEST.DOC  PAGE 1 LINE 1 COL 01                    INSERT ON

           < < <      M A I N    M E N U      > > >
      --Cursor Movement--    ¦ -Delete- ¦   -Miscellaneous-  ¦  -Other   Menus-
^S char left ^D char right !^G  char ¦ ^I Tab   ^B Reform ¦ (from Main only)
^A word left ^F word right¬!DEL chr lf¦ ^V INSERT ON/OFF   ¦^J Help  ^K Block
^E line  up  ^X line down  !^T word rt!^L Find/Replce again!^Q Quick ^P Print
     --Scrolling--         !^Y  line   !RETURN End paragraph!^O Onscreen
^Z line down ^W line up    !         ¦ ^N Insert a RETURN ¦
^C screen up ^R screen down!         ¦ ^U Stop a command   ¦

L----!----!----!----!----!----!----!----!----!----!----!--------R
Try to make a copy of this short document, reproducing all its
features as accurately as possible.  Fortunately, any mistakes
which you might make are very easy to correct.  Press [Return]
twice at the end of this sentence.                                       <
                                                                         <
     The first line of this second paragraph is indented from the
margin.  This is done with the [TAB] key.  Notice how words are
automatically moved to the next line if they are too long to fit
on the current one.                                                      .
                                                                         .
                                                                         .
                                                                         .
                                                                         .
1HELP    2INDENT 3SET LM 4SET RM 5UNDLIN 6BLDFCE 7BEGBLK 8ENDBLK 9BEGFIL 10ENDFIL
```

**Fig. 9.4** A simple document to copy

When you have finished typing, go back and proof-read your work. Any mistakes which you have made can be corrected in ways with which you will be familiar if you have read the first part of this book, namely by taking the cursor up to the point at which the error occurs, erasing any incorrect characters and inserting the correct ones.

You will notice that when you do this, the tidy right-justification of the passage on the screen disappears; under certain circumstances a line of text can grow so long that it extends off the right-hand edge of the screen; if this happens, a '+' flag appears in the right margin to warn you that some of it is out of sight.

**About flags** Apart from '+', WordStar uses several other flag symbols. Most of the time you will hardly be aware of them, but for all that there are times when they can be very helpful. For example, if you are uncertain whether or not a line ends with a 'hard return' (i.e. pressing the [Return] key), you can check whether there is a '<' flag in the right margin; if there is, then the line ends in a 'hard return'; if not, then it doesn't. All the flags used by WordStar are shown in Fig. 9.5.

```
<          line ends in "hard" carriage return, entered by user
space      this line break arose from word wrap or paragraph
             reform, and may be moved on subsequent reform
+          this line continues past the edge of the screen
-          next line will overprint this line
?          unrecognized or incomplete dot command
M          Merge-Print (optional feature) dot command
P          page break
:          this screen line is before beginning of document
```

**Fig. 9.5** Flags used in WordStar

**Reformatting paragraphs** When all the necessary corrections have been made, you can reformat the document inside its margins by taking the cursor to the top of each paragraph in turn and pressing [Ctrl]/[b] to reformat the text. Depending on the changes you have made, you may find that instead of the text being simply reformatted, the top of the screen is cleared and a notice is shown about **hyphen help**.

**Hyphen help** Hyphen help is used during reformatting whenever a word which overlaps the right margin has more than five characters to the *left* of that margin; its purpose is to prevent ugly gaps appearing in your text where there happens to be an unduly short line. Look down the screen at the body of your work, and you will see that the cursor is resting on a word which overlaps the margin.

Your choice is now either to over-ride Hyphen help by pressing [Ctrl]/[b] again, thus wrapping the word onto the following line, or to move the cursor to the left until it reaches a place where you would like a hyphen to be inserted. With the cursor at a suitable place, press [-]; the word will be broken at that point, with the portion to the right of the hyphen being wrapped to the beginning of the following line.

Hyphens of the sort which Hyphen help inserts in this way are called 'soft' hyphens; they usually appear highlighted. If the paragraph is reformed again later

178

as a result of further editing which has taken place rendering a line-break at the hyphen unnecessary, the soft hyphen will still be shown in the text; it will not be printed, however (but see the next paragraph). The hyphens which you would normally insert into the text when entering material are 'hard' hyphens.

Although it is always a good idea to reformat your text with [Ctrl]/[b] before printing it out, it is particularly important to do this if hyphen help has inserted soft hyphens, as otherwise they may occasionally be printed unnecessarily.

If you are working with a long document and would be bothered by the delays caused by hyphen help, or if you don't mind occasional short lines – and particularly if you are not using right justification – you can turn hyphen help off with [Ctrl]/[o]/[h]; this is a toggle, so the same sequence of keys will turn it on again.

**Right justification** WordStar and most if its workalikes initially expect all text to be right-justified – that is, displayed with an even right margin both on the screen and when printed out. Lines which are particularly short often look a little ungainly printed in this way, because of the large and unequal gaps which appear between words, though if your printer supports 'microspacing' then this will not happen – this is described in Chapter Ten. If you prefer, you can turn right justification off with [Ctrl]/[o]/[j]. This too is a toggle, so use the same keys to turn it back on. Once again, the factory-set default which selects right justification when the program is started can be changed at installation.

**Where the cursor won't go** You may notice while you are editing your work that there are some places to which the cursor cannot be taken; it can be moved freely over all the text on the screen and a couple of spaces past the right-hand end of a line, but nowhere else. If a line is completely blank, the cursor can only be placed in the first column.

This may cause problems if you want to line material up in tidy columns – it is often not possible to align the cursor with the point you want to match and then take it straight up or down the screen to position some other text. If you want to align only one or two items in this way, use the column counter in the Status Line; if there are several items to be aligned, do it properly with the Tab command.

# Saving your work

When you are sure that TEST.DOC is correct, and is properly aligned between the margins, save it onto disc by pressing [Ctrl]/[k]/[d]. After a short delay while the disc is working, you will be returned to the Opening Menu. It is not possible with 'standard' WordStar to print any document unless it has first been saved on disc, though this can be done with some WordStar-like programs like Sidekick's notepad.

# Printing your work

We have not yet 'installed' a printer – that is, we have not told our system what sort of printer we are using – but TEST.DOC is a straightforward document which calls for no special effects such as underlining or bold type, so there should be no real problems in making a copy of it on any reasonably standard printer.

Make sure that your printer is properly connected and turned on, and that paper has been fed in, and then select [p] at the Opening Menu. You will be asked for the name of the document to be printed, so type in TEST.DOC and then press [Esc] *not* [Return]. The reason for this is that pressing [Return] gives you access to a whole range of printer options which we shall not be using yet.

If all is well, your printer should begin printing TEST.DOC as soon as the text has been loaded from the disc. If you decide to abort the printing in the middle, you can do so by pressing [Ctrl]/[u]; [Ctrl]/[p] will make the printer pause (while you answer the telephone, perhaps); you can subsequently restart it by pressing [Ctrl]/[c].

Neither of these techniques will necessarily stop the printing immediately. This is because material which has not yet been printed is held in a 'buffer', either in the printer itself or in the computer, and until the contents of this buffer have been printed, it is not possible to stop the printer from the keyboard. In an emergency such as a paper-jam, you will have to turn the printer off at the mains; if you are unlucky, the computer may then 'lock up'; if this happens, you will have to reset it with [Alt]/[Ctrl]/[Del].

# Manipulating disc files

In WordStar, most file manipulation is carried out from the Opening Menu; it is also possible to delete disc files while you are editing or creating a different document; this is done through the Blocking and Saving Menu, which is a sub-menu reached from the editing screen by pressing [Ctrl]/[k].

This can be particularly useful if you need to make more room on the disc to store a long document on which you are working, though you should normally take care to ensure that this situation does not occur by keeping a close eye on the amount of free space which is available on your document disc. Later we shall show you can do this with the MS-DOS CHKDSK utility without leaving the word processing program.

The disc operations which can be carried out include deleting, copying and renaming files, and creating files in ASCII or Document format – i.e. with embedded control codes. It is also possible to change the currently active disc drive.

Some workalikes have an additional facility which enables files to be 'protected'; when this is done, they can be accessed – for printing, for example – but they cannot be altered unless they have first been unprotected. 'Standard' WordStar has no equivalent command, but the identical result can be achieved without leaving the program through the MS-DOS ATTRIB command. Running other programs without leaving word processing is introduced towards the end of this chapter.

# Deleting files

When you are at the Opening Menu you can delete any file by pressing [y]; you can also do this from within an editing session with [Ctrl]/[k][j]. In both cases, you will be asked to name the file to be deleted. There is generally no 'Are you sure?' check before the file is deleted, so use the command with care. Incidentally, you cannot while editing delete from disc the file which you are currently using.

# Renaming and copying files

Renaming is carried out from the Opening Menu by pressing [e], and Copying by pressing [o]; neither of these operations is available from the Block Menu.

Renaming and copying are similar in that both operations require you to specify two parameters, namely the current name of the file and either its new name (if renaming) or its new name and destination (if copying).

# Documents and Non-documents

WordStar and WordStar-like programs distinguish between two different types of file, which they call 'Documents' and 'Non-documents'. Essentially, 'Documents' are intended for printing, and thus include such features as printer control codes and extra spaces at the end of lines, while 'Non-documents' are saved in standard ASCII format. Letters, articles and other work which will be printed out would thus be classed as Documents, while data files for mail-merge, text which is to be sent through a telecommunications network, programs in BASIC, PASCAL and other computer languages, and MS-DOS Batch files should be created as Non-documents.

Documents and Non-documents are handled slightly differently; the most important differences are that the various formatting aids which are present when working with Documents are not available for Non-documents, so that it is impossible to centre or justify text, alter line spacing or margins, or use word wrap, soft hyphens or hyphen help. Page numbers are also not shown on the Status Line when you are in Non-document mode.

# Running other programs from the Opening Menu

Another interesting and useful feature of WordStar makes it possible to run a completely different program without actually abandoning word processing. This is done by leaving a small portion of WordStar still resident in the computer's memory, and returning to it automatically after running the intervening program.

This facility is intended mainly to enable you to run MS-DOS utilities such as CHKDSK.EXE. However, it cannot be used to run 'resident commands' such as COPY or ERASE, as these are not regarded as 'programs' as such.

This restriction apart, the only requirement is that a copy of the program that you wish to use must be available on the currently active disc drive; the most convenient way to do this is to store those utility programs which you expect to use on the WordStar program disc, and then make that the currently active disc (with the [l] key – that's the letter 'L') from the Opening Menu before setting out to run the new program.

The actual process of running the program is as follows: from the Opening Menu, press the [r] key, and when prompted to run the new program, type in exactly what you would use if you were running the program from the MS-DOS 'A>' or 'B>' prompt in the usual way. For example, if you wanted to find how much room was left on the data disc in Drive B, you would type in

CHKDSK B:

(You may also need a copy of COMMAND.COM on the program disc if this particular example is to work properly. COMMAND.COM is a utility which is used by some programs to enable certain MS-DOS commands to be used within programs just as if they had been typed in in the usual way.)

When the details of the disc in Drive B have been displayed, you will be prompted to 'Press any key' (i.e. the space bar, [Return] or any character key, but not [Alt], [Shift] or [Ctrl], for example) in order to return to word processing. Occasionally, if you are using a non-current version of MS-DOS or running certain awkward utilities, you may find that you are given either an error message or that you are left at the 'A>' prompt. This is mildly annoying but no worse, as you will not have lost any material; simply restart word processing with 'WS'.

## Save and continue

Because it is important to save your work onto disc at regular intervals, WordStar offers a Save and continue option from the Block Menu, which is a sub-menu of the Main Menu.

While editing, select [Ctrl]/[k]/[s], and the entire text will be saved to the currently active disc; the screen display will not change, so that you can easily continue working from the point at which the save command was issued.

Do use [Ctrl]/[k]/[s] frequently, especially if you are working on a long document; you should aim to save your work once every half hour at the very least.

## Disc and RAM space

We have already seen that some WordStar workalikes use a 'fullness gauge' to let you know how much of your computer's available memory is occupied by the document on which you are working. However, an important feature of WordStar is that it is capable of handling documents which are many times bigger than the computer's memory. This is because, when a document has exceeded a certain size, a portion of it is automatically stored on disc, thus freeing a corresponding amount of the memory.

The fullness gauge is thus in no way an indication of the maximum length which a document can reach, but rather a guide as to the point at which it will become necessary to start storing portions of the text on disc; this technique is called **paging**. You will in any case know when this starts to happen because your disc drives will be accessed more frequently; this may slow you down a little, although it is not a real nuisance.

More important than any delays you may encounter is the fact that working with long documents means that you must have ample free space on your disc. Paging may require space equivalent to three times the length of the whole document, and you will run into serious problems, possibly even involving the loss of part of your work, if you try to handle very long documents when you are running low on disc space. If the worst comes to the worst and you get a 'Disk Full Error' message, press [Esc] and then delete any unnecessary files from your disc before trying to save your work again.

If pressing [Esc] simply results in another 'Disk Full Error', you are in real trouble; you may still be able to recover some work as described in the next couple of paragraphs, but no guarantees are given. Obviously this is not a situation to get into if you can avoid it; look very carefully at how much disc space you have left and you need never see a Disk Full Error.

With luck, you may be able to recover a substantial part of your work from the disc in the form of the 'working file' that is maintained all the time that paging is being carried out. Such a file can be recognised because it will have the file-extension .$$$; it is not possible to access such a file directly – this is a precaution to prevent you from inadvertently interfering with working files or accidentally ruining a backup – so you will have to rename it first, and then see how much of your work you can recover from it.

Incidentally, .BAK files cannot be directly accessed either; they too will have to have their file-extension changed before you can load them.

# Postscript

By the time that you have reached this point, you should be able to create, edit, save and print simple documents with WordStar or its workalikes, as well as carry out some housekeeping work on your disc files. If you do not yet feel comfortable with any or all of these activities, read through the chapter again and try out the techniques described until you feel that you understand what is going on.

If you have come to 'standard' WordStar after using WordStar 1512, you may be surprised at just how different the two programs are. Actually, these differences are more apparent than real; almost everything which we have done so far with WordStar can be done just as well with WordStar 1512, and the main differences between the programs lie in the fact that the 'standard' programs rely more on your memory and less on menus, although the menus are there when you need them.

As you read on, you will find that the differences become less, rather than more, important. The dot commands which we covered in Chapter 6, for example, can be used in just the same way in standard WordStar; and although mail-merge is carried out in a slightly different way, such differences as there are lie mostly in the way the data file is constructed, rather than in the mail merge operation itself.

# *CHAPTER TEN*

# WordStar Editing Commands

## Preview

In this chapter we shall look at the various commands which are available in both WordStar and its workalikes for manipulating text on the screen and the printer. Most of these commands are entered by way of one or other of the subsidiary menus which are available from the document editing screen, usually by selecting [Ctrl] and two other keys.

Many of the commands are controlled by key sequences which strike newcomers as rather arbitrary: why, for example, is underlining reached through [Ctrl]/[p]/[s], while line spacing is accessed through [Ctrl]/[o]/[s]? The format of this chapter is intended to clarify these matters as far as possible.

The general sequence in which we shall proceed is as follows: first, we shall look at rulers and other features of the On Screen Menu, reached through [Ctrl]/[o]; next we move on to the Print Menu features, reached through [Ctrl]/[p]; after that we come to the Blocks Menu, reached through [Ctrl]/[k]; and finally we shall look at the search and replace facility and at detailed control of the printer.

## Rulers

WordStar defines margins and tabs by means of rulers (sometimes called 'ruler lines') which are composed of combinations of five symbols: the left margin is marked by an 'L'; the right margin by 'R'; ordinary tabs by '!'; and decimal tabs by '#'; all other columns are shown by hyphens, '-'. The general effect is very similar to the ruler which is shown below the Status Line in WordStar 1512; it is also possible, however, to create new rulers from within the text itself, and even, in some workalikes, to have several different rulers active in different sections of the text at the same time.

**Fig. 10.1** The Default WordStar ruler

Fig. 10.1 shows the default ruler used in WordStar. This defines a line beginning at column 1 and extending to column 65, with ordinary tab stops at column 6 and then every fifth column; there are no decimal tabs in the default ruler. This layout is designed for Pica type (10 characters per inch) on continuous-form computer stationery measuring 9½″ by 11″, though the same layout is also perfectly acceptable on single-sheet A4 paper.

# Tabs and indents

The tab settings can be changed from within the editing screen while a document is being composed. To set a new tab stop, press [Ctrl]/[o]/[i]. You will be asked where the new tab stop is to be placed, and can respond either by giving the column number of the new stop, by pressing [#] and the column number for a decimal tab, or by pressing [Esc] to insert the new tab at the present position of the text cursor.

To clear tab stops, select [Ctrl]/[o]/[n]; when prompted, either give the number of the column from which the stop is to be cleared, or press [a] to clear all tabs, or [Esc] to clear the tab from the most recent position of the text cursor, or [ ] and [Esc] to clear a decimal tab from the most recent position of the text cursor.

Both the tab set and tab clear operations can be abandoned 'in mid-stream' in the usual way with [Ctrl]/[u].

**Indents** Indents, called 'Paragraph tabs' in WordStar, are selected with [Ctrl]/[o]/[g]. To indent a paragraph which has not yet been composed, press [Ctrl]/[o]/[g] at the head of the paragraph and then enter your text in the normal way; every line will be indented to the first tab stop, and this will continue until you press [Return]. To indent a paragraph which already exists, put the cursor anywhere on the first line, select [Ctrl]/[o]/[g] and then reform the paragraph with [Ctrl]/[b]. You can abandon an indent by putting the cursor on the top line of the indented passage and pressing [Ctrl]/[b]; this will cause all text to be reformatted unindented.

**Margin release** The margins can be released temporarily with [Ctrl]/[o]/[x]. This enables you to take the cursor beyond either margin, but you must remember to cancel the margin release after you have finished with it – repeat the sequence [Ctrl]/[o]/[x]. As long as margin release is selected, a reminder to that effect is displayed towards the right of the Status Line.

Margin release is particularly useful when you are creating a new ruler from within the text, as described below.

# Changing the ruler

The simplest way to alter the margins is with the commands [Ctrl]/[o]/[l] to set the left margin and [Ctrl]/[o]/[r] to set the right margin; in each case, the margin is set to whatever position is currently occupied by the text cursor. Function Keys 3 and 4 duplicate the effect of [Ctrl]/[o]/[l] and [Ctrl]/[o]/[r] respectively, and most people find them easier to use.

**In-text rulers** A more thorough way of creating an entire new ruler is by actually 'writing' it into the text, either at the head of the document or at any point below that. All text below the line in which the new marker is made effective (which is not necessarily the same as the the line in which it is created – the difference is an important one which is explained below) will conform to the new ruler.

The first step in creating the new ruler is to put the cursor on a completely blank line at the required point in your document. If the new ruler is to extend beyond the old one at either side, release the margins with [Ctrl]/[o]/[x].

If the new left margin is to start at column 1, put a dot in that column to prevent the line being printed along with the rest of the text; lines containing dot commands are ignored during print-out, as you may remember from our comments on the use of dot commands in WordStar 1512. Then move the cursor to the right, entering hyphens wherever you want non-tab columns, [!] for ordinary tabs or [#] for decimal tabs; when you reach your intended right margin press [r].

Finally, and without moving the cursor away from the line you are working on, press [Ctrl]/[o]/[f], and the old ruler line will be replaced by the one you have just created.

If the left margin of the new ruler is to start to the right of column 1, you will have to be a little more devious to prevent the ruler being printed with the rest of your text. Put the cursor in the column intended for the left margin and press [l]; type hyphens and whatever tab symbols you require until you reach the right margin and mark this with [r]; use [Ctrl]/[o]/[f] as described above to make a new ruler from the line you have typed in; and then go back and put a dot in the first column; this will prevent the line from being printed.

Incidentally, once a new ruler has been created and activated in this way, it remains in effect until it has been deliberately replaced by another, even if you begin work on another document; the original default ruler will only reappear when you restart WordStar. This makes it easy to compose several documents which share the same non-standard settings one after the other in a single session.

**When does a ruler become effective?** When a new ruler is created in any of the ways described, it becomes effective as soon as [Ctrl]/[o]/[f] has been selected; all new text will conform to the new ruler, but text which was written previously will not be reformed to match the new margins unless you take the cursor back to it and select [Ctrl]/[b].

Such a reformatting will make everything between the current position of the cursor and the next hard return–which usually means the end of the paragraph–conform to the new ruler, rather than the one it was written with. If you are creating a document which uses a variety of different ruler settings at different places in it, you may lose track of just which ruler was used to compose a particular section, unless you take special care to avoid getting mixed up.

**Making and using a ruler file** If you need to use a variety of different rulers and do not want to go to the trouble of 'reinventing' a particular setting every time you want to compose a particular type of document, the easiest solution is to create a special file with nothing but rulers in it, and to save this on your text disc.

You can avoid needing to use the margin release facility by creating this file as a Non-document. At the Opening Menu, simply type [n] to open a non-document, giving the file the name RULERS.DOC or something similar. You can then type into it examples of all the different rulers which you think you might want, putting each one on a separate line. You can always come back and add more rulers later if necessary. Then Save the file with [Ctrl]/[k]/[d].

To call up a ruler from this file while you are in the middle of composing another document, place the text cursor on a blank line at the place where the new ruler is to be located and enter the sequence [Ctrl]/[k]/[r]; this command inserts a new file into your document at the position occupied by the text cursor.

You will be prompted for the name of the file to be inserted; answer RULERS.DOC, or whatever your file is called, and press [Return], and all the rulers in that file will be inserted into your text; the fact that RULERS.DOC is a Non-document does not matter.

Delete all the rulers except for the one you want, using the line-delete command [Ctrl]/[y]; then activate the remaining ruler with [Ctrl]/[o]/[f].

This may seem rather a long-winded procedure; actually it takes much longer to describe than to carry out; it can be a real time-saver, especially if you need to reproduce a particular ruler which has a complicated structure of ordinary and decimal tabs.

# Print menu features

Several useful effects are available including character overprinting, underlines, bold type and the like; the menu which controls these features is called the Print menu. We show this in Fig. 10.2.

```
        < < <    P R I N T    M E N U    > > >
------ Special  Effects -------  | -Printing  Changes- |  -Other  Menus-
(begin and end) |  (one time each) | A Alternate pitch  | (from Main only)
B Bold D Double | H Overprint char | N Standard pitch   |^J Help  ^K Block
S Underscore    | O Non-break space | C Printing pause   |^Q Quick ^P Print
X Strikeout     | F Phantom space   | Y Other ribbon color|^O Onscreen
V Subscript     | Q Phantom rubout  |    User  Patches    |Space Bar returns
T Superscript   | RET Overprint line | Q(1) W(2) E(3) R(4) |you to Main Menu.
```

**Fig. 10.2** The WordStar Print Menu

This menu is reached from the editing screen by selecting [Ctrl]/[p]. In a few cases you can select a Print Menu command without the [Ctrl]/[p] combination by using the Function Keys.

Four different groups of commands can be reached through the Print Menu. The first group comprises 'Begin and end' commands; the second group is made up of 'One time each' commands; third are 'Printing changes'; and last are 'User patches'.

# The appearance of the commands

Because of the need to make the programs compatible with many different types of screen, neither WordStar nor its workalikes expects to show boldfaced text, for example, actually emboldened on the screen. On most screens, however, affected text is shown highlighted – generally in reverse video, with black characters displayed against a white ground, though some programs use a coloured background.

In addition to any highlighting which your screen may display, print features are shown on the screen by displaying a two-character code, the first character of which is a caret (^) and the second an upper-case letter which is the same as the code letter used to select the feature. Although this code occupies two character-spaces on the screen, it is treated as a single character, and can be deleted by a single keystroke; furthermore, although it makes the line of text in which it appears on the screen seem longer than it really is, this extra length is ignored when the line is fitted between the margins.

# Begin and end commands

Begin and end commands are those which are grouped in pairs around some part of your text; the first occurrence of the command turns some feature on, and the second turns it off. The features which are controlled in this way are Boldface, Double Strike, Underscore, Strikeout, Subscript and Superscript. Two or more features can be selected simultaneously if you wish, resulting for instance in bold superscript, though many printers are not capable of reproducing all possible combinations.

It is very important to ensure that every Begin command has a matching End. This is easily checked if your screen highlights all the text which is located between paired commands; otherwise, do take care to check that every one of these commands really is properly paired before you start printing the completed document. If you do not, sooner or later you will leave the printer running while you go off to do something else, and only discover when you come back that the whole of the second half of your printout has been produced with unwanted underlines.

**Boldface type and Double strike** Boldface type is selected with [Ctrl]/[p]/[b], and Double strike with [Ctrl]/[p]/[d]. On most keyboards the former is also available from a function key, usually Function Key 6. A section of text to be emboldened will appear ^Blike this^B on the screen, and **like this** when printed.

The difference between double strike and boldface varies from printer to printer. On some printers, boldface is struck three times and double strike is literally struck twice; on others, boldface is produced by shifting the print head fractionally sideways before restriking, while double striking is done without moving the print head; on yet other printers, only one style is available, and is accessed by both commands.

**Underscore** Underscoring is turned on and off with [Ctrl]/[p]/[s]; it can also be selected by pressing Function Key 5.

Onscreen, text to be underscored will appear ^Slike this^S; when printed it will look like this.

A point to note about underscoring is that although all individual words which occur between the first and second Underscore commands will be underlined, the spaces which appear between them will generally not be so treated. If you wish to underline *everything*, this can be done by using underline characters in your document '_' instead of spaces.

An awkward problem may then arise if you want your work to be printed right-justified; if a line is to appear completely underlined, with underline characters inserted between every word, that line will not be printed right-justified; if only a portion of the line is to be underlined, then no extra 'pad' spaces will be inserted into the underlined section; instead, they will all be concentrated into the other parts of the line. This may make the line look rather unbalanced.

The best rule to follow is this: if you want every character to be underlined, don't also try to justify the text; if underscoring words alone is acceptable, then the text can be fully right-justified without problems.

**Strikeout** Strikeout is turned on and off with [Ctrl]/[p]/[x]. It prints a hyphen through the middle of every character except spaces, and is most frequently used in the preparation of legal documents, particularly those which are built up out of boilerplates.

**Superscript and subscript** Superscript and subscript characters are selected and deselected with [Ctrl]/[p]/[t] (superscript) and [Ctrl]/[p]/[v] (subscript).

They are usually reproduced as half-height characters placed respectively above and below the ordinary characters in the same line of text, to produce such effects as '$e=mc^2$' or '$H_2O$'. These would appear onscreen as '$e=mc\wedge T\wedge T2$' and '$H\wedge V2\wedge VO$'.

Some printers print subscripts and superscripts as full-size characters and place them on separate lines, and some others are incapable of producing them at all.

# One time each commands

One time each commands are used singly, not in pairs, to produce several different effects. They effect only the character which appears immediately after them or the character which they themselves represent.

**Overprinting single characters** Overprinting enables two or more characters to be printed in a single position. The most obvious use of this facility is to produce accented characters, which are not otherwise available; many other useful characters can also be produced in this way.

Character overprinting is selected by pressing [Ctrl]/[p]/[h] between the two characters which are to be superimposed on each other; the characters themselves can appear in any order. For example, to print 'Noël', you would enter either 'Noe[Ctrl]/[p]/[h]"l' or 'No[Ctrl]/[p]/[h]el'; the former would appear onscreen as 'Noe^H"l', and the latter as 'No"^Hel'.

There are a couple of points to note here. First, [Ctrl]/[p]/[h] is actually a backspacing command, and the overprinting is usually carried out by physically moving the print head back the equivalent of one character space and then printing the next character on top of the first; if the [Ctrl]/[p]/[h] sequence is used twice instead of once, the print head will move two spaces back.

Second, the diaeresis was produced by using the double-quotation marks; this is necessary because the standard keyboard lacks a proper diaeresis character. You may need to employ a little ingenuity to build up all the characters you need from elements available on the standard keyboard, and what is available will in any case depend on the shape of the characters produced by your printer. For example, if your printer produces an apostrophe which is 'comma-shaped' rather than vertical, it can do double duty as an acute accent.

Several other characters can be printed by the creative use of the overprinting facility. For example, the left and right arrows '←' and '→' can be made from a combination of hyphens and the Greater than and Less than signs '<' and '>', and c-cedilla can be made up of 'c' or 'C' and a comma ','. More advanced work may involve using superscripted and subscripted characters; the Plus or minus sign '±' can be created on most printers by printing a subscripted hyphen, an overprint character and the Plus sign '+' .

The IBM expanded character set cannot be reached from inside standard WordStar in the same way as it can in WordStar 1512.

**Overprinting whole lines** Very occasionally you may need to overprint complete lines. To do this, type in the line in the usual way, then select [Ctrl]/[p] [Return] at the very end of the line. Then type the material which you want to overprint the first line, ending it with an ordinary [Return]. The first line will be marked with a – flag, and during printing the second line will overprint the first.

**Phantom space and rubout** The elements used in daisy-wheel printers often, though not invariably, have two extra symbols in addition to the normal ASCII printable characters.

These non-standard, or 'phantom', characters are available from the Print Menu, one of them by pressing [Ctrl]/[p]/[f] and the other by pressing [Ctrl]/[p]/[g]. The first of these prints whatever character is available on the element at position 32 (which is 20 in hexadecimal), often called 'Phantom space', and the second prints the character at position 127 (hex 7F), called 'Phantom rubout'. If you are using a daisy-wheel printer, the manual supplied with it, or the information sheet usually enclosed with additional elements, will show what characters your equipment will print at those positions. The most common characters are '£' at phantom space and a double underline at phantom rubout.

If you are using a dot-matrix printer, or if no characters are available at those positions on your daisy-wheel elements, a space will be printed instead.

**Non-break spaces** Non-break spaces are special spaces which you have inserted between characters where you do not want line-breaks to occur.

To understand why this is necessary, it is helpful to have some idea of what constitutes a 'word' as far as WordStar is concerned. To oversimplify slightly for the sake of clarity, a 'word' is any group of characters which are not separated from each other by spaces. This means, for example, that a phrase like 'Flight BA472' is regarded as comprising two words, although most humans would probably think of it as one word followed by a series of letters and numbers which do not constitute a word.

Occasionally, we need to prevent separate words (by the computer's definition) from appearing on different lines. For example, it is not usually acceptable to have 'Mr.' at the end of one line and 'Smith' at the beginning of the next.

The trick is to use a special 'non-break space' instead of the usual kind. The command to select this is [Ctrl]/[p]/[o]; this appears on screen as '^O', and as an ordinary space during printing – you should not enter an ordinary space as well as the non-break space. You would thus type 'Mr.[Ctrl]/[p]/[o]; the screen would display 'Mr.^OSmith', and this would be printed as 'Mr. Smith'

# Printing changes

WordStar offers four 'Printing changes' from the Print Menu. These are single commands which control the printer while a printed copy is being produced; the changes which they create remain in effect until cancelled by a different Change command.

**Changing Pitch and Pausing the printer** Pica type, which is 10 cpi, is the Standard Pitch for both programs; this can be changed to Elite type (12 cpi) by selecting Alternate Pitch by pressing [Ctrl]/[p]/[a] at the Print Menu; Standard Pitch can be reselected by pressing [Ctrl]/[p]/[n].

If you are using a dot-matrix printer, no further commands are needed to change pitch. However, nearly all daisy-wheel printers need to be stopped so that a different element can be inserted, and on many daisy-wheel printers it is also necessary to adjust a switch on the front panel.

To stop the printer, use the Printer Menu command [Ctrl]/[p]/[c] either immediately before or immediately after the pitch change command. The printer can be paused in the same way to allow an element containing italic or other characters to be inserted.

Remember that changing the pitch usually means that the margins will need to be changed as well; because margins are set in terms of the number of characters in a line, rather than being measured in inches from the edge of the paper, this means that margin settings which will create a line, say, 6½" long for Pica type (using a line 65 characters in length) will set a line-length of only 5½" for Elite type.

**Ribbon colour** Some printers are able to use two-coloured ribbons and to change automatically from one colour to the other; to do this, use the command [Ctrl]/[p]/[y]. The command is a toggle, so the same key combination is used to return to the first ribbon colour.

Usefully, dot-matrix printers which don't use two-coloured ribbons may recognise the same command as an instruction to change to or from an italic font.

# User patches

In computer terms, a **patch** is a short piece of programming tacked on to a larger program, originally in order to correct an error in the main program – hence the name. WordStar is designed to have special 'patch' additions made to it by a knowledgeable user so that, for example, the full facilities of a particular printer can be made available to them.

Four such 'User patches' are available to control the printer; the precise way in which these are used depends on the facilities which are available with any particular printer, but they might be used to control such features as double-width printing or a cut-sheet feeder.

The four 'free' codes which are available for these purposes are [Ctrl]/[p]/[q], [Ctrl]/[p]/[w], [Ctrl]/[p]/[e] and [Ctrl]/[p]/[r]. If no corresponding 'patch' has been added to the program, then these commands will be ignored at print time.

Patches are really beyond a book of this sort; if you feel that you would like to make use of a facility which your printer has but which you cannot control directly from your program, either ask an experienced machine-code programmer to help you or be prepared to spend a long time learning about the program and what you can do with it; always do your patching on a *copy* of your program, or you are very likely to find that it can no longer be made to work properly, or even at all.

# Additional Options from the Onscreen Menu

The Onscreen Menu offers a variety of options, some of which we have already met: these include selecting and deselecting justification, hyphen-help and soft hyphens, as well as setting margins and tabs.

```
                < < < O N S C R E E N   M E N U > > >
-Margins & Tabs-  ¦ -Line  Functions- ¦  --More Toggles--  ¦  -Other  Menus-
L Set left margin ¦C Center text       ¦J Justify    now ON ¦ (from Main only)
R Set right margin¦S Set line spacing  ¦V Vari-Tabs now ON  ¦^J Help  ^K Block
X Release margins ¦                    ¦H Hyph-help now ON  ¦^Q Quick ^P Print
I Set  N Clear tab¦    ---Toggles---   ¦E Soft hyph now OFF ¦^O Onscreen
G Paragraph tab   ¦W Wrd wrap now ON   ¦D Prnt disp now ON  ¦Space Bar returns
F Ruler from line ¦T Rlr line now ON   ¦P Pge break now ON  ¦you to Main Menu.
```

Fig. 10.3 The Onscreen Menu

Margins and tabs affect the way a document appears on the screen; it is this 'onscreen' aspect which distinguishes it from the Print Menu. If double line-spacing is selected through the Onscreen Menu, for example, then the text on the screen will itself be double-spaced, and will also be printed that way. The Onscreen Menu is shown in Fig. 10.3.

## Preview Commands

The first group of Onscreen Menu commands which we shall look at are sometimes called Preview Commands. They remove non-printed characters, such as print control commands, from the screen, and thus make it easier for you to see how your work will appear when it is printed out. This can be particularly useful when you are proof-reading documents which have a large number of such extraneous symbols embedded in them.

**Hiding print control commands** The Print Display command [Ctrl]/[o]/[d] removes print control commands from the monitor screen. The commands are only hidden, of course, and are not removed from the document – if you print a document which contains hidden commands, they will still function just as if they were visible.

It is not a good idea to hide the commands until you have finished most of your work on a document and are almost ready to print it, because when the commands are hidden it is impossible to check whether they are actually in the right place, and – more important – whether both elements of any paired commands really are present.

**Hiding the ruler** The ruler line can be hidden with the command [Ctrl][o]/[t].

Unless you are preparing a document which uses complicated tab and margin arrangements, you will probably not need to see the ruler displayed at the top of the screen; and you can gain an extra line of screen space for displaying your document if you remove it. Clearing the ruler from the screen makes no difference to the way in which your document will be laid out.

A final preview command, [Ctrl]/[o][p], has different functions in WordStar and some of the workalikes: in WordStar, it removes page boundary markers from the screen; in some workalikes, it hides dot commands.

These commands are all toggles, so the same sequences can be used to display the codes on screen once more.

# Turning word-wrap on and off

Word-wrap can be turned on and off with the toggle command [Ctrl]/[o]/[t].

For almost all word processing work, most users prefer to have the word-wrap feature turned on, so that any word which extends over the right margin is transferred to the beginning of the next line. There is, however, one case in which you may find it useful to turn word-wrap off, namely when you are working on a document in which there are a number of columns, and you want to avoid accidentally wrapping an item which should appear in the right-hand column onto the beginning of the following line.

When word-wrap is turned off, the right margin is not effective and every line must be ended by pressing the [Return] key; this in turn means that justification and paragraph reforming (with [Ctrl]/[b]) are not possible while word-wrap is off.

If only a very few lines are likely to extend over the right margin, it is probably easier to select simple margin release with [Ctrl]/[o]/[x] than to deselect word-wrap.

Word-wrap is in any case turned off when a Non-document is being composed.

# Formatting commands

Hyphen-help and right-justification were introduced in Chapter Nine. Toggles are available at the Onscreen Menu to select and deselect these features. Justification is turned on or off with [Ctrl]/[o]/[j], and hyphen-help with [Ctrl]/[o]/[h].

# Line spacing

To alter line spacing from the default of single-spacing, select [Ctrl]/[o]/[s]; you will be prompted for a new value between 1 and 9.

Some users find these numbers confusing. If '1' is chosen, then the document will be single-spaced – that is, there will be no blank lines between the lines of text; if '2' is chosen, the text will be double-spaced, with *one* blank line between each line of text, and so on.

Once a new value has been entered, all new text will conform to this spacing, both on screen and during printing; text which is already written will not be affected unless it is reformatted with [Ctrl]/[b].

By no means all word processing programs follow the example of WordStar in displaying double-spaced text actually double-spaced on screen. This is because the amount of text which appears on screen is significantly reduced when double or treble spacing is used, and many users prefer to be able to see more of their work on screen at once.

The simplest solution is to compose a document with single-spacing and then to double-space it before printing. This means that the entire document must be reformatted with [Ctrl]/[b], one paragraph at a time, which can be rather time-consuming.

Many printers, particularly daisy-wheel printers, have line-spacing switches on the front panel; if these are used, it quickly becomes impossible to accurately predict where page divisions will occur.

# Centering lines

To centre a line, place the cursor anywhere upon it and select [Ctrl]/[o]/[c]. The line will be repositioned midway between the margins of the current ruler.

If the line is too long to fit between the margins – having perhaps been composed according to a different ruler, or with the margin released – then it will not be affected by the centering command.

# Block commands

WordStar and its workalikes allow sections of text to be marked out as a block which can then be erased, moved, copied or saved to disc. Almost all monitors show a defined block by highlighting it or displaying it in a different colour.

The WordStar Block Menu, shown in Fig. 10.4, also controls the saving and abandoning of text and the selecting and deselecting of Column Mode. It is reached by pressing [Ctrl]/[k].

```
            < < <   B L O C K   M E N U   > > >
-Saving Files- ! -Block Operations- ! -File Operations- !  -Other  Menus-
S Save & resume ! B  Begin  K  End   ! R  Read  P  Print  ! (from Main only)
D Save--done    ! H  Hide / Display  ! O  Copy  E  Rename ! ^J Help   ^K Block
X Save & exit   ! C  Copy   Y  Delete! J  Delete          ! ^Q Quick ^P Print
Q Abandon file  ! V  Move   W  Write ! -Disk  Operations- ! ^O Onscreen
-Place Markers- ! N  Column  now OFF !L Change logged disk! Space Bar returns
0-9 set/hide 0-9!                    !F Directory now OFF ! you to Main Menu.
```

Fig. 10.4 The WordStar Block Menu

## Using block markers

To define a block, place the cursor at the point where the block is to begin and select [Ctrl]/[k]/[b]; then move to the end of the intended block and enter [Ctrl]/[k]/[k]. If you wish, you can define the end of the block first and then move back to the beginning, but you must always make sure that the end block marker is physically later in the document than the begin block marker.

The first marker to be inserted is shown on the screen by a special symbol: '<B>' for the beginning of a block and '<K>' for the end of a block. Once both markers are in place, these symbols disappear from the screen, but the block itself is shown highlighted.

To change the position of a marker, simply put the cursor at the place to which you want the marker to be moved, and re-enter the marker command. To clear a marker once it has been placed, put the cursor immediately *after* the marker and re-enter the marker command. Incidentally, the text cursor treats the block markers in a rather odd way: it will not rest on them, but instead skips directly over them.

Block markers and highlighting can be hidden with the command [Ctrl]/[k]/[h], but this does not itself remove the markers – it merely renders them invisible and ineffective; you can restore them with [Ctrl]/[k]/[h] again.

197

# Block manipulation commands

The various block commands which are mentioned in this section and the next can be used to re-order sections of text, to incorporate sections from one document in another – perhaps to move material from one chapter of a report to another – and to delete large chunks of text.

It is very easy to get confused when shunting blocks of text around inside a single document, and these problems are even more marked when two or more different files are involved. In order to avoid getting totally lost, it is a good idea to make extra back-up copies (on different discs) of the files you are going to alter before you start the cutting and pasting operations; in this way, you always have your original copies to fall back on if necessary.

Putting the copies on different discs is a useful precaution because, as you move from one document to another, you will perforce have to Save the document on which you are currently working; after a couple of Saves, the original document will no longer be present even as a .BAK file, and so you will have no way of aborting a cut-and-paste operation which has gone wrong and beginning again from scratch. If you are carrying out a particularly complicated block operation involving several different documents, it is also very helpful to make brief notes with pen and paper to help you keep track of just where you are.

**Scissors and paste** To delete a block completely, use [Ctrl]/[k]/[y]. To move a block from one place to another, simultaneously erasing it from the original position, place the cursor at the point to which the block is to be moved and enter [Ctrl]/[k]/[v].

To copy a block without deleting or moving the original, put the text cursor at the place at which the copy is to appear and enter [Ctrl]/[k]/[c]; the markers will be moved with the block, and if they are to be deleted, this will have to be done from the place in which they now appear.

**Saving and inserting blocks** Blocks of text can be saved onto disc using the command [Ctrl]/[k]/[w]; you will be prompted to give a name to the block, and it will then be saved in the usual way. Block markers are not removed after this operation, so once a block has been saved to disc, it can very easily be erased from its original document.

To insert text from disc into a file, place the text cursor at the point where the inserted text is to be located and press [Ctrl]/[k]/[r]. You will be prompted for the name of the file which is to be inserted, and this file will then be read into the document. This is the same command as we met earlier for inserting a ruler file into a document.

If you are operating in Column Mode there are special restrictions on the insertion of text; these are described in the section on Column Mode below.

**Other disc commands from the Blocks Menu** To save the document on which you are working and then return to carry out more work on it, use

[Ctrl]/[k]/[s]; this command should be used frequently in order to safeguard against the possible effects of power failures, etc.

To save the document on which you are working and return to the Opening Menu, use [Ctrl]/[k]/[d]. Any block markers which are still current in the document will be lost when it is saved, so it is not possible to mark out a block during one working session, save your work to disc, and then resume working on the same block after later reading the file from disc.

To abandon the current document and return to the Opening Menu, press [Ctrl]/[k]/[q]. If the document is new, or if you have altered it since it was read off disc, you will be asked if you want to abandon the changes you have made.

Disc operations which can be carried out from the Blocks Menu include Copying a file from one drive to another, renaming a file, printing a file and changing the logged (current) disc drive.

**Copying files** Copying a file is done with [Ctrl]/[k]/[o]. This command is used most often to make a copy of a file on another disc in order that it can be erased from the current text disc, thus freeing disc storage space for the program you are working on.

You will be prompted for the name of the program which is to be copied and then for a name under which it is to be stored. If you are using a two-drive system, the simplest way to do this is to first copy the file onto the RAM Disc, Drive C, by putting 'C:' in front of the file-name when asked for the name under which the file is to be stored, and then later copying it from the RAM Disc onto another real disc in Drive B using another Copy command. Once the file has been safely copied, you can erase it from the original disc and thus create more room.

**Renaming files** A file can be renamed with [Ctrl]/[k]/[e]; you will be asked for the name of the file to be renamed and the new name which it will be given. A file which is not on the current disc can be renamed by putting the Disc Drive name and a colon in front of the file-name; for example, if Drive B is the current drive, you can rename a file on Drive C by putting 'C:' before the name.

It is not possible to rename the file on which you are currently working.

**Changing the logged disc drive** The current disc drive can be changed with the command [Ctrl]/[k]/[l]; you will be prompted for the drive which is to be used instead.

If you have loaded a document off the logged drive, it will still be saved onto the same drive even though that may no longer be regarded as the current drive. The same is true of a new document – it will still be stored on the disc which was current when it was created, even though that may no longer be the logged disc.

**Printing a file while editing** WordStar permits a file to be printed while editing is in progress; this provides another way of getting a file 'out of the way' so that you can erase it and save disc space, but it also makes it possible to speed up your work considerably by printing one document while another is being prepared. Printing in this way is called **background printing**.

It is possible to print the document which you are currently editing provided that there is a version of it on disc; however, if you do so, what will be printed will be the last version on the disc, not incorporating any changes which you may have made since but which have not yet been saved; you will also not be able to save the current version of the document to disc while the previous version is being printed.

Once you have started to print a document from the Block Menu, you will be returned to the normal editing screen. Depending on how your system is configured, this can cause a noticeable slowing down of the operation of WordStar, especially when disc operations are being performed – typically, running the printer will need about 10% of the computer's time, leaving 90% for your word processing, so the degradation in performance is not very great.

To abort or pause the background printing of a document, first return to the Print command with [Ctrl]/[d]/[p] and then enter [Ctrl]/[u] to abort printing or [Ctrl]/[p] to pause the printer; [Ctrl]/[c] will start the printer again after a pause. As we have already seen, the printer may not stop immediately a pause or abort command is given because some text may be stored in the printer buffer, and this will be printed out before the stop command is acted upon; in an emergency, you may have to turn the printer off at the mains.

## Working with columns

WordStar has a Column Mode which can be used when tables of data are being entered or manipulated. Enter Column Mode from the Blocks Menu with the command [Ctrl]/[k]/[n]. Column Mode does not actually make the entering of data much easier, but it does make the handling of columns through the Blocks Menu much easier.

Figure 10.5 shows a short but typical document laid out in columns – temperature, hours of sunshine, wind speed and rainfall are all laid out in columns for five different dates.

```
L------------#------------------#----------------#----------#----------R
   Date   Sunshine        Wind speed        Rainfall    Temp.

June 1      8.2             3.2              0         68.3
June 2      1.6            10.4               .43      52.8
June 3      2.5            12.4               .62      50.2
June 4      7.9             2.3              0         73.4
June 5      8.6             1.1              0         75.6
```

**Fig. 10.5** A document laid out in columns

Each column in this document is marked out with a tab stop – we have used the '**#**' symbol to select decimal tabs, as our columns consist of numbers which will be tidily aligned by decimal points; columns of text could be similarly aligned using ordinary tabs.

Data is entered *across* the page, rather than down each column in turn; for example, all the data for June 1st is entered first, then the data for June 2nd and so on. Be very careful that none of the entries are word-wrapped onto the next line, as this will confuse the column layout which we are creating; if necessary, move past the right margin by using [Ctrl]/[o]/[x].

**'Blocking' columns** With Column Mode turned on, it is possible to set up column blocks; for example, it is possible to begin a block to the left of the Temp. column in Fig. 10.5, and to end it to the right of the bottom of the same column, so that all the items in that column are included in the same block, without any other area being included.

Column blocks can be erased, moved and copied like any other kind of block. WordStar does not allow files to be inserted into a file while Column Mode is turned on; insertion can take place (using [Ctrl]/[k]/[r]) if Column Mode is turned off, but the layout will then be lost.

# Search and replace operations

WordStar's Search and Replace operations are accessed through the Quick Menu: [Ctrl]/[q]/[f] is used to find a 'string' of characters, and [Ctrl]/[q]/[a] to find and replace a string.

Unlike WordStar 1512, which requires you to stipulate at the Change Settings Menu whether searches are to be case-sensitive and whether they are to apply to whole words or not, 'standard' WordStar prompts you with a series of options at the time that the Search or Replace command is given.

If you are unfamiliar with search and replace operations, please read the relevant passage in the WordStar 1512 section between pp. 72-74; computers set about these tasks with a mindless determination which can be very disconcerting to an inexperienced user. Before beginning any wholesale modification of a document it is always wise to save it to disc (with [Ctrl]/[k]/[s]) so that if things go wrong, you can always get back to where you were to begin with.

When you enter either [Ctrl]/[q]/[f] (to find) or [Ctrl]/[q]/[a] (to find and replace), you will be prompted to give the search string – the set of characters that you want found or altered. Once this has been entered, you can either press [Return] to begin the search, or enter one or more option letters before pressing [Return]. Options may be entered in any order, and are separated from each other by a space.

The options which are available in WordStar are as follows:

[b] –This stipulates a backwards search beginning at the present cursor position; lines are scanned from right to left and from the position of the cursor backwards towards the start of the document. This would normally be used when you are looking for something which you know is at an earlier point in the document than you are currently at, or if you are already at the end of the document.

[w] –This is a search for whole words only. If you were looking for occurrences of 'sing', specifying a whole word search would avoid finding incorrect 'hits' in such words as 'bles*sings*'.

[u] –This ignores case; capitals and lower-case letters are regarded as equally acceptable if this option is chosen, so that a search for 'Butter' would also find 'butter' and 'BUTTER'.

[g] –This is the 'whole file' option; the cursor is taken to the beginning of the file (or to the end, if a backward search is chosen) before any search or replace operation is started. If this option is not chosen, searches begin at the current position of the cursor. During replace operations, the cursor will be immediately taken to the next occurrence of the target string as soon as the current replacement has been accepted or rejected.

[n] – Replace without asking. When carrying out a search and replace operation, WordStar normally pauses with the cursor on the first character of the string to be replaced and prompts with 'Replace? Y/N'. If you press [y], then the string will be placed; otherwise it will be left as it stands. The [n] option means that every hit will be replaced automatically without a prior request for confirmation.

[*n*] – Find the *n*th occurrence. A number *n* will cause the *n*th occurrence of the search string to be found, in the direction and starting at the point defined by the other options.

If you are not using the [g] or [r] options, the search or replacement operation will stop after the first hit; it can be restarted by pressing [Ctrl]/[l] (that's the letter 'L' ). [Ctrl]/[l] can be used at any time after a search or replace has been started, even if deletions have taken place or other material has been added to the document in the meantime.

# Printing a document

It is not possible to print a document which has not been saved onto disc. Printing is chosen from the Opening Menu by pressing [p] and giving the name of the file to be printed; this can be preceded by the name of the disc drive (followed by the usual colon) if the file is not on the currently logged-on disc.

Once you have named the file to be printed, and assuming your printer is loaded with paper and ready to go, you can begin printing immediately by pressing

[Esc]. If you do this, all the default values of the program (either as set at the factory or as changed during installation) will apply.

If you press [Return], then the various print options will be displayed, one at a time. You can either input a suitable response and press [Return], or press [Return] without making any response (to accept the default for that particular option), or press [Esc] (to accept all the remaining defaults). If you want to abort printing before it has started or while it is taking place, press [Ctrl]/[u].

# The WordStar Print Options

```
NAME OF FILE TO PRINT? test.doc
For default press RETURN for each question:
    DISK FILE OUTPUT (Y/N): N
    START AT PAGE NUMBER (RETURN for beginning)?
    STOP AFTER PAGE NUMBER (RETURN for end)?
    USE FORM FEEDS (Y/N): N
    SUPPRESS PAGE FORMATTING (Y/N): N
    PAUSE FOR PAPER CHANGE BETWEEN PAGES (Y/N): N
```

**Fig. 10.6** The WordStar Print Options

The various WordStar Print Options are shown in Fig. 10.6.

**Disc file output** If Disk File Output is accepted, the document is not printed onto paper in the usual way, but is instead 'printed' onto the disc. This is particularly useful when you are preparing a complex mail-merge operation and want to be sure that it is set up properly; you can 'print' a few personalised letters (or whatever) on disc, and then call them up as if they were ordinary WordStar documents in order to see that they have been processed correctly. if everything is in order, you can start a normal 'print' on paper; if not, correct the errors and try again.

You will realise from this that dot commands are 'obeyed' when a file is 'printed' on the disc; it is thus easy to check whether such features as Header and Footer text and page numbers occur in the places where you want them before you waste paper actually printing your file. You would probably not bother with this for straightforward work, but it can be a great help if you have been working on a complicated document.

Another use for the facility is if you have a computer at home and another in the office; at home you can prepare and 'print' a file on disc, setting it up with the appropriate codes for the (presumably more powerful) office printer, and then take it to work the following morning ready to be printed immediately.

**Start at Page/End at Page** The Start at Page Number and Stop at Page Number options enable you to print only a portion of a longer document. Pressing [Return] at both questions will cause printing to begin with the first page and end with the last.

An important use of the Start at Page option is if you have had to abandon printing a document in the middle, perhaps because of a paper-jam; you can then start reprinting just before the point at which the break occurred.

**Use Form Feeds** Use Form Feeds is for those printers which 'know where they are' on a page. Usually, WordStar advances the paper at the end of a page by sending an appropriate number of line-feeds. Many printers, however, keep a record of their current position on the page, and these usually have a Form Feed (sometimes called TOF, or Top Of Form) facility for advancing the paper, and this is often quicker than individual line-feeds.

You may also need to select Form Feeds if you have a printer with an automatic cut-sheet feeder, as these often require a TOF signal before feeding a new sheet. If you have a sheet-feeder and it is not working as it should select this option.

**Suppress Page Formatting** The Suppress Page Formatting option should be selected for those occasions when you want to print a document exactly as it stands – that is, with dot commands reproduced *as dot commands* rather than 'working'.

All page formatting features, such as margins and page numbers, are completely ignored, and the printer will print across the folds between the pages of continuous stationery. However, commands to underline and embolden text and the like will be acted upon.

The Suppress Text Formatting command can be used to make a printed copy of a document which has already been 'printed' on a disc using the Disc File Output option described above.

**Pause for Paper Change** If you are using single-sheet stationery, press [y] in answer to the Pause for Paper Change (Y/N) option. The printer will stop at the end of every page for you to insert a new sheet, and the message 'Print Paused' will appear on the Status Line. To restart printing when the new sheet is in place, press [p] again.

# Postscript

Before you feel completely at ease with all the commands introduced in this chapter, you will need to spend a considerable amount of time actually using your program, whether it is WordStar or one of its workalikes. The concepts which underlie the commands are not themselves difficult, and almost all of them have already been introduced in the section of the book dealing with WordStar 1512; such difficulties as there are derive from the need to become familiar with a multitude of two and three-character commands.

The key to acquiring a full working knowledge of these commands is constant practice; after a surprisingly short time, you will find that even if you are not consciously aware of knowing the commands, most of them will be familiar to your fingers, so that you will be able to use most features of the program quite automatically.

# CHAPTER ELEVEN

# Dot commands and Mail-Merge in WordStar

## Preview

If you have read Chapters Five and Seven, you will know that in WordStar 1512, dot commands are special commands inserted into your text to control print formatting and the insertion of material during mail-merge work. They always begin in Column 1; the first character is always a dot or full stop, and this is followed by a two-character code which is itself usually followed by a space and either a number or some text.

The dot commands which are used in 'standard' WordStar are identical in principle to those used in WordStar 1512; indeed, most of the commands already introduced work in precisely the same way in WordStar and its workalikes. However, these programs have some extra commands of their own, and lack some of the commands found in WordStar 1512.

Mail-merging is an optional extra with standard WordStar.

## WordStar Dot Commands

The following commands can be used in both WordStar 1512 and 'standard' WordStar.

.. Comment line
.av Ask for variable (mail-merge)
.cp Conditional page break
.cs Clear screen (mail-merge)
.dm Display message (mail-merge)
.fi File insert (mail-merge only except in WordStar 1512)

207

.fm Footer margin
.fo Footer text
.he Header text
.hm Header margin
.ig Ignore comment
.lh Line height
.lm Left margin (mail-merge only except in WordStar 1512)
.ls Line spacing
.mb Bottom margin
.mt Top margin
.oj Justification on (mail-merge only except in WordStar 1512)
.op Omit page number
.pa Unconditional page break
.pc Page number column
.pf Print formatting
.pl Page length
.pn Page number
.po Page offset
.rm Right margin (mail-merge only except in WordStar 1512)
.rp Repeat operation (mail-merge)
.sv Set value (mail-merge)

Full details of all the above commands are given in Chapters Five and Seven.

# Commands peculiar to 'standard' WordStar

In addition to the dot-commands mentioned above, there are a few additional commands which are used by WordStar but which are not used in WordStar 1512.

**.bp — Bidirectional printing** If you want to prevent your printer from printing bidirectionally, you can do so with the command

.bp off

Bidirectional printing can be restored with the command

.bp on

Reasons for turning off bidirectional printing are that some printers produce higher-quality output when they are working unidirectionally, or that they cannot produce accurate column work while printing bidirectionally. The factory-set default is for bidirectional printing to be turned on, but you can change this during installation if you want.

**.cw — Character width** Many printers are capable of 'micro-spacing'– that is, of moving the print head a smaller distance than single characters. With such printers, it is possible to use the character width command to adjust the distance that the print-head moves in increments of 1/120″. The format of the command is

.cw *n*

where *n* is the character width in units of 1/120″.

There is a relationship between a particular size of type and the character width, but it is not necessarily a fixed one. For example, Pica type (10 characters per inch) usually has a character width of 12/120″ and Elite type (12 cpi) usually has a character width of 10/120″.

```
This line is printed in Pica type in normal width.

This  is  also  in  Pica  but  with  a  width  of  15.

This line is printed in Pica but with a character width of 10.
```

Fig. 11.1 Using non-standard character widths

By setting a character width larger than the standard for the type-face you are using, you can space letters out a little more, for emphasis; by setting the width a little smaller than the standard, you can squeeze more characters on a line. In Fig. 11.1, we show the effects of printing a line of Pica type first with its standard character width, then with a width of 15, which spaces the characters out, and finally with a width of 10, which compresses the line. Some printers print expanded characters very slowly.

Non-standard character widths have an effect on margin settings similar to changing the type-size.

Selecting either the normal or the alternate type face with [Ctrl]/[p]/[n] or [Ctrl]/[p]/[a] will cause the character width to revert to the standard value for the type size you have chosen; therefore, if you want to change both the type face and the character width, always set the type face first and the character width second, as if the character width command comes first it will be ignored.

**.df and .rv—Data file and Read values** These commands are described in the section on mail-merge below.

**.sr—Superscript and subscript roll** This command sets the distance that superscripts and subscripts are printed above or below the remainder of the line.

Printers with variable line pitch can advance the paper in vertical steps of one forty-eighth of an inch; normally, lines are spaced 8/48″ apart, i.e. 6 to the inch and superscripts and subscripts are 'rolled' 3/48" up or down — i.e. 3/8 of the standard line pitch.

To change this value, use the command

.sr *n*

where *n* is the size of the roll in steps of 48ths of an inch.

If your printer is not able to print superscripts and subscripts rolled up or down to such an 'intermediate' position', it will normally print them on the previous or following lines, if those lines are blank; if they are not blank, superscripts and subscripts will be printed on the same line as the remainder of the text.

**.uj — Microjustification** Microjustification is a way of inserting spaces (in steps of 1/128") between characters in order to improve the appearance of your work. This is particularly useful when text is being printed right-justified, as it eliminates the unsightly appearance of lines justified by inserting extra full-character widths between adjacent words.

To turn microjustification off, use the command

.uj off

and to turn it back on again, use

.uj on

You might want to turn microjustification off if you were preparing work to be printed in columns, as these are not usually properly shown when microjustification is on, or if you want your document to be printed quickly — some printers microjustify very slowly.

The factory-set default is for microjustification to be set on, but it can be deselected during installation.

# Mail-merging with WordStar

Essentially, 'standard' WordStar handles its mail-merging operations in the same way as WordStar 1512, except that there is no built-in database from which the details to be merged in are taken. This very important exception apart, the use of merged variables enclosed in ampersands (&) is almost exactly the same in all three programs.

If you are not familiar with mail-merge, begin by looking at the description printed in Chapter Seven; all the information contained there is relevant here, except that you will have to use a data file as described in the next section instead of the database or masterfile described in Chapter Seven.

# Creating a data file

Because standard WordStar does not use a pre-defined database, it follows that you will have to create a special data file of your own. On a sheet of paper – not while you are sitting at the computer – list, in some order which appears reasonable to you, all the various items which you think you might want to incorporate in mail-merged letters. A typical list would consist of a title; forenames or initials; surname; and five lines of address – house, street, town, county and postcode. To this you should add any other details which you might reasonably find useful, such as a telephone number – perhaps two, to allow for home and business phones.

When you have drawn up your list, Create a non-document to hold it (press [ n ] from the Opening Menu) and name it something like ADDRESS.DAT; the file-extension .DAT will serve as a handy reminder to you that this is a data file, but it is not essential for the operation of the mail-merge.

# Data file formats

A typical entry containing the items mentioned above might look like this:

Mr, J.P., Smith, 52 New Street, Blistover, Hampshire, SO56 8VR

Every item – or **field**, to give it the correct name – has been separated from its neighbour by a comma; the comma therefore acts as a **field separator**. There is also a space before every field except the first; this is ignored when you come to use the data file, but makes the file easier to read when you are checking your work.

**Including commas in field names** There are times when you have to use commas as part of a field; a company might be called 'Jones, Martin, James and Son', for example, and you would not want this to be treated as three separate variables. The way around this is to enclose the field in double quotation marks, "Jones, Martin, James and Son". Everything inside double quotes is treated as a single field, regardless of any enclosed commas. Actually you can put commas around any field, but there isn't much point in doing it unless you have to.

**Missing fields** There are times when some fields are blank for some entries; for example, the county name can often be left out of an address. Where such blank fields occur, they *must* be represented by an extra comma, as in this example:

Mr, R.P., Holloway, 45 East Bank, Manchester,,M32 5TG

If you do not put in an extra comma wherever a record has a missing field, the file will get out of step when you are merge-printing letters, and you will probably end up printing something like "Dear 45 East Bank".

# The matrix file

The main document – the one which contains the text of the letter which is to be mail-merged and which 'calls' the data-file – makes use of some special dot commands which enable the correct items to be fetched from the data file and inserted as appropriate. Remember that the dot commands go in the matrix document – the form-letter or whatever – and *not* in the data file.

**.df – Data file** The command to name the file from which the information will be taken would normally be placed at or near the very top of the form letter; obviously it must occur before any attempt is made to actually insert any information from that file.

The form of the basic command is as follows:

.df *filename.extension*

where *filename.extension* identifies the data file. The program will look for the named file on the current disc drive, but this can be changed by specifying a different drive name, followed by the usual colon, immediately before the filename. Thus to force the program to find a data file called LETTERS.DAT on Drive B, you would use the command

.df B:LETTERS.DAT

If LETTERS.DAT is on a different disc from the one which is already in the drive, use this form of the command:

.df B:LETTERS.DAT change

The command 'change' causes a prompt to be displayed on the screen telling you to insert a disc containing the file into the specified drive, and then to press [ Return ]. Obviously the fact that the data file does not have to be on the same disc as the matrix document means that you can make more efficient use of your discs.

**.rv – Read value** Once you have specified the data file and said where it is to be found, you must then tell the matrix program what to call the various fields which it finds. This is done with the .rv command.

For example, a command to insert the information which we entered into the data file on p.211 could look like this:

.rv title, initials, name, house, street, town, county, postcode

**About variables** The names given to these variables are entirely arbitrary – you could make them almost anything you wanted, but obviously it makes sense to pick variable names which will mean something to you when you come back to your file next month or next year.

There are three main rules about variable names, though you probably won't find that any of them really restrict the names you use: first, variable names are limited to 40 characters in length; second, they always begin with a letter; and finally, variable names consist of letters, numbers and hyphens *only*; be especially careful not to try to use any other form of punctuation.

**Matching variables and values** There must be exactly the same number of items in the list after the .rv command as there are in each record in the data file. If there are more items after .rv than exist in one line of the data file, then .rv will begin to poach items from the next line; if there are more items in one line of the file than there are names after .rv, the extra will be ignored. Either way, you will find that your matrix file will quickly get out of step with your data file.

One consequence of this is that even if a variable is not going to be used in the matrix document, it must still be listed in the .rv command.

If the 'tail' of the .rv command is too long to fit on one line, you can simply use a second .rv command on the next line; the first command will read values for as many variables as are listed in its 'tail', and the second command will read the rest.

# Writing the matrix document

Part of a typical matrix document to work with the data file shown above might look something like this:

```
.op
.df LETTERS.DAT
.rv title, forename, surname, housename
.rv street, town, county, postcode
&title& &forename& &surname&
&housename&
&street&
&town&
&county& &postcode&


Dear &title& &surname&


Thank you for your letter applying for a Bodgers' Store Card. Your
application is being processed at the moment, and within the next week
you should receive your new card.
.pa
```

Applying this to the first name inserted into the data file would produce a letter reading as follows:

Mr. J. P. Smith
52 New Street
Blistover
Hampshire
PO5 8VR

Dear Mr. Smith,

Thank you for your letter applying for a Bodgers' Store Card. Your application is being processed at the moment, and within the next week you should receive your new card.

This simple example should make the general principles quite clear: the initial .op command prevents the program from printing a page number on each letter; the two lines of .rv commands read values from the file named in the .df command which precedes them; and the variable names, enclosed in ampersands, '&' , are included in the letter wherever a value from the data file is to be included. These values can be used as often as you want, and in any order – there is no need to put them in the same sequence as they are placed in the data file, or, indeed, to use any particular value at all. Finally, .pa forces each successive letter onto a new page.

Of course, there is no need to restrict mail-merge variables to the inside address and salutation of a letter – you can use them freely anywhere inside a matrix document.

**Empty matrices** You can also create 'empty' matrices – that is, documents which have no text of their own. The following. for example, will take information from a data file like the one we have listed above and use it to print sticky address labels – you may have to adjust the number in the tail of the .pl command to accommodate different sizes of label.

```
.op
.pl 9
.df LETTERS.DAT
.rv title, forename, surname, housename
.rv street, town, county, postcode
&title& &forename &surname&
&housename&
&street&
&town&
&county& &postcode
.pa
```

# Merge-printing

To print a mail-merge document, press [ m ] at the Opening Menu. You will be prompted for the name of the document which is to be merge-printed. As always when printing, you can move directly on by pressing [ Esc ] at any stage; otherwise you will be asked the same questions which you would be asked during normal printing.

You will also be asked for the number of copies which are to be produced; WordStar does not do this with ordinary printing. This means the number of copies *of each letter* – mail-merge expects to produce one document for every record in the data file, and if you tell it to make 10 copies, for example, it will produce 10 letters for every record in the file.

If you don't want to produce a document for every record in the file, read the section on conditional merge-printing below and in Chapter Seven.

## Variables that don't come from a data file

It is not always convenient to refer to a data file for values for variables, and WordStar makes it possible to enter values in other ways.

**.av – Ask for value** The letter which we have just used was undated. It would, of course, have been quite possible to insert a date into it in the ordinary way, but it will probably be easier to treat it as a variable and insert it into the matrix document.

To do this, insert among the other dot commands at the top of the letter the command

.av date

followed by the variable '&date&' at the point in the letter where you would like to have the date printed. When the letter is being merge-printed, it will pause when the .av command is found, and the prompt 'DATE?' will appear on the screen. Type in the date in any format you wish, and it will be inserted at the point occupied by the variable &date&.

**.sv – Set value** The Set value command is used to give a particular value to a variable. For example

.sv date, January 23 1988

will cause 'January 23 1988' to appear in the document wherever the variable '&date&' is placed.

# Conditional merging

Conditional merging is used to print documents for some records but not for others as well as to modify what is printed depending on the value of variables in the data file or input *via* the .av command. It is thus an extremely powerful way of generating several non-identical documents while merge-printing.

Apart from the fact that WordStar 1512 uses a fixed database, and therefore does not need the .df and .rv commands, mail-merging with WordStar 1512 and 'standard' WordStar are almost identical with each other. The use of inserted files (with .fi) and conditional merge-printing (with .if, .ef and .ex) works in precisely the same way with 'standard' WordStar as it does in WordStar 1512. The .sv and .av commands are also used in the same way in both programs. You should therefore refer back to Chapter Seven for fuller details of all these commands.

The .if and .ef commands are more important in 'standard' WordStar than they are in WordStar 1512, because standard WordStar lacks WordStar 1512's facility to preselect which records will have documents printed for them, using the Search feature. With 'standard' WordStar, the same effect can only be achieved with conditional merge-printing; for example, to print letters for all records which have London in the 'town' field, you might create a matrix document like the following:

```
.op
.df LETTERS.DAT
.rv title, forename, surname, housename
.rv street, town, county, postcode
.if &town& <> "London" goto end
&title& &forename& &surname&
&housename&
&street&
&town&
&county& &postcode&

Dear &title& &surname&

Thank you for your letter applying for a Bodgers' Store Card. Your
application is being processed at the moment, and within the next week
you should receive your new card.
.pa
.ef end
```

Notice that here the .pa command occurs *before* the .ef; this is so that the printer doesn' t attempt to advance the paper after records which have not been printed.

# Postscript

There is very little difference between the use of dot commands and mail-merge in 'standard' WordStar on the one hand and the same facilities in WordStar 1512 on the other, so even if you are not using WordStar 1512 at all, you will still find it very useful to read the relevant chapters in the earlier section of the book and to work through the examples given there.

The most important differences between WordStar 1512 and the other programs centre on the in-built database, which does make it very easy to set up a permanent data file for mail-merge work.

# *APPENDIX*

# The Data Protection Act 1984

Readers in the United Kingdom now need to be aware of the implications of the Data Protection Act 1984. Because of the uncertainty created by the Act, and the erroneous view still held by many micro-computer users that it has nothing to do with them, this appendix is devoted to a rapid canter through some of the Act's requirements. This is not meant to be a legally water-tight account of the Act and its provisions – for that you should speak to your solicitor; it is intended only as an explanation of some of the consequences of the legislation. As far as the Act is concerned, data processed on computers and word processors, and relating to a living individual who can be identified from it, or from other information, falls under the scope of the Act. Even if data is referenced by number and not by name, it is still personal data under the Act.

A **data user** is a person who holds data and:

The data forms part of a collection intended to be processed by that person or on his behalf, and

The person controls the content and the use of the data either jointly or separately, and data are in a suitable form for processing or in a form into which they have been converted after processing with a view to subsequent reprocessing.

## Data Protection Principles

The Act lays down eight principles of data protection, as follows:

The information to be contained in personal data shall be obtained, and personal data shall be processed, fairly and lawfully.

Personal data shall be held only for one or more specified and lawful purposes.

217

Personal data held for any purpose shall not be used or disclosed in any manner incompatible with that purpose or those purposes.

Personal data held for any purpose or purposes shall be adequate, relevant and not excessive in relation to that purpose or those purposes.

Personal data shall be accurate and where necessary kept up-to-date.

Personal data held for any purpose or purposes shall not be kept for longer than is necessary for that purpose or those purposes.

An individual shall be entitled:

> (a) at reasonable intervals and without undue delay or expense to be informed by any data user whether he holds any personal data of which that individual is the subject, and to have access to any such data held by a data user, and

> (b) where appropriate to have such data corrected or erased.

> Appropriate security measures shall be taken against unauthorised access to or alteration, disclosure or destruction of, personal data, and against accidental loss or destruction of personal data.

From May 1, 1986, all U.K. Data Users have been required to register the details of the personal data they handle with the Data Protection Registrar, using Form DRP1, Parts A and B. It is a criminal offence to hold computerised personal data unless there is a corresponding entry in the register.

Further information and registration forms can be obtained by writing to the Data Protection Registrar, Springfield House, Water Lane, Wilmslow, Cheshire SK9 5AX, or by telephoning the Registrar's office on Wilmslow (0625) 535777.

# INDEX

221